Recognition theory and contemporary French moral and political philosophy

Manchester University Press

REAPPRAISING THE POLITICAL

Simon Tormey and Jon Simons · series editors

The times we live in are troubling, and as always theory struggles to keep pace with events in its efforts to analyse and assess society, culture and politics. Many of the 'contemporary' political theories emerged and developed in the twentieth century or earlier, but how well do they work at the start of the twenty-first century?

Reappraising the Political realigns political theory with its contemporary context. The series is interdisciplinary in approach, seeking new inspiration from both traditional sister disciplines, and from more recent neighbours such as literary theory and cultural studies. It encompasses an international range, recognising both the diffusion and adaptation of Western political thought in the rest of the world, and the impact of global processes and non-Western ideas on Western politics.

already published

Rethinking equality: the challenge of equal citizenship
Chris Armstrong
Radical democracy: politics between abundance and lack
Lars Tønder and Lasse Thomassen (eds)
The biopolitics of the war on terror: life struggles, liberal modernity and the defence of logistical societies
Julian Reid
Time and world politics: thinking the present
Kimberly Hutchings
Unstable universalities: post structuralism and radical politics
Saul Newman

EDITED BY

Miriam Bankovsky and Alice Le Goff

RECOGNITION THEORY AND CONTEMPORARY FRENCH MORAL AND POLITICAL PHILOSOPHY

Reopening the dialogue

Manchester University Press

Copyright © Manchester University Press 2012

While copyright in the volume as a whole is vested in Manchester University Press, copyright in individual chapters belongs to their respective authors, and no chapter may be reproduced wholly or in part without the express permission in writing of both author and publisher.

Published by Manchester University Press
Altrincham Street, Manchester M1 7JA, UK
www.manchesteruniversitypress.co.uk

British Library Cataloguing-in-Publication Data is available

ISBN 978 1 5261 1696 3 *paperback*
ISBN 978 0 7190 8356 3 *hardback*

First published by Manchester University Press in hardback 2012

This edition first published 2017

The publisher has no responsibility for the persistence or accuracy of URLs for any external or third-party internet websites referred to in this book, and does not guarantee that any content on such websites is, or will remain, accurate or appropriate.

Printed by Lightning Source

Contents

Preface	page vii
List of contributors	ix
Acknowledgements	xiii

Part I: French contributions to recognition theory   1

1. Deepening critical theory: French contributions to theories of recognition   3
   Miriam Bankovsky and Alice Le Goff
2. The relevance of contemporary French philosophy for a theory of recognition: an interview   23
   Axel Honneth, interviewed by Miriam Bankovsky

Part II: Agonistic identity construction   39

3. Impossible recognition: Lacan, Butler, Žižek   41
   Catherine Malabou
4. The politics of suffering and recognition: Foucault contra Honneth   54
   Lois McNay
5. Sartre and Honneth on conflict and recognition   70
   Alice Le Goff
6. Tully, Foucault and agonistic struggles over recognition   88
   David Owen

Part III: Embodiment and vulnerability   109

7. The theory of social action in Merleau-Ponty and Honneth   111
   Jean-Philippe Deranty
8. Between gender and subjectivity: Iris Marion Young on the phenomenology of lived experience   127
   Marie Garrau

Part IV: Systematic oppression and the productivity of power   141

9. Conflicts of recognition and critical sociology   143
   Christian Lazzeri
10. Systematic misrecognition and the practice of critique: Bourdieu, Boltanski and the role of critical theory   160
    Robin Celikates

Contents

Part V: Justice-to-come: questioning equality and the presumption of finality — 173

11 Habermas and Derrida on recognising the other — 175
    Isabelle Aubert
12 Honneth, Lyotard, Levinas — 191
    Jean-Michel Salanskis
13 Justice-to-come in the work of Axel Honneth and Nancy Fraser — 208
    Miriam Bankovsky

References — 226
Index — 241

Preface

There is a long history of cultural stereotypes of different national philosophies: Montesquieu, Marx, Nietzsche and even Deleuze and Guattari put forward variations on the idea that 'nationalitarian' characteristics or styles of thought flourish in particular regional cultures. Within this history, the differences between French and German thought have long been one of the most intractable barriers to a more ecumenical European thought. These differences persist even outside of Europe, where conferences, departments and journals of so-called 'continental philosophy' are often characterised by their French or German tendencies. A key focus of this divide in recent years has been the concept of recognition, which has assumed an increasingly significant place in social and political philosophy since the publication in 1992 of Charles Taylor's *Multiculturalism and the politics of recognition* and Axel Honneth's *Kampf um Anerkennung: Zur moralischen Grammatik sozialer Konflikte* (*The struggle for recognition: the moral grammar of social conflicts*, 1995).

Recognition was widely supposed to be a German obsession, derived from Hegel's philosophy. Insofar as French thinkers concerned themselves with it at all, it was to insist on the inescapability of misrecognition in interpersonal relations and to assert the impossibility of authentic recognition. While there are undoubtedly different attitudes towards the 'problem' of recognition on either side of the Rhine, a primary achievement of this volume is to show that it is much too simple to suggest that only German thinkers have contributed to the recent development of recognition theory. This is not only because there is widespread interest in the theory and politics of recognition among French thinkers, several of whom are represented in this volume, but also because the work of key German theorists of recognition, in particular that of Honneth, drew upon the thought of a number of paradigmatically 'French' thinkers such as Sartre, Levinas, Foucault and Derrida. Whether or not that impact exhausts the resources available in the work of these French thinkers, or whether it amounts to coercive reinterpretation and assimilation within a different paradigm, is one of the questions explored in several of the chapters included here.

Honneth's work is a central thread that links many of these chapters. His efforts to develop a comprehensive concept and ideal of recognition that would encompass the legal, affective and cooperative spheres of social relations carry the promise of a new master concept and new foundations for critical theory. The translation of his work into English, along with the discussions and dialogues it has provoked, has brought his ambitious programme to the forefront of contemporary debates in political theory, sociology, feminism and

Preface

...ilosophy. Over the same period, concepts of recognition have been taken up and developed by others such as Judith Butler, Nancy Fraser, James Tully and Iris Marion Young, often alongside and in concert with ideas drawn from a wide range of post-war French thinkers. The rich and complex debates that have unfolded over two decades have exposed a number of internal tensions in the concept of recognition. Some of these tensions might be summarised in a paraphrase of Amartya Sen's question about equality: recognition of what? Is recognition ultimately a matter of the conditions required for the full expression of our human subjectivity or is it primarily a question of the intersubjective norms by which we are governed? Other tensions, such as that between a naturalistic social and psychological concept of recognition and a non-naturalistic moral or normative political concept, are arguably shared by other varieties of post-Marxist thought, as Jean-Michel Salanskis shows in the case of Lyotard. In each case, these are tensions that bear on the meaning and precise political significance of recognition. These questions are far from settled. As this remarkable volume shows, recognition remains a highly fruitful but also widely contested concept.

A major achievement of many of the chapters published here lies in the suggestions made for the further development of theories of recognition. Some of the contributors point to ways in which Honneth's concept might be improved by further engagement with aspects of post-war French phenomenology, such as Merleau-Ponty's efforts to develop a philosophy of praxis or Sartre's analyses of everyday reification. Others point to the more or less explicit and often positive role of recognition in the work of post-phenomenological French thinkers such as Bourdieu, Derrida, Foucault and Lyotard. They also suggest potential contributions that might be drawn from Bourdieu's concept of *habitus*, Derrida's fundamentally asymmetric conception of the relation to the other or Foucault's concept of power and his practice of genealogy. In this manner, by showing how both the promise and the shortcomings of the concept of recognition are usefully explored by engagement with diverse currents of contemporary French social and political thought, this volume makes a valuable contribution to the dissolution of 'nationalitarian' borders and the promotion of a more cosmopolitan approach to philosophy.

Paul Patton

List of contributors

Isabelle Aubert is currently lecturing in philosophy at the Université Paris I – Panthéon Sorbonne. She is completing a German – French 'cotutelle' PhD at Johann Wolfgang Goethe University (Frankfurt/Main) and University of Paris I – Panthéon Sorbonne, under the supervision of Professor Axel Honneth and Professor Jean-François Kervégan. Her thesis focuses on the scope of Jürgen Habermas' critical theory, reconstructing the different kinds of subjectivity that his communicative paradigm both presupposes and produces.

Miriam Bankovsky is Lecturer in Politics at La Trobe University in Melbourne, Australia. Informed by French, German and American traditions, her work revolves around the implications of undecidability for theories of justice. With an Australian – French 'cotutelle' PhD from the University of New South Wales, Sydney (2009) and Université Paris Ouest-Nanterre (2008), Miriam has a book forthcoming with Continuum, *Perfecting justice in Rawls, Habermas and Honneth: a deconstructive perspective*.

Robin Celikates is Associate Professor of Social and Political Philosophy at the University of Amsterdam and an associate member of the Institute for Social Research in Frankfurt/Main. His research interests include critical theory, democratic theory and the philosophy of the social sciences. He is the author of *Kritik als soziale Praxis: Gesellschaftliche Selbstverständigung und kritische Theorie* (Campus, 2009) and he co-edited *Philosophie der Moral* (Suhrkamp, 2009) and *Socialité et reconnaissance* (L'Harmattan, 2007).

Jean-Philippe Deranty is Associate Professor in Philosophy at Macquarie University, Sydney. He has published extensively on French and German philosophy, including, most recently, *Beyond communication: a critical study of Axel Honneth's social philosophy* (Brill, 2009) and, as editor, *Jacques Rancière: key concepts* (Acumen, 2010). His current research is dedicated to work, its impact on subjectivity and its role in modern society.

Marie Garrau lectures in philosophy at Université Paris Ouest-Nanterre, while completing a PhD in political philosophy that focuses on the notion of vulnerability in contemporary political thought. Her work deals with theories of care, recognition and capabilities, studying their attempts to redefine the concept of justice with reference to the category of vulnerability. She has published a number of articles on ethical and political philosophy, including a book, co-authored with Alice Le Goff, entitled *Care, justice et dépendence: une introduction aux théories du care* (Presses Universitaires de France, 2010).

Alice Le Goff is Assistant Professor in Social Philosophy at Université Paris Descartes (Paris V). Her research interests include theories of recognition and democracy. Her publications include a special edition on 'La reconnaissance. Perspectives théoriques', co-edited with Marie Garrau in *Le temps philosophique* (Paris Ouest-Nanterre publications, 2009), *Care, justice et dépendence: une introduction aux théories du care*, co-authored with Marie Garrau (Presses Universitaires de France, 2010) and *La démocratie délibérative: textes fondamentaux*, co-edited with Charles Girard (Hermann, 2010).

Axel Honneth is Professor of Social Philosophy at Johann Wolfgang Goethe-University and Director of the Institute for Social Research in Frankfurt/Main. His central idea is that intersubjective relationships of 'recognition' play a formative role in the constitution of individuals and societies. His many publications include *Social action and human nature* (Cambridge University Press, 1988, with Hans Joas), *The critique of power* (MIT Press, 1991), *The struggle for recognition* (Polity, 1995), *The fragmented world of the social* (SUNY, 1995), *Redistribution or Recognition?* (Verso, 2003, with Nancy Fraser), *Disrespect* (Polity, 2007) and *The pathologies of individual freedom: Hegel's social theory* (Princeton University Press, 2010).

Christian Lazzeri is Professor of Political Philosophy at Université Paris Ouest-Nanterre and Director of the SOPHIAPOL (*Sociologie, philosophie, anthropologie politiques*), a research centre for philosophers and sociologists working on recognition theory. His research interests include recognition theory, critical theory, conflict theory and neorepublicanism, with recent publications including *La reconnaissance aujourd'hui* with Alain Caillé (Editions CNRS, 2009), *Reconnaissance, identité, intégration sociale* with Soraya Nour (Paris Ouest-La Défense Editions, 2010), 'Pourquoi se révolte-on? Identité, intérêt et action' (*Revue du MAUSS*, 2009) and 'Réification et reconnaissance: une discussion avec Axel Honneth' (*Revue du MAUSS*, 2010).

Catherine Malabou is Professor at the Centre for Modern European Philosophy, Kingston University London. Central to her work is the concept of 'plasticity', inspired by Hegel and by research on neuro-biological responses to trauma. Drawing on contemporary German and French philosophy, critical theory and work in the neurosciences, Malabou has authored numerous books, including *The future of Hegel* (Routledge, 2004), *What should we do with our brain?* (Fordham University Press, 2009) and *Plasticity at the dusk of writing* (Columbia University Press, 2009). Her most recent book is entitled *Changing difference* (Polity Press, 2011).

Lois McNay is Professor of the Theory of Politics at Oxford University. The author of a number of books, including, most recently *Against recognition* (Polity, 2008), she is currently working on a book entitled *The misguided search for the political*.

David Owen is a Professor of Social and Political Philosophy at the University of Southampton. He has published nine books, most recently, *Nietzsche's genealogy of morality* (Acumen, 2007), *Multiculturalism and political theory* (co-edited with Tony Laden, Cambridge University Press, 2007) and *Recognition and power* (co-edited with Bert van den Brink, Cambridge University Press, 2007). He has published articles on various aspects of moral, social and political philosophy, and is currently working on Nietzsche and political theory, transnational citizenship and the ethics of migration.

Jean-Michel Salanskis is Professor in the Philosophy of Science, Logic and Epistemology at Université Paris Ouest-Nanterre. Dealing with a variety of traditions, including the philosophy of mathematics, phenomenology, Jewish thought, twentieth-century French philosophy, and analytic philosophy, he has authored twenty books, edited or co-edited eight collected editions and published numerous articles. His recent books include *Le constructivisme non standard* (Presses du Septentrion, 1999), *Talmud, science et philosophie* (Les Belles Lettres, 2004), *Territoires du sens* (Vrin, 2007), *Usages contemporains de la phénoménologie* (with F. D. Sebbah, Sens et Tonka, 2008) and *La gauche et l'égalité* (Presses Universitaires de France, 2009).

Acknowledgements

The editors would like to acknowledge the research centre SOPHIAPOL (*Sociologie, philosophie, anthropologie politiques*) at Université Paris Ouest-Nanterre, and its directors Christian Lazzeri and Alain Caillé, for sponsoring a conference on 'Theories of recognition and contemporary French philosophy' in Paris which gave birth to the idea for this collection. Our thanks also go to Alexandra Day for her proof-reading assistance. This was made possible by a grant from the Faculty of Humanities and Social Sciences at La Trobe University, who also financed translation work associated with the project. We are grateful to both Paul Patton and Jon Simons for their sound advice at various stages. We also acknowledge Axel Honneth for contributing his valuable time to this project. Finally, we thank Manchester University Press, and the editors of the series *Reappraising the political*, for supporting our book.

PART I
FRENCH CONTRIBUTIONS TO RECOGNITION THEORY

1

Deepening critical theory: French contributions to theories of recognition

Miriam Bankovsky and Alice Le Goff

THE chapters in this volume not only study the impact of French theory on the recent revival of recognition theory but also suggest new ways in which French thought might continue to inform its evolution. The resurgence of theories of recognition since the 1990s has taken a number of forms, including 'Hegelian approaches' which understand recognition as central to the development of 'authentic identity' (Taylor and Honneth); 'theories of justice' which frame demands for recognition as calls for the restitution of both impartiality and the equal status of individuals (Fraser); and the 'critique of oppression' which interprets struggles for recognition as attempts on the part of social movements to contest their oppression, requiring attentiveness to the complexity of social processes which produce group-subjugation (Young). It has often been noticed that the work of Hegel and Mead, among others, has been an important resource for recognition theory, particularly in the early phase of its revival. Although French moral and political theory has also had a significant effect on the categories of recognition theory, its role has, for the most part, been neglected. The chapters in this volume aim to respond to this neglect, highlighting the different contributions that French thought has already made to recognition theory, while also suggesting avenues for further engagement, identifying ways in which French thought assists in thinking through aspects of the recognitive process that are often ignored.

We will begin by mapping out the main elements of the recent renewal of theories of recognition, briefly indicating the different ways in which French theory has already influenced the construction of recognition theory outside of France, while also drawing attention to the inverse and productive impact that recognition theories have themselves had on the French scene in recent years. This map should also provide the reader with a broad summary of the main concerns of recognition theory in its different forms, as well as an account of why the relation between recent theories of recognition and contemporary French theory is worthy of study.

French contributions to recognition theory

With this background work completed, we will then undertake a close analysis of the main themes which French thought promises to contribute to recognition theory, thereby framing the chapters which make up this volume. In particular, we will explore the importance for recognition theory of French accounts of agonistic identity construction; embodiment and vulnerability; systematic oppression and the productivity of power; ethical obligation; and reflexive theory construction. In so doing, we hope that this volume will contribute to a continuing dialogue between recognition theory and contemporary French thought, supporting the intentions of critical theory with a nuanced attention to elements of the recognitive process which have often been overlooked.

The role of French theory in the revival of recognition theory

Recognition: a recent evolution

As we mentioned above, in the years since 1990, there has been a revival of theories of recognition, with the work of Charles Taylor, Axel Honneth, Nancy Fraser, Iris Marion Young and James Tully, among others, gaining increasing attention around the globe. Situated within the broader context of 'critical theory', for which the concept of human emancipation provides the standard with which to critically assess actual social structures, theories of recognition claim that practices of intersubjective recognition condition and facilitate the development of a subject's practical freedom. If, as Horkheimer claims, the goal of critical theory is 'to liberate human beings from the circumstances that enslave them' (Horkheimer, 1982: 244), then the contribution of recognition theorists is to understand 'enslavement' in terms of norms which are not yet mutually recognised and which consequently prevent a person from being able to view themselves as free.

The early revival of recognition theory, inspired for the most part by Hegel and advanced by Taylor and Honneth, brought new energy to 'critical theory', promising insights into the way in which norms of recognition stifle or facilitate the development of 'authentic identity'. This early 'Hegelian approach' established a new goal for critical theory, namely, the achievement of a practical concept of self, undistorted by instituted norms of recognition. As Christopher Zurn explains, in contrast to both moral philosophy (which deals with questions of individual obligation and right action) and political philosophy (which attends to questions of law and fair distribution), 'Hegelian approaches' are best described as 'social philosophy' because they focus the analysis on the structural and social conditions which damage human subjectivity and, as such, require a standard of social normalcy or 'authentic identity' against which to conduct their evaluation (Zurn, 2000: 118).

In Honneth's work, for example, we discover a rather elaborate account of the formal conditions for a healthy identity, a standard which extrapolates from all particular substantive conceptions of the good life in developed societies: 'a formal conception of ethical life' (Honneth, 1995a: 171–9). This formal and quasi-universal ideal of healthy identity then serves as Honneth's standard for his therapeutic diagnosis and critique of pathological social practices, that is, social practices which involve norms of recognition which inhibit the development of 'authentic identity'. For Honneth, real and effective freedom requires the development of certain practical relations-to-self which are themselves dependent on the validation of one's capacities by one's peers. Drawing on the distinction Hegel makes within 'Objective Spirit' between the family, the State and civil society, Honneth identifies three specific practical relations-to-self which are necessary for real and effective freedom, each of which receives recognitive validation within three different spheres of life. The first relation-to-self is self-confidence or the ability to trust in one's own feelings and desires, insofar as these are validated by the recognition accorded by the solicitude of others (in the sphere of intimate, affective relations of love and friendship). The second is self-respect or the belief that one has an authority equal with others to make claims and demands, insofar as this authority is validated by the respect of others (who mutually recognise each other's egalitarian rights). The third is social esteem, social achievement, or the feeling of belonging, insofar as this feeling is validated (in the sphere of civil society) by relations of solidarity where others share one's own beliefs and thereby recognise the value of one's contribution to social life (Anderson and Honneth, 2005: 127–31, 138, 142–5).

Hegel hereby allows Honneth to present social struggle for recognition as the moral driver of social progress. Now equipped with a substantive concept of ethical life (a concept of social normalcy), Honneth is able to systematically identify forms of social pathology in terms of deficits in the norms of recognition responsible for healthy subjectivity, thereby grounding social struggle in the dynamic experiences of disrespect in a manner which strongly contrasts with the Marxist reduction of social conflict to economic interests. Social movements are now understood as motivated by a 'moral grammar', historically variable in being structured by a particular denial of the intersubjective conditions of self-confidence, self-esteem and self-respect, that is, a denial of the conditions of 'authentic identity' or 'social normalcy'. More specifically, the theory identifies three avenues for critiquing the norms that regulate interactions between subjects because moral claims can be raised in each of the spheres of intersubjective relation (affective, reciprocal or cooperative) (Honneth, 2004: 358). In the affective sphere, appeal to mutually attested love can ground a demand for the affective recognition of newly developed or previously unconsidered needs in what Honneth refers to as 'a different or expanded kind of care' (Fraser and Honneth, 2001: 144). In the sphere of egalitarian right, appeal to the basic idea of equality can ground a demand for the legal recognition of previously excluded groups or of previously neglected facts (Fraser and Honneth, 2001: 144). In the sphere of cooperative and social recognition, appeal to the achievement principle can ground a demand for the consideration of hitherto neglected or underappreciated activities and capacities which contribute to the common good and are deserving of greater social esteem and material resources (Fraser and Honneth, 2001: 144). In each case, the goal is to secure the conditions of mutual recognition under which undistorted identity formation can take place (Fraser and Honneth, 2001: 174).

However, critical theorists were naturally wary of this 'Hegelian approach' precisely due to its dependence on a standard of 'authentic identity', the concept of individual good upon which the theories of Taylor and Honneth are constructed. Many, like Nancy Fraser, felt that a quasi-universal notion of 'authentic identity' or individual good could not provide an appropriate basis for a political theory of justice upon which citizens themselves (with their own very different accounts of the good life) might agree. Eliding the vocabulary of 'the good life', and dismissing notions of 'social normalcy', 'substantive individual good' and 'authentic identity', Fraser instead proposes to frame demands for recognition with a concept of 'justice', along with all of its associated Kantian ideas of fairness, impartiality, neutrality and equality. For Fraser and the 'theorists of justice', the moral value of demands for recognition is not a question of individual good but rather a matter of fairness. Beginning with a radical liberal postulate of the equal value of constructions of identity and difference (Fraser, 1997: 30), Fraser is able to designate certain norms of recognition as unjust or unfair if they systematically deny equality to certain identities on account of their difference alone. In other words, where the early 'Hegelian approaches' to recognition lay claim to a model of authentic identity as the goal of critical theory, the 'theorists of justice' instead focus their analysis on unfair evaluations of 'social status', that is, on evaluations of 'social status' which do not treat different social identities as equal peers. For the 'theorists of justice', misrecognition is best described as 'status subordination' or prevention from participating as a peer in social life. For Fraser, such injustice still requires a politics of recognition, but one that is no longer reduced to the denial of an 'authentic identity'. Instead, status subordination requires a politics aiming to re-establish the misrecognised individual as a full member of society, so that the advantages and disadvantages of norms of recognition are distributed neutrally and impartially among different individuals. For 'theorists of justice', all individuals are entitled to fair and impartial conditions under which to pursue their very different conceptions of their own individual good, and this requires recognising the subordinated individual as capable of participating on a par with the rest.

For thinkers like Iris Marion Young, however, neither the 'Hegelian approaches' nor the 'theories of justice' capture the essence of demands for recognition. Such demands, put forward by new group-based social movements (feminism, Black liberation, American Indian movements, gay and lesbian liberation and so on) are essentially claims for the specific difference of each group identity to be validated, a demand which is clouded by both the Hegelian's focus on an individual's 'authentic identity' and by the emphasis on impartiality that characterises the 'theories of justice' (Young, 1990: 3–4). For Young, neither approach pays sufficient attention in an explicit manner to the specificity of systematic oppression and domination, which coalesce in complex ways to produce shared experiences of injustice which members of certain social groups together undergo. It is these shared experiences of oppression, rooted in a specific group-based difference, which produces the demand for recognition (Young, 1990: 3). In other words, struggles for recognition originate in the experience of group-based oppression. In what we here refer to as a 'third' stage in the evolution of the revival of recognition, namely, the 'critique of oppression', Young draws attention to what she sees as the very phenomenon granting the call for recognition its normative weight, namely, 'a cry of suffering or distress, or feeling distress oneself' (Young, 1990: 5). The struggle for recognition is born out of an oppression which is suffered on account of the difference which characterises a certain group (Young, 1990: 4, 5). Although Honneth's theory certainly attempts to identify pathological social practices, the contribution of the 'critique of oppression' is to shift the language of the analysis away from a vocabulary centred on the conditions of 'authentic, healthy identity' towards a vocabulary focusing on the specific experiences of dominated groups. For Young, the quasi-universal Hegelian notion of individual 'authentic identity' clouds the very group-difference which cries out to be recognised, and the 'theories of justice' fail to notice that partiality (not impartiality) is needed to overcome deep-rooted oppression. For Young, the nature of domination cannot be defined in advance of an engagement with the dominated, and this requires hearing and heeding a call rather than in asserting and mastering a state of affairs. Beginning, instead, with the concept of domination, the 'critique of oppression' focuses on the relation between norms of recognition and subjugation in specific, concrete, social institutions and consequently displays a heightened sensitivity to relations of power and subsequent oppression. Including sociological analysis of complex social structures, the 'critique of oppression' shifts the focus of critical theory onto those hidden social processes which produce oppressed subjects, processes to which both 'Hegelian approaches' and 'theories of justice' pay insufficient attention.

These three types of recognition theory draw on a variety of sources to facilitate their reflections and analyses. However, in each case, it has rarely been remarked that French philosophy serves as a valuable resource. It is to this theme that we now turn.

French theory: a valuable resource

It is, of course, natural that readers of Taylor and Honneth would initially focus on the main driver of their approach, namely, Hegel and, to a great extent, George Herbert Mead. However, drawing attention to the role that French thought plays in the development of the 'Hegelian approach' promises to throw light on certain aspects of each thinker's theory which remain relatively unexplored.

In 'The politics of recognition' (1994), for example, Taylor develops a critique of the universalism of the politics of equal respect, using the politics of local difference to which certain minorities lay claim. Reflecting on the difficulty in articulating the first standpoint with the second, Taylor draws not only on Hegel but also Jean-Jacques Rousseau, developing a dialogical conception of intersubjectivity which ascribes importance to both equality and difference-recognition in the construction of a society of authentic individuals who are also characterised by a unity of purpose. In Rousseau's terms, I must both 'obey myself' while also being a member of the common project, the 'general will', caring about the esteem which society grants me when I lead a socially virtuous life (Taylor, 1994: 48; see also 29–30, 35, 44–51).

In Honneth's work, we discover an elaborate theory of recognition, developed well beyond the question of multiculturalism, an account which again draws not only on Hegel but also on contemporary French theory. It is well known that the central motor of Honneth's theory is his re-reading of the Hegelian legacy through the lens of Mead's sociological pragmatism. Mead enables Honneth to offer a naturalist reading of Hegel's theory, allowing him to sketch out his own concept of healthy subjectivity. This, in turn, forms the basis of a normative social theory which explains social transformation as a function of the normative expectations structurally inscribed in relations of recognition. While much secondary literature has focused on Honneth's use of Hegel and Mead, his deployment of the contemporary French tradition has received very little attention. However, as the contributions to this volume make clear, the French tradition clearly forms an important backdrop, providing resources which inform Honneth's efforts to develop a social theory which is not exhausted by the horizon of Habermasian deliberation and mutual understanding.

The existentialism of Jean-Paul Sartre and the phenomenology of Jacques Derrida and Emmanuel Levinas allow Honneth to explore the ethical and moral importance of what he refers to as non-deliberative intersubjective relations. For Honneth, Sartre offers a presentation of the existential meaning of recognition which grasps the ways in which recognition relations affect our capacity for practical action. Moreover, Derrida's and Levinas' ethical concern for the other person allows Honneth to think through the need to supplement Habermas'

Deepening critical theory: French contributions

framework of equal treatment with a principle of unilateral care (Honneth, 1995c; see also Chapter 2 of this volume).

French social theory also assists Honneth in his defence of a normative conception of human needs. In this, Honneth inherits the concerns of Sorel by highlighting the affective and emotional dimension of struggles for recognition and drawing attention to collective feelings of humiliation (1995a: 145–59).

Still more recently, Honneth makes use of the work of Michel Foucault and Louis Althusser, as well as the ideas of French social theorists Luc Boltanski, Pierre Bourdieu and Laurent Thévenot, so as to think through questions of social structure and power. Foucault's account of the reproductive aspect of power assists Honneth in explaining how certain forms of recognition reproduce regulative patterns of social domination (Honneth, 2008; see also Chapter 2 of this volume).

Furthermore, it is clear that the categories deployed by the 'theories of justice' and the 'critique of oppression' are also enriched by the contemporary French tradition. Nancy Fraser, for example, makes use of deconstruction when expounding her concept of 'transformative recognition', a strategy which seeks to remedy the very evaluative structure responsible for the misrecognition of subordinate groups. Deconstructive strategy, she states, has the capacity to change everyone's sense of self so as to achieve an ideal in which all groups are satisfied with the value that they are granted (Fraser and Honneth, 2001: 75, 106). As 'transformative recognition', deconstruction deploys a radical principle of the equality of differences, thereby supporting a 'utopian cultural ideal of fluid, shifting differences (Fraser and Honneth, 2001: 106; see also Chapter 13 of this volume).

Moreover, Lasse Thomassen is correct to point out that Iris Marion Young pursues her 'critique of oppression' in a manner sympathetic to both deliberative and deconstructive projects (Thomassen, 2007: 23–4), arguing that the domain of communication be enlarged to include not only deliberative argument but also different styles and terms of communication such as rhetorical language, narrative, and the activist politics of civil disobedience (Young, 2000: Chapter 2; 2001; 1996; 1997). For Young, the worthwhile project of elaborating a communicative ethics which recognises difference and particularity is impeded when moral respect is portrayed uniquely as a relation of symmetry between self and other. Drawing on the work of Lyotard (Young, 1990: 5) and Levinas (Young, 1997: 340), Young argues that, while comparing the situation of agents according to some standard of equality is ultimately necessary for theorising justice, symmetrical reciprocity cannot alone account for the moment of respect for the particular, embodied, other person which characterises deliberative exchange. This leads Young to argue that the ideal of communication must be enlarged to include different ways of communicating which allow one to 'listen' and learn from the other person, so as to approach an ideal of ever-widening conversation among participants who seek mutual understanding across their differences. Moreover, as Chapter 8 of this volume points out, Young also draws heavily on the tradition of French phenomenology, particularly that of Merleau-Ponty and Simone de Beauvoir, so as to develop an account of the 'lived experience' of oppressed groups which is far more nuanced than a purely deliberative approach.

Recognition theory, then, in its different forms, claims a close alliance with contemporary French thought, an interest that is shared by an increasing number of moral and political theorists in the English-speaking world.

This relation of recent theories of recognition with contemporary French philosophy is worth identifying and studying, for a number of reasons. A primary reason lies in the need to question the view, popular within the Anglophone and German worlds, that contemporary French philosophy has little to offer the tradition of moral and political philosophy. This view tends to inherit, in a fairly uncritical manner, Habermas' early critique of the contemporary French tradition in the 1980s, professing to defend reason from the jaws of its radical critique by the French thinkers (Habermas, 1990a; see also Chapter 13 of this volume). As Honneth himself points out, we cannot underestimate the effect of the criticisms which Habermas brought to the French tradition in the 1980s, for these produced a series of rather polemical encounters that 'had a very damaging effect and placed the Franco-German relation under the heading irrationality versus rationality' (Critchley and Honneth, 1998: 34). We share Honneth's regret that this 'fruitless' dualism has contributed to 'a certain and still growing underestimation of the French tradition' (1998: 34). We believe that recognition theory offers the chance to reopen the dialogue under new terms of reference because of its unusual interpretations of the relevance for critical theory of contemporary French accounts of identity construction, vulnerability and embodiment, oppression, ethical obligation and finitude.

A further reason for undertaking this study is to lend support to those in the Anglophone world who, since the 1980s, are using French theory to bring new ethical orientations to critical theory more generally. We are thinking, in particular, of the work of an increasing number of thinkers who are progressively strengthening the influence of French thought on moral and political theory, including, for example, thinkers like Chantal Mouffe, William Connolly, Judith Butler, Drucilla Cornell, Bonnie Honig, Paul Patton, Lasse Thomassen and Simon Critchley, just to mention a few. Our volume adds critical mass to such work, while also bringing a new element into the equation, namely, a particular focus on theories of recognition and their relation to contemporary French thought.

Finally, and even more importantly, a study of this type also promises to identify and clarify certain dimensions of the recognitive process which have often been ignored. In this sense, the volume does not simply aim to reconstruct the ways in which contemporary French philosophy has already been used by recognitive theorists. It also intends to identify ways in which French theory promises a more nuanced attention to elements which have been overlooked: in particular, the far-reaching implications of agonistic and conflictual identity construction; the effects of embodiment; the impacts of systematic oppression on the recognitive process; and the significance of ethical obligation with respect to reflexive and future-oriented theory construction.

An inverse relation: the productive impact of recognition theory on the contemporary French scene

However, before discussing the above themes more carefully, it is also worth pointing out that not only has contemporary French thought influenced the construction of recognition theory outside of France, the inverse is also true. The revival of theories of recognition has itself produced important effects on the contemporary French intellectual scene. The first proof of this is Paul Ricoeur's book *The course of recognition* (2007) published in French in 2004, in which Ricoeur examines the various meanings of the term 'recognition' (namely, description or identification of objects; self-assertion or recognition of one's self and one's capacities; and agreement or mutual recognition). He does so in order to determine the extent to which the concept of recognition might be the object of a unified philosophy. Ricoeur's response to his question is negative: instead of offering a way to unify our different relations to the world, 'recognition' resists unification. Not only can neither concept be reduced to the other, the very agreements or 'states of peace' which count as 'mutual recognition' among parties are often achieved in a manner which maintains an essential asymmetry in the relation between those parties. Undertaking an analysis of actual experiences of 'states of peace', Ricoeur discovers that practices of giving and receiving of gifts facilitate actual agreements, and he concludes that mutual recognition always involves some form of gratitude on the part of the receiving party (a central meaning of the French word, 'reconnaissance'), a gratitude which is difficult to resolve with recognition as identification or self-assertion and which maintains the original asymmetry of self and other.

In this sense, it is primarily in the domain of French social theory that the impact and productivity of the revival of the theory of recognition is most visible. A number of current trends in France have emerged in an attempt to develop and deepen Honneth's theory in the direction of a 'politicisation' of the ethics of recognition. The work of Emmanuel Renault pursues such politicisation, further developing the details of the theory as it concerns three phenomena, namely, institutions, collective identity and social suffering (2004; 2008a, 2008b; see also Deranty and Renault, 2007). Attempting to account for the institutional dimension of existence, Renault no longer conceptualises the relation between institutions and recognition relations as expressive but rather constitutive: in other words, he argues that institutions actually shape recognition relations rather than merely expressing or reflecting them. Renault's concerns converge with those of Jean-Philippe Deranty who questions (and attempts to overcome) the interpersonalist reduction of recognition in Honneth's work by revitalising the originally naturalist character and materialist designs of recognition theory (Deranty, 2005; 2009; and Deranty and Haber, 2009). Moreover, since 2002, work conducted by the research centre SOPHIAPOL (*Sociologie, philosophie, anthropologie politiques*) at Université Paris Ouest-Nanterre has also contributed to the renewal of critical theory in France, by bringing together philosophers, sociologists and anthropologists so as to explore the intersections between recognition theory and the sociology of the gift developed by MAUSS (*Mouvement anti-utilitariste dans les sciences sociales*) (Caillé, 2007; Lazzeri, 2010).

Reflecting on the impact of contemporary French theory outside of France and on the inverse influence of recognition theory upon the contemporary French scene invites us to consider the question of the interest of a dialogue between the theory of recognition and contemporary French thought, the very aim of our book. It is with this aim in mind that we will now attempt to identify the main themes which characterise this dialogue, themes which, as previously mentioned, have the potential to illuminate aspects of the recognitive process which are often overlooked. Drawing attention to these less visible aspects of the recognitive process, French thought has the capacity to contribute to the development of a more nuanced and differentiated account of recognition, an account which is more sensitive to the positive and negative effects of recognition on intersubjective life.

French contributions

Agonistic identity construction

A first contribution of contemporary French thought is its wariness of the notion of 'authentic identity' upon which the early phase of the revival of recognition depends. Where the 'Hegelian approaches' of Taylor and Honneth think that mutually recognised norms facilitate the production of 'authentic identities', the French authors studied in this volume are sensitive to elements which restrict or block this productive process. This sensitivity to the negative or reifying aspects of mutually recognised norms leads to an understanding of identity construction as 'agonistic'. By 'agonistic', we mean that mutually recognised norms contain competing elements which are polemic and combative, and consequently produce identities marked by tension and conflict. Norms of recognition are at once facilitative and reifying, such that identity construction is both self-determining *and* determined, 'authentic' *and* 'inauthentic'.

Deepening critical theory: French contributions

It is worth pointing out that in Chapter 2 of this volume Honneth himself identifies what he sees as a contrast between the German tradition, which emphasises the positive and emancipatory dimension of recognition in the production of 'authentic identity', and the French tradition, beginning with Rousseau, which identifies such recognition with negative forms of objectification or reification. Rousseau, for example, insists that another's look can distract the self from recognising its true beliefs and desires, thereby producing an 'inauthentic self' and contributing to social decline (Rousseau, 1984). Pursuing the German – French contrast still further, Honneth even suggests that French thinkers like Lacan, Sartre and Althusser have inherited Rousseau's negative account of recognition insofar as each thinker identifies recognition with reification and appropriation. For Althusser, 'interpellation' *is* misrecognition (Althusser, 1971: 127–88).

The reflections on French contributions to the concept of recognition in this volume tend to suggest that the opposition Honneth establishes between the German and French tradition is only partly correct. On the one hand, supporting Honneth's distinction, it often turns out that French theory does lend weight to the view that recognition involves forms of subjugation to norms which pre-exist identity construction, encouraging a critique of the essentialist model of 'authentic identity' on which the Hegelian approaches are founded. On the other hand, the French acknowledgment that recognition relations involve forms of domination does not always prevent social theory from pursuing mutual recognition as a worthy ideal, and, in this sense, Honneth's distinction between a positive German and a negative French tradition no longer appears to be so clear-cut.

To explain further, this French identification of recognition with domination and subjugation can take two forms, either a radical or a moderate critique, of which only the first supports Honneth's distinction. On the one hand, the radical critique of 'authentic identity' calls into question the very usefulness of mutually recognised norms. Catherine Malabou pursues this line in Chapter 3, presenting a comparative reading of the concepts of recognition defended by Lacan, Žižek and Butler, which leads her to reject the very notion of 'authentic identity'. Malabou argues that we can never have our 'true' subjectivity recognised because the modes in which we present ourselves are already structured in advance by a prior and passive acceptance of norms.

On the other hand, the moderate critique of 'authentic identity' says that the fact that recognition involves some form of domination should not entail its complete and radical rejection. Although this moderate form of criticism also draws attention to the ways in which supposedly mutual recognition relations become impregnated by the spectre of reification, such critique views the ideal as useful nonetheless. In other words, such critique commits to the project of achieving mutual recognition in spite of its inherent difficulties affirming, in this way, the agonistic dimension of the idea of mutual recognition, that is, its uneasy status as both facilitative and reifying.

The analyses of Alice Le Goff in Chapter 5 draw on Sartre's work so as to develop a moderate critique of the notion of 'authentic identity', suggesting that Sartre's *Being and nothingness* (1993a) can be interpreted as a phenomenology of everyday reification, wherein recognition relations inevitably involve forms of objectification. Le Goff does not delve into the detail of Honneth's own reading of Sartre's work (which criticises Sartre for a strictly negativist account of intersubjectivity where mutual recognition is impossible) but instead focuses on the way in which Sartre indicates the importance of the subjective need for recognition, while also indicating a way of critiquing the concept of 'authentic identity'. Sartre's work is used by Le Goff in an attempt to overcome the opposition between construing recognition as a question of authentic identity (Honneth and Taylor) or a question of justice (Fraser). Drawing on Nikolas Kompridis' analysis of the debate, Le Goff calls for an account of recognition which produces a practice of freedom that is agonistic – both constructed and creative – in line with Tully's account of the democratic freedom to oppose oppressive, exclusive and assimilative norms of mutual recognition (Tully, 2004: 98–102).

The contributions of Lois McNay and David Owen (Chapters 4 and 6) also discover in Foucault's work resources for a moderate critique of the notion of 'essential freedom' associated with the idea of authentic identity that characterises the Hegelian approaches. For Owen, Foucauldian freedom is 'agonistic', both produced and productive. Owen develops his account of agonistic freedom by outlining Tully's use of Foucault to defend a practice wherein freedom modifies the rules governing relations between individuals. Instead of the 'finality' of the idea of authentic identity implied by the achievement of mutual recognition, freedom should rather be understood as constructing itself out of constructed norms through a process of dialoguing, responding and recreating new norms. This is an account of processual and ongoing struggle, with a view to speaking and acting differently. In a similar manner, Lois McNay uses Foucault to question the possibility of actually realising the authentic identities of which Honneth speaks, suggesting instead that Foucault provides a more nuanced account of the 'phenomenology of suffering', exploring the way in which supposedly authentic identities are always produced by power-relations which precede their construction. She calls on recognition theory to take more seriously the idea that freedom itself is constructed, drawn out of individuals who are governed by social practices.

In so doing, McNay does not reject Honneth's decision to focus on the debilitating experience of suffering, because she believes that a phenomenology of suffering has the capacity to help us identify emerging forms of oppression. However, using Foucault's more complex account of the ambivalent effects of individualising governmentality, McNay nonetheless calls on us to consider the limitations of Honneth's reduction of the dynamics of power to a simplistic dualism of genuine and ideological modes of recognition. In this sense, McNay's use of Foucault to sustain a 'moderate' critique of recognition allows her to oppose Foucauldians such as Wendy Brown, who prefer to use Foucault to dismiss the politics of identity and recognition outright as 'suffer-mongering'. For Wendy Brown, the politics of recognition commits individuals to regressive assertions of victimhood, and she uses Foucault to highlight the way in which the subjugating force of disciplinary power in effect produces 'normalised' individuals whose sense of identity through recognition blinds them to more imaginative possibilities of action. McNay seeks to use Foucault against this Foucauldian rejection of the politics of recognition, instead highlighting the potential of the phenomenology of suffering to assist in identifying and resisting certain forms of subordination.

Embodiment and vulnerability

The development of a more nuanced approach to recognition appears to require not only an emphasis upon the ambivalence of 'self-realisation' due to the way in which the construction of 'authentic identity' is always inscribed in power-relations, but also the development of a phenomenology of the recognitive process and its role in the formation of identities. This phenomenology would also consider the embodied aspects of the processes of subjectivation, aspects which produce reason as material, interdependent and vulnerable.

Jean-Philippe Deranty's and Marie Garrau's contributions to this volume, in Chapters 7 and 8, reflect on the possible contributions of French phenomenology for a theory of recognition drawing, in particular, on Merleau-Ponty's phenomenology of the social to highlight the primordiality of corporeality. For Deranty, Merleau-Ponty's account of the social reveals that the production of the subject of recognition is, in fact, conditional on pre-linguistic processes which produce reason as embodied and material. Deranty wishes to remind Honneth that his theory of recognition, in fact, shares with Merleau-Ponty an account of the corporeal dimension of the process of recognition. Deranty encourages Honneth to make his proximity with Merleau-Ponty more explicit, defending the view that a phenomenology of the body and its vulnerability with respect to the world could serve to enrich an account of recognition which appears, at times, to provide a rather truncated version of interaction. As Deranty points out in his book *Beyond communication* (2009), Honneth reduces the experience of interaction to interpersonal exchange, failing to acknowledge the way that the subject develops through interaction with the material world, mediated by the body.

Marie Garrau further extends Deranty's analyses, noting the convergence between the work of Simone de Beauvoir and that of Merleau-Ponty who together develop a phenomenology of lived experience and of the body-proper, thereby offering a response to the question of the empirical referent of critical social theory. In this way, Garrau defends, with Iris Marion Young, the need to articulate a critical sociology attentive to the structural factors of oppression, by means of an analysis of the lived experience of the oppressed.

Systematic oppression and the productivity of power

Garrau's chapter not only elucidates the possible contributions of the phenomenological approach of Beauvoir and Merleau-Ponty, sensitive to the material, embodied character of reason. It also highlights the attentiveness displayed by the 'critique of oppression' towards the structural factors of domination. These are complex processes that produce vulnerable subjects, processes to which the 'Hegelian approach' of Honneth and Taylor pays insufficient attention. Although, as we mentioned at the start of this chapter, Honneth's theory does seek to overcome pathological social practices, grounding social struggle in the dynamic experiences of disrespect, the contribution of the 'critique of oppression' explicitly shifts the focus of analysis away from individual experiences of disrespect and their negative impact on the development of 'authentic, healthy identity' and instead focuses the analysis on group experiences of subjugation. Although Honneth is, of course, also concerned with group subjugation and the contestation of oppression by social movements, the logic of this analysis is presented more clearly by the 'critique of oppression' interpretation of recognition, in its explicit shift from a focus on the conditions of 'healthy subjectivity' to a focus on the precise forms of 'group oppression'. Following Young, the nature of domination cannot be defined in advance of an engagement with the dominated, and this means that critical theory would do well to draw on the insights of Beauvoir in conducting an analysis of the lived experience of the oppressed, along with an identification of possible ways to respond to oppression. Garrau's attentiveness to the materiality of oppression maps onto yet another theme that characterises the dialogue between recognition theory and contemporary French thought, pursued in this volume. As we explained earlier in this chapter, the influence of the revival of recognition theory is particularly visible in the domain of French social theory, which displays a heightened sensitivity to systematic oppression and the pervasiveness of power, elements which operate within the consensual horizon of the idea of mutual recognition, thereby producing the effect of reconciling oppressed subjects to their social world rather than encouraging them to critique it. Developing the 'critique of oppression' still further, French social theory concerns itself with the underlying structural difficulties and social factors that produce marginalised subjects who are unfortunately resigned to accept their condition. The nuanced account of power and structure provided by French social theorists such as Bourdieu and Boltanski provides resources for questioning the assumption, among many recognition theorists, that subjugated subjects will automatically enter into conflict when denied sustaining forms of recognition. A more realistic approach to struggles for recognition would, in this sense, need to account for the factors that inhibit and frustrate marginalised subjects, preventing them from wanting to engage in conflict over unjust norms.

The contributions of Christian Lazzeri and Robin Celikates in Chapters 9 and 10 make use of French social theory to develop such concerns. Lazzeri focuses in particular on the possible contributions of the critical sociology of Pierre Bourdieu, exploring the structural impediments to subjects engaging in recognitive struggle. Celikates' chapter echoes that of Lazzeri by comparing critical sociology, on the one hand, with the sociology of critique, on the other. Celikates argues that critical sociology in the tradition of Bourdieu tends to view agents as complicit in the domination they suffer whereas the sociology of critique in the tradition of Boltanski emphasises the reflexive capability of actors to participate in a critique of their own society. For Celikates, critical sociology is too pessimistic and the sociology of critique too optimistic, and he instead claims that a theory of recognition concerned with a 'critique of oppression' must find a balance between both approaches for its critical analysis of social conflict to be persuasive.

These concerns, discovered in French social theory, complement those expressed by Simon Thompson in his book *The political theory of recognition* (2006: Chapter 7) where he uses James Tully's reflections on the unpredictable nature of struggle to show that Honneth's three-stage account of engaging in struggle is not as straightforward as it seems. In stage one, hurt feelings are meant to produce a sense of injustice which, for structural reasons, Thompson points out, does not always occur. In stage two, this sense of injustice is meant to trigger a struggle for recognition that, as Thompson indicates, structural reasons can again prevent. In stage three, the struggles are meant to contribute to the moral development of society which, as Thompson states, no longer appears to ring true, given that only the hurt feelings of certain types of subjects – those with sufficient resources, both psychological and other – produce the intended effects. Similar concerns are expressed elsewhere, in the work of Christian Lazzeri, which constructs a dialogue between the theory of recognition and theories of mobilisation. Lazzeri points to the way in which theories of recognition tend to presuppose a certain automaticity and, drawing on his own tradition of French social theory, he undertakes a careful analysis of the obstacles and cultural factors which prevent subjects from taking part in a critique of their own society (Lazzeri, 2009).

Justice-to-come: questioning equality and the presumption of finality
A further theme of contemporary French philosophy concerns the emphasis it places on the ethical importance of non-symmetrical and unequal responsibili-

ties, a useful counterpoint to the privilege that contemporary 'theories of justice' grant to the idea of equal respect. It is precisely this idea that Honneth takes from Levinas and Derrida in 'The Other of justice: Habermas and the ethical challenge of post-modernism' (1995c). Here, Honneth argues that the later Derrida follows Levinas in developing a notion of moral responsibility for the concrete other which conflicts with the norm of equal treatment and instead supports an ethics of care much like the one that Carol Gilligan defends (Gilligan, 1993; Honneth, 1995c: 306–19). To the principle of impartial justice, deconstruction adds an asymmetrical (and non-reciprocal) principle of unilateral help and, in so doing, reveals the limits of Habermas' ethics of discussion, which has a tendency to underestimate the importance of asymmetrical responsibilities in our relations with others. As a counterpoint to the perspective of the 'theories of justice' offered by Habermas and Fraser, deconstruction emphasises the ethical nature of 'unequal' and non-reciprocal responsibility, manifest in the caring treatment of another person (Honneth, 1995c: 306–19).

The Derridean and Levinasian idea that ethics is not exhausted by a principle of reciprocal equality overlaps with an important current in French sociology which also informs Honneth's work, namely, the sociology of gift, originally presented by Marcel Mauss and revitalised since the 1980s by French academics associated with MAUSS working at the intersection of sociology, anthropology, philosophy and economics. The work of this group (which includes the likes of Jean Baudrillard, Vincent Descombes, Bruno Latour, Claude Lefort, Philippe Chanial and even Cornelius Castoriadis) presents this ethics, modelled on gift-giving, as an important alternative to both the utilitarian account of intersubjective relations and to the paradigm of rational choice in the social sciences, which tend to account for cultural and economic relations in the instrumental language of rational self-interest (see, in particular, the summary of the research undertaken by MAUSS provided by Chanial, 2008). The concern to include the normative value of gift-giving in an account of moral relations distinguishes Honneth's work from Habermasian ethics, and converges with Iris Marion Young's attempt to make space in communicative ethics for asymmetrical relations. As we indicated earlier, Young remains sympathetic to both the deliberative and Levinasian project, arguing that the worthwhile project of elaborating a communicative ethics that recognises difference and particularity is impeded when moral respect is portrayed uniquely as a relation of symmetry between self and other. Prior to this relation of symmetry, a moment of respect for the particular, embodied, other person is needed, wherein the relation of self towards the other is asymmetrical, irreducible and irreversible. As Lasse Thomassen points out, Young attempts to include asymmetrical relations by enlarging the domain of communication to include not merely deliberative argument but also different styles and terms of communication more appropri-

Deepening critical theory: French contributions

ate to the specificity of the other (rhetorical language, narrative and the activist politics of civil disobedience).

Quite clearly, then, the non-symmetrical ethical relation, visible in both the work of Derrida and Levinas, and in the French sociology of the gift, has informed recognition theory's attempt to correct the Habermasian framework of equality so as to develop a plural account of justice which ascribes ethical weight not just to equality but also to asymmetrical relations of love, friendship and care. In this sense, as Honneth himself makes clear in his contribution to this volume, French thought has nourished the account of principles in the spheres of affective need and social cooperation, but not in the sphere of juridical relations, these being already regulated by the Habermasian principle of equal respect.

In a simple sense, the idea is that instead of determining the relation to other people in advance through the lens of norms which the self assumes the other person also recognises, the self must rather learn from the other person beyond any initial expectations about what might be learnt. This idea describes an attempt to mark a difference between the 'actual' (those norms which currently regulate social interaction, receiving justification of their validity by reference to their being mutually recognised) and the 'possible' (an as yet unactualised world which has the potential to affect the actual if only actors would orient themselves ethically). This concern to avoid 'colonising' the possible is the final theme explored in this volume; the concern that theory maintain a critical perspective on its own production, recognising its located nature and attempting to respond to its inevitable finitude.

As Isabelle Aubert explains in Chapter 11, the tension between Habermas' and Derrida's account of the relation to the other person concerns, on the one hand, an understanding of interaction as an ordinary everyday practice and, on the other hand, an account of welcoming the other which respects the *exceptionality* and unique nature of his or her arrival. Aubert's comparison establishes the way in which the full recognition of another person requires a rather complex articulation of the modalities of 'fellow citizen' and 'foreigner', modalities which are in tension with one another because they require the recognition both of those general characteristics that a person shares with their fellow citizens, and of those particular, distinct characteristics that mark individuals out as different to their fellows. The Derridean approach to alterity is thereby presented using the theme of openness onto a world beyond the 'actual', a world irreducible to the modality of the 'shared'. The preoccupation to avoid unduly constraining the 'possible' with the 'actual' thereby constitutes a further contribution of contemporary French philosophy for theories of recognition.

On a level that is more ontological than ethical, the contribution of certain French philosophers studied in this volume consists in their concern for the way in which possibilities become overly narrowed within a horizon of mutual recognition. For Jean-Michel Salanskis (Chapter 12 of this volume),

French contributions to recognition theory

Jean-François Lyotard's post-Marxist period is particularly relevant here in helping to articulate a concern with respect to the regulatory, consensual horizon of both Habermas' and Honneth's theory which ultimately situates individuals equally, sharing the same mutually recognised norms. For Salanskis, Lyotard's primary aim in *The differend: phrases in dispute* (1988) is to prevent an economy of shared understanding and mutual recognition from predetermining the arrival of the 'possible'. For the Lyotard of *The differend*, a 'wrong' consists in the inability to express a phrase within the province of the dominant regime or genre. As soon as a phrase from another regime is expressed in the dominant regime, it loses its distinctive character and is 'wronged'. As Salanskis puts it, the social and political problem is that phrase regimens or genres of discourse are totalising with their procedures and stakes. The regulatory horizon offered by Habermas and Honneth forgets the role Lyotard ascribes to the socio-political, namely, its role as 'guardian' of the possible. This transcendent guardianship of the possible leads to a new political task, namely, artistically creating new idioms in an effort to avoid predetermining the possible so as to bear witness instead to the wrong (see also Garrau and Le Goff, 2010).

In a similar vein, Salanskis argues that the value of Emmanuel Levinas' account of the self's irrevocable responsibility before the other person does not so much equate to Honneth's idea that individuals have needs which must be cared for (since this idea reformulates the asymmetry of the self – other relation as a symmetrical account of individual needs), but rather consists in the attempt to constantly critique the residual and inevitable immorality of all general norms and laws which, as mutually recognised, ascribe moral value and political legitimacy only to shared understandings and not to the unique, particular perspectives which individual others promise to bring.

The concern that theory avoid 'colonising' the possible is also reflected in Miriam Bankovsky's contribution in the final chapter of this volume (Chapter 13). After reconstructing the different ways in which Fraser and Honneth incorporate deconstructive insights into their respective theories in the form of either transformative recognition or care, Bankovsky contrasts these forms to what she sees as the productive aspect of deconstruction, namely, its attention to the failure of general norms to respond to specific forms of harm, the very condition of Honneth's concern to diagnose and overcome social pathologies (Honneth, 2007a: 80–96). She argues that her own understanding of deconstruction's attention to failure finds a correlate not in Honneth's and Fraser's respective understandings of deconstruction but rather in their commitment to the idea of progress in history (on a par with 'democracy-to-come'), by means of which they implicitly concede that the application of their theories cannot guarantee justice in the present. Honneth's idea of moral progress effectively admits that the institution of norms which are mutually recognised does not

Deepening critical theory: French contributions

include every possible norm worthy of mutual recognition, and this concession is the source of Honneth's idea that claims for recognition contain a 'surplus' of validity, that is, a claim which is valid even though it is not formulated as a norm that all subjects mutually recognise. Likewise, Fraser is unable to provide absolute criteria to negotiate the tension between competing demands for economic and redistributive justice, on the one hand, and for cultural and recognitive justice, on the other, and must also engage, at least implicitly, with a deconstructive idea of progress (see also Bankovsky, forthcoming).

Such reflections are intended to converge with Tully's critique of the 'finality presumptions' of much recognition theory, which assumes that there are definitive and final solutions to struggles over recognition, in both theory and in practice (Tully, 2004: 91, see also 95–8; Tully, 2008: 306). As David Owen points out in his contribution to the debate (Chapter 6 in this volume), Tully's rejection of the orientation to finality should remind us that no matter what procedures for the exchange of reasons are applied to proposed norms of mutual recognition, in either theory or practice, an element of 'reasonable disagreement' or 'reasonable dissent' will always remain.

We hope, with such reflections, to encourage recognition theorists to engage more explicitly with the constitutive gap between the 'actual' and the 'possible'. As Drucilla Cornell correctly points out, this gap is critical to the very concept of justice itself because it makes possible the essential transformability and perfectibility of the actual, without which the project of justice would make no sense. By keeping open the essential possibility of determining justice in view of as yet unimaginable possibilities, responding to specific forms of harm, deconstructive justice is, states Cornell, 'more utopian' (Cornell, 1992: 182).

Concluding reflections: reopening the dialogue

We have now identified a number of themes which contemporary French thought promises to contribute to the theory of recognition, with a view to furthering the goal Horkheimer ascribes to critical theory, that of 'liberat[ing] human beings from the circumstances that enslave them' (1982: 244). In so doing, we have not only shown that French philosophy has already served as an important resource for theories of recognition, but we have also identified the different ways in which French philosophy promises to illuminate aspects of the recognitive process which are often ignored. French philosophy's wariness of the notion of 'authentic identity' on which the Hegelian approaches depend generates a heightened sensitivity to the negative or reifying aspects of norms of recognition. This sensitivity also carries over into an awareness of the phenomenal and embodied nature of subjectivation processes and the manner in which structural factors impact upon the lived experience of the oppressed. French social theory in turn draws attention to underlying social forces which prevent marginalised subjects from wanting to engage in a critique of their society, thereby contributing a nuanced account of power to the 'critique of oppression'. French philosophy also brings a critical perspective to the notion of symmetrical equality often associated with norms of recognition, highlighting the importance of asymmetrical relations of care. Finally, French theory encourages recognition theory to maintain a critical perspective upon itself, recognising that the project of justice makes little sense without the recognition of the essential transformability and perfectibility of the actual (which includes theory itself).

In closing, we would like to consider the idea that the openness of recognition theorists to French philosophy in fact represents something about the very theory itself, namely, an attempt (expressed in the very construction of its theory) to recognise the other's difference, in this case, the French other, rather than colonising that relation in advance. We mentioned earlier that in the context of the dominant Anglophone and German tradition, contemporary French thought has often been presented as having little to offer to a constructive account of morality and politics and, in a sense, the popular rejection of French concerns could be viewed, from the perspective of recognition theory, as a denial of recognition in Honneth's third sphere, that is, a denial of the potential value of French contributions to civil society. What is striking about Honneth's ecumenical approach to theory construction is his attempt to recognise the distinct contributions which each tradition (including the French tradition) makes to social life. In this sense, and as Honneth himself explains in the interview published in this volume (Chapter 2), his openness to French philosophy is 'deliberative' in orientation, enlarging the public space of intellectual deliberation to include the French tradition while, in so doing, questioning that very orientation itself by drawing on contemporary French insights which place importance on the non-deliberative nature of certain forms of intersubjective relations.

It is our hope that this volume will contribute to a continuing dialogue between recognition theory and contemporary French thought and, in this way, support the ends of critical theory, with important implications for constructing creative solutions to our ethical and political problems in a manner that is sensitive to the complexity of our intersubjective life.

2

The relevance of contemporary French philosophy for a theory of recognition: an interview

Axel Honneth, interviewed by Miriam Bankovsky*

THIS interview clarifies the role that the reference to contemporary French philosophy plays in the construction of the categories that define Honneth's theory of recognition. On different occasions, and with different purposes in mind, Honneth has drawn on the theories of Sartre, Foucault, Lyotard, Derrida, Levinas and even Merleau-Ponty. Here, Honneth explains his main reasons for thinking that these French theories are valuable for critical theory, while also distancing himself from certain aspects of their accounts. In so doing, Honneth identifies new avenues for dialogue between contemporary French philosophy and the German tradition of critical theory.

The interview is divided into two parts. First, Honneth clarifies the ways in which he has used contemporary French philosophy to develop his theory of recognition, and he compares this use with Habermas' relation to contemporary French philosophy. Next, Honneth identifies the relevance of contemporary French philosophy for his more recent attempts to articulate the relation between his ethics of recognition and a normative 'plural' theory of justice.

French philosophy and the ethics of recognition

Sartre: recognition as an existential and practical relation towards others
M. B. – In *The struggle for recognition,* you argue that Sartre's *Being and nothingness* presents the 'struggle for recognition' as a uniquely conflictual relation that characterises all forms of social interaction. You criticise this view for excluding the possibility of resolving conflict in interpersonal and mutually recognised forms of reconciliation (Honneth, 1995a: 141–60; see also 1995b: 158–68).[1] You then praise the implicit revision of this theory presented by Sartre's political writings, arguing that, in his *Anti-Semite and Jew* (Sartre,

1995), the struggle for recognition no longer represents an inescapable structural feature of human existence but can be overcome when recognition relations are affirmed by both parties (Honneth, 1995a: 156–9; Honneth, 1987: 82 and Honneth, 1992: 217). How does this double-edged interpretation of Sartre inform your ethics of recognition?

A. H. – Of all the post-World War II French writers, Sartre is still the most important for my work. For almost thirty years, his work has been of extreme importance for me. Indeed, I continue to rework my views on Sartre's *Being and nothingness*.

When I wrote *The struggle for recognition* (1995a), I wanted to oppose the negativism of Sartre's concept of recognition. By negativism, I mean that Sartre does not think that a stable form of mutual recognition is possible. Instead, he thinks that recognition relations between subjects are always conflictual. In contrast, I have maintained that mutual recognition is both possible and necessary. The elaboration of my own theory reflects this major difference.

However, since writing *The struggle for recognition*, I have discovered a new way of reading the famous chapters on recognition in *Being and nothingness*. I now think that these chapters provide one of the most convincing presentations of the socio-ontological and existential meaning of recognition. By this, I mean that Sartre presents recognition not so much as a state of cognition but rather as an existential relation towards others, which affects our capacity for practical action. Of course, this idea that recognition relations condition our capacity for action also informs my own work. As I became aware of the important distinction between, on the one hand, recognition viewed simply as a certain cognitive state and, on the other hand, recognition as an existential, socio-ontological stance towards others, I realised that I needed to reshape my whole interpretation of *Being and nothingness*. Sartre is one of the first to stress that recognition is not simply an epistemic stance but is part of a deeper sphere of our being-in-the-world, namely, an existential stance which we take towards others and which affects our being-in-the-world. My own account of forms of recognition as the condition for the development of self, in particular, the development of practical relations-to-self, is to some extent informed by the Sartrean idea that recognition relations play a constitutive role as concerns one's capacity to situate oneself existentially and practically in the world.

Having said that, although I learnt from Sartre's account of recognition as an existential relation, his presentation of recognition as irreducibly conflictual overlooks the ways in which conflict can be resolved into stable and positive forms of recognition which are mutually affirmed by both parties to the conflict. It is clear that Sartre's ontological framework, which takes conflict as incapable of being eliminated, prevents him from presenting recognition in a positive form, that is, in a form which is enabling for both parties.

On one level, as I have already indicated in *The struggle for recognition*, I believe that Sartre's political writings contrast with *Being and nothingness* because they imply that the strongly conflictual and negative account of recognition presented in the earlier work *can* be resolved, to some extent, in positive forms of non-conflictual, mutual recognition. In writings like *Anti-Semite and Jew* (1995), Sartre reflects on the ways in which mutual recognition among groups can actually be realised. Admittedly, he is dealing, here, with recognition relations between groups and not between individuals. However, the point is still relevant. With a view to criticising anti-Semitism as a form of social disrespect, Sartre tries to overcome the negativity of his earlier account of merely conflictual recognition by allowing for, or at least indicating, the possibility of a positive form of mutual recognition between groups, one which resolves the initial conflict.

On another level, however, it is fair to say that Sartre never managed to bring these two elements together: he could not reconcile his concept of existential negativism, on the one hand, with the promise, implied by his political writings, of sublimating conflict into positive forms of mutual recognition. Indeed, Sartre's late book on morality, *Notebooks for an ethics* (1992), is quite disappointing in its treatment of recognition, returning to the merely negativistic account wherein alienation is an inescapable condition. Moreover, in my view, the later *Critique of dialectical reason* (Sartre, 2004 and 2006) no longer presents recognition as an existential stance, as per *Being and nothingness*. It is precisely the existential account of recognition which has drawn my attention back to *Being and nothingness* in recent times.

In summary, in spite of a fruitful account of recognition as an existential stance in *Being and nothingness* and the promise of an account of positive, mutual recognition among groups in *Anti-Semite and Jew*, both of which I have drawn on and developed when elaborating my own concept of intersubjectivity, Sartre does not attempt to defend the possibility of positive forms of recognition which mark intersubjective experience and freedom. I defend this possibility and this remains a central difference between our approaches to recognition.

M. B. – Could I ask you to clarify the difference between your own concept of conflict and that of Sartre? On the one hand, you distance yourself from Sartre's concept of conflict. On the other hand, the notion of conflict and struggle is fundamental to your own theory; you continually draw attention to the moral importance of conflict. Could you say a little more about how your own understanding of conflict differs with what you call Sartre's 'conflictual negativism'? Is there any equivalent to Sartre's conflictual existentialism in your own concept of conflict?

A. H. – There is nothing equivalent to Sartre's conflictual negativism in my own work. While the idea of conflict is certainly central to my theory, it has a completely different sense to Sartre's concept of conflict.

French contributions to recognition theory

Sartre presents the idea that all forms of recognition by others are immediately, and at the same time, forms of objectification. This is an essential part of his theory, at least in *Being and nothingness*. In fact, in my view, Sartre's notion that the other 'takes my world away' is characteristic of a certain French tradition which begins with Rousseau. For Rousseau, recognition distracts people from an awareness of their own true convictions and desires, leading to social decline (Rousseau, 1984). Continuing in this line, Lacan, Sartre and, most clearly, Althusser also present the idea that recognition objectifies. For Althusser, 'interpellation' is misrecognition (Althusser, 1971: 127–88). The framework which Sartre offers in *Being and nothingness* further develops these concerns. For Sartre, recognition *reduces* subjects to certain capacities or to certain existential choices. In the French tradition, then, recognition is usually identified with objectification or reification.

In contrast, the German tradition never viewed recognition as objectifying or negative. Following Hegel and Fichte, we present recognition as positive and enabling. Recognition, mutual recognition, allows subjects to view themselves as having certain capacities, enabling them to actually realise their freedom. I am clearly a representative of the German tradition, whereas Sartre's work forms part of the French tradition or the certain French sub-tradition which I have just described.

Consequently, the accounts of 'conflict' which Sartre and I offer are very different. Sartre's version of 'conflict' is ontological and existential: it cannot be overcome. In contrast, I view conflict as something which *can* be overcome. Conflict must be sublimated in new forms which are mutually recognised by both parties. In this sense, although it is clear that I disagree with Sartre's existential account of conflictual recognition, it had an enormously fruitful impact on the formation of my own thinking, especially for my later work on reification (Honneth, 2008a). I ascribe a moral imperative to those conflictual situations in which the other 'steals' my world from me (Sartre, 1958: 279, 386). Sartre's ontological idea that the other always and necessarily 'steals' my world becomes, in my theory, a situation to be overcome. In so doing, I try to learn from Sartre while avoiding the negative consequences which accompany his merely conflictual concept of recognition.

M. B. – Your positive appreciation of some aspects of Sartre's work contrasts with Habermas' negative dismissal of the latter. Habermas writes that 'intersubjectivity remained something, if not entirely foreign, secondary for Sartre' and that *Being and nothingness* does not achieve the necessary break with the traditional philosophy of consciousness (Habermas and Wolin, 1992: 497). Could you say a little more about the difference between your interpretation and Habermas'?

The relevance of contemporary French philosophy

A. H. – Habermas never dealt carefully with Sartre's work. He would have read Sartre early on in the 1950s, when so many people in Germany were reading Sartre. However, Habermas soon came to believe that Sartre's approach is limited by a certain, outdated philosophical tradition, namely, the philosophy of consciousness. He rejected Sartre's work, shifting his own analyses from monological structures of consciousness to intersubjective forms of action.

Habermas' dismissal of Sartre requires that one accept a black and white distinction between philosophy of language and philosophy of consciousness. I do not accept this distinction. The main difference between our views is that Habermas believed, and still believes, that our *only* access to phenomena of consciousness is by means of a language, by what is linguistically articulated. Consequently, his analyses focus uniquely on the structure of language itself. In my view, this premise is no longer correct. We have learnt, in the last twenty years, that we have other forms of access to phenomenological consciousness which do not require that language itself be the sole object of analysis. For example, I believe that it is possible to give a relatively accurate description of certain emotional reactions, without necessarily focusing the analysis on their linguistic representation. Phenomena which are not automatically mirrored in linguistic articulation can then be analysed, for example, emotions felt at the level of the body, and even the direction and cognitive content of such emotions. The view that we can only understand the activity of consciousness by analysing its representation in language presumes that only linguistic facts are accessible to us. However, this view is unconvincing. If we generalise our analyses slowly and carefully, phenomenological description can attain a validity which extends beyond the perspective of the observer.

The medium of language has a far greater priority for Habermas than for myself. It is precisely the phenomenological aspect of the French tradition which I find appealing. This is also why I am interested in the philosophy of mind which is not dissimilar to the early phenomenological tradition. Habermas does not share this attraction.

Foucault: the productivity of power

M. B. – **As with Sartre, your relation to Foucault is both critical and positive. From which aspects of Foucault's work do you distance yourself? Conversely, which aspects of Foucault's work have had a positive impact on your theory of recognition?**

A. H. – In *The critique of power* (1991) and *The fragmented world of the social* (1995b), I praised Foucault for drawing attention to the conflictual dimension of social interaction, conceived as a network of strategic actions. However, I also voiced the following concern. When Foucault systematically explains social interaction in systems-theoretic terms, he overlooks the fact that subjects have the capacity to participate, themselves, in the normative self-critique of their own society. Unfortunately, Foucault views subjects as atomistic, monological individuals who are constitutively isolated from each other and fully determined by their place in the power system (Honneth, 1991: 99–203; 1995b: 121–34; 1996: 392–3). I distance myself from Foucault's view of individuals, insisting instead on the fact that subjects are intersubjectively related to each other within recognition relations which condition practical freedom.

As I did with Sartre, I continued to develop my relation to Foucault, becoming more and more aware of the fruitfulness of his concept of power (Honneth, 1991: xiii – xxxii and 2003: 15–26). I still think that Foucault runs into difficulties with his theory of power, the very same systems-theoretical and structural difficulties which I described in the aforementioned texts and which prevent Foucault from ascribing intersubjective agency to subjects themselves. However, this no longer prevents Foucault's writings from being the source of productive insight for my own work.

I have since learned that Foucault's concept of power is much more productive than I had initially thought. Power has an enabling character: power is a certain way of organising things by means of which subjects are able to relate to themselves in specific ways and to act in certain ways. I have learnt a lot from Foucault's descriptions of society's mechanisms for reproducing itself, for organising power, and for organising state authority by decentralised instances of power. Indeed, this concept of power is very similar to certain Wittgensteinian ideas. Both Wittgenstein and Foucault think that ways of life, images and discourses constitutively determine what we are able to think and do. In this sense, Foucault's account of the productivity of power provides an access to the idea of ideology, which I was not so aware of in my early work. In some of my more recent writings, I enrich my own theory of the social by using Foucault's notion of productive power to explain how certain forms of recognition, certain public displays of social value, can, in fact, reproduce regulative patterns of social domination, whereby individuals are encouraged to adopt a particular conception of themselves, voluntarily conforming to the established system of expectations instead of seeking liberation from domination (Honneth, 2007b: 343). In an article on some of the paradoxes of contemporary capitalism, co-authored with Martin Hartmann, I implicitly make use of Foucault's idea of regulative power in order to show how some of the emancipatory ideals of the social democratic period have since become ideological instruments of capitalist accumulation (Hartmann and Honneth, 2006: 41–58).

In sum, while rejecting those aspects of Foucault's work which deny the way in which intersubjective recognition relations can permit the internal critique of society by subjects themselves, I have nonetheless drawn on his analyses of power's formative role in reproducing subjects and societies.

M. B. – Habermas appears to share your concern that Foucault overlooks the capacity for subjects to participate in the critique of their own society. While Habermas agrees with Foucault that reason is a 'thing of this world' and not of a subject, he nevertheless criticises the latter for not affirming the implications of the 'performative contradiction' of using reason to criticise reason (Habermas, 1990a: 238–326). Does your own reading of Foucault add anything further to that of Habermas? Or do you share this view of Foucault?

A. H. – Habermas and I wrote our respective criticisms of Foucault at around the same time, which means that the criticisms that I voiced in *The critique of power* (1991) were developed independently of Habermas' critique of Foucault. Having said that, we do appear to bring the same criticism to bear on Foucault, both of us warning against explaining social interaction in purely systems-theoretic terms, as Foucault is wont to do. Foucault tends to present the subject as completely determined by power in the structuralist sense, eliminating inter-subjective agency.

On the other hand, I try to remain much more open than Habermas to the many fruitful elements in Foucault's writing. Our difference lies in the use which each of us make of Foucault. I place more emphasis than does Habermas on the productive aspect of power which Foucault theorises and I make use of this Foucauldian insight when analysing the structure of modern societies.

Lyotard, Derrida and Levinas: supplementing equality with asymmetrical responsibility

M. B. – In 'The Other of justice: Habermas and the ethical challenge of postmodernism' (Honneth, 1995c: 289323), you deal with the normative relevance of the work of Lyotard, Derrida and Levinas. On one hand, you argue that Lyotard's ethics brings nothing new to Habermas' moral principle of equality. On the other hand, you suggest that Derrida, following Levinas, defends a principle of unilateral, disinterested care and that this should supplement Habermas' framework of reciprocal equal treatment. How does your ethics of recognition incorporate both demands, that is, equal treatment and unilateral care? Also, what are the central differences between your own and Habermas' relations to Lyotard and Derrida?

A. H. – First, there is an important difference in the way in which Habermas and I relate to the philosophical approaches of Lyotard, Derrida and Levinas. Habermas comes at these writers from the perspective of the philosophy of language. Believing that deconstruction's account of language as free play threatens his own presentation of language oriented toward mutual understanding, he turned to deconstruction with a view to defending his own theory from Derrida's account (Habermas, 1990a: 184–210). And given that he did not see any real alternative theory of language in Lyotard's account, Habermas never gained any sustained interest in Lyotard.

My own interest in Lyotard and Derrida does not turn on their philosophy of language. In contrast, I came to their writings because I wanted to work out the implications of an ethical principle which is *not* uniquely oriented toward mutual understanding but which instead emphasises asymmetrical responsibility for others. I wanted to explore the ethical and moral importance of the possibility of non-deliberative, non-consensual interrelations.

I soon lost my interest in Lyotard when I realised that he cannot but end up with an approach much like discourse ethics itself. Against Lyotard's own intention, he remains committed to the horizon of a deliberative consensus. The normative intention of Lyotard's account of bringing 'silent' disputes to ethical awareness is precisely the idea of reciprocal and mutual recognition among persons from a standpoint of equality.[2]

In contrast, my interest in Derrida grew because he helped me to see the importance of a completely different ethical concept, namely, the obligation to treat people *unequally* (if I can put it like that). This is the idea that there exists a certain one-sided obligation for others in our life-world. I fully appreciated the radicality of the idea which Derrida, following Levinas, was attempting to delineate: the asymmetry of true ethics, respect before its symmetrisation. I realised that Habermas had overlooked the importance and the simple fact of asymmetries in our lives; ethical relations which cannot be articulated in terms of mutual respect or equal treatment but must be expressed in terms of unilateral, affective relations like care or love. There were other French writers who helped me to the same degree, not only Levinas, but also Paul Ricoeur, who for a certain period had similar ideas.

My interest in Derrida's non-reciprocal ethics of the gift also complements my interest in the French sociologist Marcel Mauss' idea of gift-giving. I have always been interested in the intersubjectivity of the idea of the gift, an idea which plays a big role in French thinking even today. This differentiates me from Habermas, who never developed an interest in the sociology of the gift. Although Habermas is very familiar with the work of French sociologist Emile Durkheim, he did not study the tradition which Durkheim indirectly founded via Mauss and others. I try to make a place for the importance of the gift and gift exchange within my own intersubjectivist framework.

In this way, I have used what I see as deconstructive ethics to deepen Habermas' theory of freedom, insisting that mutually recognised norms can only succeed in expressing the freedom of participating subjects if these norms allow subjects to present themselves in intersubjective structures of public life without shame. It is not enough to be able to participate as equals who, on the Habermasian model, mutually accord each other egalitarian rights. One also needs the solicitude of others in the affective relations of love and friendship, that is, unilateral, unconditional care. The realisation that I needed to supplement Habermas' principle of equal treatment with a unilateral principle of care was even a path to something that I would later formulate as 'pluralistic justice' (Honneth, 2004: 358 and 352–3; Fraser and Honneth, 2001: 170, 174–5, 180-1).

M. B. – When you say that, unlike Habermas, you were *not* interested in deconstruction as a philosophy of language, do you mean that you view deconstruction as a theory of existential relations between persons?

A. H. – Yes, I am interested in deconstruction because of its account of asymmetry as a fundamental existential category. I was aware that by approaching deconstruction from this perspective, I was doing some harm to Derrida's work by not dealing with the deepest elements of his thinking. However, I decided to situate him within the phenomenological tradition rather than the philosophy of language. Doing so even allowed me to see a certain similarity between Derrida and Ricoeur who, I'm sure, didn't really have a lot in common.

M. B. – It seems to me that by reformulating the notion of existential *inequality* in terms of a normative ethics of care, you are effectively determining the moral content of deconstruction once and for all. Derrida, the champion of the im/possible, would probably remind us here that concepts like 'care' and 'love' cannot fully determine the ethical relation and indeed remain themselves deconstructible. Shouldn't one also affirm (against your own interpretation) that the deconstructive imperative is *not* exhausted by an ethics of care and love?

A. H. – I agree. Derrida would probably object to my use of deconstruction. He would remind me that deconstruction is *not* fully equivalent to the ethics of care and love which I identify with deconstruction. However, my aim was to take from Derrida what was most useful for my own work, namely, an alternative ethical principle to Habermas' principle of equality. My relation to Derrida is more or less instrumental: I do not concern myself with deconstruction's deeper mission. Derrida would not have been entirely happy about the use which I make of deconstruction because he would have been suspicious of the positive notion of care which I identify with the idea of a non-reciprocal ethics of the gift.

However, drawing on a philosopher's work with a view to developing one's own project is often the most productive way to deal with some writers. Again, this meant that my interest in Derrida was never as deep as my interest in Foucault and especially in Sartre, whose perspectives have a greater overlap with my own work.

French philosophy and the spheres: care and cooperation

M. B. – You share, with Habermas, a commitment to a moral and political ideal of undistorted communication relations in social and public life. As you mentioned earlier, you deepen Habermas' ideal with the idea that mutually recognised norms can only succeed in supporting freedom if they allow subjects to participate in social and public life without shame. On your view, communication relations are undistorted only if all parties can take part, with self-confidence, self-respect and self-esteem, in three spheres of intersubjective relations, these being affective, legal and cooperative.

Has the work of these French philosophers contributed to your elaboration of these three spheres of interrelations? Would it be correct to say that you use the French philosophers to develop the affective sphere of love and care (necessary for self-confidence) and the sphere of cooperative relations (necessary for self-esteem), but *not* the sphere of legal reciprocal relations (necessary for self-respect) since this latter sphere has already been adequately developed by Habermas?

A. H. – It is completely true to say that I have used French philosophy to elaborate the spheres of intimacy and social esteem but not the sphere of equal respect. The phenomenological tradition of French thinking has always been relatively weak as concerns the sphere of equal mutual respect. This weakness is curious, especially when one considers the strong role which the idea of equal respect plays in the French republic. It would be interesting to consider the reasons why the concern with equal respect is only marginal for the French phenomenological tradition which we have been discussing. Perhaps the focus on the ethical relevance of asymmetry, inequality and conflict is a product of a certain critical spirit of rebellion against the dominant moral values of the French republican tradition.

Consequently, I find that the work of Sartre, Foucault, Levinas and Derrida is most interesting and fruitful for my work not only as concerns the sphere of love and care, but also social esteem. Sartre, Levinas and Derrida deepen our understanding of the first sphere, that is, the non-reciprocal relations of love and care, of social intimacy and dependence. They do so by emphasising the value of asymmetrical responsibility. Moreover, Foucault and, once again, Sartre deepen our understanding of the question of social esteem, the third sphere. Foucault tries to explain how the discursive background of social esteem – namely, value orientations and ethical perspectives – is established and altered by the mechanisms of regulative power. And Sartre's later work broadens our understanding of the mechanisms of collective action and social cooperation in which social esteem is rooted.

However, one finds very little, in the work of each of these philosophers, on the middle sphere of equal respect and rights.

The relevance of contemporary French philosophy

French philosophy and justice

Freedom

M. B. – In your 2008 seminar series in Germany and France, you identified two concepts of freedom with their associated concepts of justice, distinguishing these from a third concept, namely, your own Hegelian concept of social freedom with its associated concept of justice. You explain that the first concept, negative freedom or the absence of constraint, found in the work of Hobbes, Locke and Nozick, is associated with a concept of justice conceived as a contract among consenting individuals who desire to protect their negative freedom. The second concept you identify is reflexive freedom that occurs in two forms, that is, reflexive self-legislation (Kant, Rousseau, Habermas, Rawls) or reflexive self-articulation (Herder, Humboldt, Taylor). As self-legislation, freedom is taken up by a procedural account of justice where principles are the result of all individual acts of self-legislation, that is, procedures of cooperative will-formation. As self-articulation, freedom is associated with the teleological goal of articulating one's self in cooperation with others in a community.

You then claim that your own account of 'social freedom' fixes the deficiencies of both negative and reflexive freedom by adding a further component, namely, the co-imbrication of freedom and intersubjective, social relations. The concept of 'social freedom', you state, requires a 'plural' concept of justice, wherein claims can be made in reference to any one of the three types of intersubjective relation necessary for freedom (affective, reciprocal, or cooperative).

We have just discussed your positive use of Sartre, Foucault, Derrida and Levinas. Do you think that these thinkers affirm a concept of freedom which falls into the three-fold typology of freedom which you are laying out (negative freedom, reflexive freedom as self-legislation or self-articulation, or your own social freedom)? Have you drawn on the concepts of freedom which Sartre, Foucault and Derrida defend when elaborating your own concept of social freedom?

A. H. – It is not easy to work out the nature of the concept of freedom which Derrida, Foucault or Sartre use. I do not think that these thinkers have been particularly useful to my task of elaborating upon the notion of freedom which is of highest importance to me, namely, the Hegelian notion of social freedom.

I do think one finds some elements of social freedom in the later Sartre's *Critique of dialectical reason* insofar as he makes the realisation of individual freedom dependent on participation in collective and cooperative action or in institutionalised practices. That said, the notion of freedom which Sartre uses in *Being and nothingness* is strictly and radically negative: the other in the social life-world steals my freedom. Sartre's account is typical of a purely negative concept of freedom. In contrast, my own theory affirms the ways in which intersubjective relations of recognition between self and others enable the self to realise its freedom. The relation between self and other is not negative but enabling.

It is more difficult to specify Foucault's notion of freedom. To a certain degree, and even against his own self-understanding, Foucault has an idea of what I refer to as a type of reflexive freedom. His is 'aesthetic freedom', that is, self-articulation and self-discovery. This is especially clear if you look at his later writings on articulating the self. Here Foucault develops an account of how the subject might become independent of those dominant expectations which inform conceptions of self, by carefully articulating one's own way of relating to the world. This process is described in aesthetic terms; self-articulation provides access not only to independent opinions and convictions, but also to new forms of conduct including bodily behaviours and desires. In this sense, the later Foucault can be said to move in the direction of the romantic idea of reflexive self-articulation that we find in the work of Herder and Humboldt. However, I remain critical of Foucault's notion of freedom. Foucault overlooks the social bases of self-articulative freedom, partly because his concept of the subject is too atomistic. Once again, on its own, Foucault's concept of freedom is not equivalent to the Hegelian notion of freedom which I defend because it does not highlight the intersubjective and social bases of freedom.

Derrida's is the most complicated case. Defending the view that we cannot even formulate a positive content for freedom, Derrida instead tries to identify all the various problems which prevent one from being able to realise, or even give content to, freedom. The deconstructive machinery is probably intended to make us aware of the difficulties involved in claiming that one is free. In contrast to Derrida, I assume that freedom can be given a positive content and that it can be realised. This is very different to Derrida's account.

So, to summarise, the concepts of freedom which Sartre and Foucault affirm can, in some senses, be said to fall into the typology of freedom which I am laying out; Sartre's concept is negative, whereas Foucault's is reflexive, in the form of self-articulation. My own Hegelian concept of social freedom moves beyond both of these concepts. Social freedom is not negative but positive and enabling. Social freedom is not atomistic self-articulation but rather an intersubjective pursuit.

Derrida is unique in that his concept of freedom appears not to fall into my typology because he does not believe that we can even formulate a positive content for freedom.

To answer the second part of your question, I do not draw on Sartre's or Derrida's concepts of freedom. One must distinguish between, on the one hand, ideas of freedom and, on the other hand, theories of the social fabric which makes freedom possible. I have not made use of Sartre's negative concept of freedom, but I have used elements of his account of the substance or social fabric of the spheres, that is, the social fabric of the spheres necessary for freedom (the spheres of recognition relations which bear on intimacy and social esteem). In this sense, I have learnt less about the idea of freedom by which the spheres of intimacy and social esteem are constituted and more about the social fabric of the spheres themselves.

Similarly, with Derrida, I have not made use of his analyses concerning the difficulties involved in claiming that one is free, but I have used elements of his account of the social fabric of the sphere of affectivity, intimacy and care. I have drawn on his account of ethics as care so as to argue that asymmetrical responsibility towards another allows this other to develop the ability to trust in their own emotions and to have confidence in their assessment of their own needs. When I realised that Habermas' principle of equal treatment needed to be supplemented by deconstruction's asymmetrical principle of care, I also recognised that a theory of justice would have to affirm a number of different and even conflicting principles, one for each sphere of intersubjective relation. This was the path to what I now call 'plural justice'. To repeat what I have stated elsewhere, if a moral claim is shaped by an appeal to love then the principle of need has priority; in legally shaped relationships the principle of equality takes priority; and in cooperative relationships the principle of merit drives the formulation of validity claims (Honneth, 2004: 358 and 352–3; see also Fraser and Honneth, 2001: 170, 174–5, 180–1).

With Foucault, it is the other way around. From the later Foucault, Herder and Humboldt, I have learnt about the importance of the idea of self-articulation and of the distinctions one has to be aware of when reconstructing the idea of freedom as self-articulation. However, Foucault is not so useful to the task of specifying the social fabric or substance of the spheres of realised freedom because he does recognise that self-articulation is, in fact, dependent on intersubjective relations of recognition. Consequently, I have learnt less from Foucault about the social fabric or substance of the spheres of freedom and more about the core idea of freedom by virtue of which the spheres are constituted, that is, self-articulation. Foucault does not provide an account of how freedom as self-articulation actually works between subjects, that is, at an intersubjective and social level.

To summarise, then, I have drawn on Sartre and Derrida when elaborating the substance or social fabric of the spheres. However, I have not learnt much from them about the social freedom which, following Hegel, I defend. Conversely, Foucault's core idea of freedom as self-articulation is similar to my own, but I have learnt nothing from him about the intersubjective social fabric of this idea because Foucault, in contrast to me, does not appear to view aesthetic freedom as an intersubjective pursuit.

Deconstructive justice and 'progress'

M. B. – Do you think there is an aspect of Derrida's concept of justice that coincides with the commitment to 'progress' which informs your plural concept of justice? I am wondering whether Derrida's presentation of justice as a regulative idea which is both possible and impossible resembles your commitment to 'progress' in the quality of recognition relations. On the one hand, as you said earlier, one has to assume that mutual recognition is possible, for otherwise it cannot be pursued as a meaningful goal. On the other hand, your commitment to continual 'progress' in the quality of recognition relations suggests that one *cannot* achieve mutual recognition: progress is always possible because mutual recognition is never fully possible. Is mutual recognition a regulative idea which is both possible *and* impossible in the Derridean sense? Is your theory open-ended in the deconstructive sense?

A. H. – I would say that yours is a correct description of my ideas. There is a certain element of unattainability in my account of making and responding to normative demands concerning recognition relations in each of the three spheres. The core normative principles of these spheres (the obligation to respond to deficits in the conditions for self-confidence, self-respect and self-esteem) will always have surplus meanings and there will exist validity claims that we cannot fully satisfy by our social practices. But we nonetheless have an understanding of what constitutes that surplus of validity. This understanding makes mutual recognition possible even if it cannot be fully satisfied within our intersubjective relations.

By 'surplus validity', I mean that all institutionalised normative principles express an ideal which is never satisfied by the already given social forms of its fulfilment or realisation; there is always something which has not yet been realised, so that the principle motivates us to continue our efforts to search for its institutional realisation. I'm not fully sure whether this resembles Derrida's idea of possibility and impossibility. Sometimes one finds formulations in Derrida which appear to be similar. For me, we need to identify and overcome the difference which exists between those principles which we think should have a normative role for social practice and those which are already built into our social practices. This is a distinction between the regulative and actual; the idea that we have certain normative principles which already function in our social practices (like the idea of care, or equal justice, or social esteem) and that we also have to become aware of, and draw attention to, the endless surplus meaning of these principles. This is a Kantian idea: the idea of the idea, in Kant. Kant's practical ideas serve the function of motivating us to continue our struggle for social emancipation. Derrida might well have had a similar distinction in mind. If this is the picture Derrida tries to present in his writings on the im/possibility of democracy and justice, then my own account of the normative goal of recognition might be close to it.

M. B. – As we discussed earlier, you have argued that Habermas' commitment to the norm of equal treatment must be supplemented by the deconstructive commitment to a principle of moral responsibility for the needs of the concrete other (Honneth, 1995c). It is foreseeable that moral claims raised in the affective sphere by an appeal to love and need might conflict with claims raised in the reciprocal sphere subject to the principle of equality. When claims in different spheres conflict with each other, how are we to decide which principle is to take priority? Do we find, here, a moment of what Derrida might refer to as 'undecidability', that is, the notion that a decision must be made without any absolute criteria?

A. H. – I think that the notion of 'undecidability' is often too exaggerated, too hyperbolic. In my view, 'undecidability' simply refers to the unavoidable fact that, in cases of conflict, there are no universally acceptable solutions. This means that we have to take it on ourselves to find a solution. We are responsible for finding a solution because we live under the constraints of action. There has to be a decision, but this decision might not be justifiable in a more general way. It seems to be an existential fact of our lives that in certain situations we have to take it upon ourselves to make a decision between conflicting spheres of recognition.

Concluding reflections

M. B. – In contrast to Habermas, whose relation to contemporary French philosophy is almost exclusively critical, your own work seems to consciously attempt to reflect on the potential utility of French philosophy for a critical theory of society. Do you think that your own openness to contemporary French philosophy is fundamentally 'deliberative' in orientation, that is, do you see yourself as enlarging the public space of intellectual deliberation? Or do you have other reasons for wishing to draw on French philosophy? Does your positive engagement with French philosophy instead indicate a critique of the uniquely 'deliberative' orientation?

A. H. – On one level, there is certainly a deliberative element to my openness to French philosophy. The intention of broadening the horizon of critical theory by incorporating traditions from many other countries is a deliberative intention.

However, my openness to French philosophy was also motivated by what I see as a non-deliberative and pre-reflexive rebellion of a younger man against his teachers (see also Critchley and Honneth, 1998: 34). To a certain degree, my interest in the French tradition, which I had from very early on, was a reaction to a certain overemphasis on the importance of the American and English tradition for German philosophy. This interest equates to a rebellion, among representatives of a younger generation, against those teachers who directed their attention towards America and England, and who still believe that German philosophy can only learn from the Anglo-Saxon and analytical tradition. I believe that there is a lot to learn from the French tradition.

Moreover, on another level, and as I said earlier, I turned to writers like Derrida with a view to working out the ethical importance of an asymmetrical ethical principle which is not uniquely oriented toward deliberation and mutual understanding. As I indicated, I wanted to explore the ethical and moral importance of the possibility of non-deliberative intersubjective relations. It is primarily the phenomenological aspect of contemporary French philosophy which interests me, because it does not assume, as Habermas does, that our *only* access to phenomena of consciousness is by means of an analysis of language.

Notes

* The questions were prepared by Miriam Bankovsky with assistance from Christian Lazzeri, Alice Le Goff and Isabelle Aubert. The interview took place at the University of Frankfurt on Tuesday, 2 December 2008. Honneth and Bankovsky then modified, clarified and developed certain points in a written exchange.
1 Honneth is referring, in particular, to Part III, Chapter 1 of *Being and nothingness* (Sartre, 1958: 271–370).
2 For an alternative reading, which questions the reduction of Lyotard's ethics to the horizon of deliberative consensus, see Jean-Michel Salanskis' contribution to this volume, 'Honneth, Lyotard, Levinas' (Chapter 12).

PART II
AGONISTIC IDENTITY CONSTRUCTION

3

Impossible recognition: Lacan, Butler, Žižek

Catherine Malabou*

IN *Giving an account of oneself*, Judith Butler argues that the process of recognition presupposes, as its condition of possibility, a normativity of the visual field, 'a framework for seeing and judging ... a set of norms that exceed the perspectives of those engaged in the struggle for recognition' (Butler, 2005: 29). Recognition, as conceived by Hegel and as we find it in the *Phenomenology of spirit* (1977), cannot take place without this precondition, a normativity which Hegel himself does not take into account. The face-to-face between consciousnesses thus loses its transcendental status, its value as originary structure, and is supplanted by something anterior to it, the sense *of the gaze*.

Butler, therefore, but also Lacan and Žižek, view Hegel as an important thinker, whose work cannot be ignored, while in each case addressing to him the same critique: there can only be recognition between consciousnesses if the meaning of the gaze of the consciousnesses engaged in this scene is already fixed or determined in advance in a non-dialectical fashion. What does this mean? The sense of the gaze, or the normativity of the visual field, is constituted through

> not only an epistemological framework within which the face appears, but an operation of power as well, since only by virtue of certain kinds of anthropological dispositions and cultural frames will a given face seem to be a human face to any one of us ... There is a language that frames the encounter, and embedded in that language is a set of norms concerning what will and will not constitute recognisability. This is Foucault's point and, in a way, his supplement to Hegel when he asks ... in 'What is Critique?' 'What, therefore, am "I", I who belong to this humanity, perhaps to a piece of it, at this point in time, at this instant of humanity, which is subjected to the power of truth in general and truths in particular?' (Butler, 2005: 29–30)

Recognisability would therefore be the necessary precondition for recognition, a regime of truth and power that fixes the norm and the manner in which a face is exposed to view. Social and ideological vision is therefore primary in relation to phenomenological vision.

It is this hierarchy that I would like to examine here, and more specifically the importance of the normative framework which, if we follow Foucault, the concept of humanity assumes in the process of recognition. What is the normative vision of the human which makes possible the phenomenological and political recognition of this or that singularity? Must consciousness always be identified beforehand as 'human' in order to assert itself as a recognisable agent?

Lacan, Butler and Žižek examine precisely this normative value of humanity. Who determines its rules? What does it hide? Which interests does it serve? Why does this normativity figure in Hegel's text, without Hegel realising it, as it figures in all Western traditional political philosophy? This norm of the 'humanity' of consciousness functions neither as a universal – a precondition for each particular act of recognition – nor as a purely relative and empirical concept of the human, which would constitute a fragile and precarious horizon where, on an ad hoc basis, one or another process of recognition would take place. The norm enjoys precisely this specific status, which situates it between the universal and the singular.

Our three authors point out that this norm, which is presupposed by Hegelian discourse, consists in subordinating the status of the phenomenology of recognition – the other as they appear to another consciousness – to a logical decision, which both sets out and situates the anthropological context of appearance. As for this context, it remains invisible. These writers ask themselves how this invisibility can be made visible, how the logical and ideological norm can be made manifest, how a deeper form of recognition might be set out, which allows recognition's condition of possibility to be recognised. Is it possible to see the concept of humanity which the Hegelian logic puts into play, if it is this very concept which allows the other's consciousness to be seen, which renders visible the other's consciousness, when it appears facing me?

I will set out the responses to these questions elaborated by each of these three authors. They all contrast something like an oblique line with the face-to-face of consciousnesses as Hegel presents it: the presupposition of a concept of the human. They show how, in determining vision, it does not come into the field and remains invisible. We can only see it, says Butler, if we turn around – a theory of retrospective vision related to interpellation. We see it, says Žižek, by inventing a parallax view, a displacement of the apparent position of a body due to a change in the position of the observer. We see it from behind, says Lacan.

Remaining faithful to this series of inversions, we will commence with the latter affirmation. I begin by outlining the celebrated *mise en scène* elaborated by Lacan in the chapter of *Écrits* entitled 'Logical time and the assertion of anticipated certainty' (Lacan, 2006: 161–75). The problematic of recognition is presented there in the form of a logical puzzle. The sub-title of the article is, moreover, 'A new sophism':

Impossible recognition: Lacan, Butler, Žižek

> A prison warden summons three choice prisoners and announces to them the following: ... There are three of you present. I have here five disks differing only in colour: three white and two black. Without letting you know which I will have chosen, I will fasten one of them to each of you between the shoulders, outside, that is, your direct visual field – indirect ways of getting a look at the disk also being excluded by the absence here of any means by which to see your own reflection. (Lacan, 2006: 161)

The prisoners will therefore have to examine each other and deduce their own colour on the basis of what they see on the back of their companions. 'The first to be able to deduce his own colour', the warden continues, will be freed, 'but his conclusion must be founded upon logical and not simply probabilistic grounds. Keeping this in mind, it is agreed that as soon as one of you is ready to formulate such a conclusion, he will pass through this door so that he may be judged individually on the basis of his response' (Lacan, 2006: 161–2). Lacan continues: 'This having been agreed to, each of our three subjects is adorned with a white disk, no use being made of the black ones, of which there were, let us recall, but two. How can the subjects solve the problem?' (Lacan, 2006: 162)

For the prisoners, who know nothing, the only possible combinations are the following: either all three are white, or there is one white and two blacks, or there are two whites and one black.

In fact, none of the three errs. The first solution is the correct one, all three of them having a white disk on their backs. After regarding each other for a moment, they all leave together at the same time, giving the warden the correct response: 'I am a white.' Separately, each presents the following reasoning:

> I am a white, and here is how I know it. Since my companions were whites, I thought that, had I been a black, each of them would have been able to infer the following: 'If I too were a black, the other would have necessarily realised straight away that he was a white and would have left immediately; therefore I am not a black.' And both would have left together, convinced they were whites. As they did nothing of the kind, I must be a white like them. At that, I made for the door to make my conclusion known. (Lacan, 2006: 162)

The three prisoners are therefore released at the same time upon explaining the same line of reasoning.

As soon as one reflects on it or tries to explain it clearly to someone else, this situation becomes dizzying. In order to accept the line of reasoning involved, it is important to see that it rests on the simultaneity of the responses. Each person makes the same argument at the same time: I see two whites, and say to myself: 'If I was a black, the other two would see a white and a black. Then they would have to conclude that one of us would leave immediately, identifying themselves as a white, since there are only two black disks. Since this does not occur, there must be three whites.'

What strikes Lacan in this scene is the simultaneity that exists between the phenomenological and sensible apprehension of the subjects (the concrete vision of the disks), and logical structure – the rationale that underlies this vision, identical for each of the prisoners. In fact, this simultaneity is a hierarchy. Logic predominates and paradoxically precedes sensible vision. In this fiction of recognition, Lacan affirms, 'the instance of the gaze' plays a central role, but this gaze slips away, subject to 'a formal exigency' (Lacan, 2006: 166), the phenomenological eclipsed by logic. Something more than just the empirical vision of the disks is in play, namely an excess of logic – hence the fact that the prison warden insists so strongly on the importance of reasoning. For each prisoner, reasoning is 'an *intuition*', Lacan writes, 'by which the subject *objectifies* something more than the factual givens offered him by the sight of the two whites' (Lacan, 2006: 168). This something more, this excess, is what Lacan calls '*the time for comprehending*' (Lacan, 2006: 168). Each prisoner 'find[s] the key to his own problem in the inertia of his semblable' (Lacan, 2006: 168).

What is experienced by each of the prisoners is the act of recognition, which goes hand in hand with a fundamental *passivity:* I see the other, and deduce from this his or her colour and then my own. The *subject* of recognition is in fact its *object*. The subject is seen from behind, behind his or her back. The subject is both the origin of an act (reasoning) and, at the same time, subordinate to the act of the other (the object of the reasoning of the other). The subject sees him- or her-self as an element or step in the logical deduction. 'If in this race to the truth one is but alone, although not all may get to the truth, still no one can get there but by means of the others' (Lacan, 2006: 173). The logic which precedes the concrete vision of the colour of the disks is the apprehension of the simultaneous condition of the subject and the object. Now, this condition is that of humanity, which precedes all effective recognition. True reasoning, presented by Lacan at the very end of his article, is the following: '(1) A man knows what is not a man; (2) Men recognise themselves among themselves as men; (3) I declare myself to be a man for fear of being convinced by men that I am not a man' (Lacan, 2006: 174).

There is therefore a logical genesis of phenomenological vision through which the subject, subjected to the gaze of the other, both knows and discovers one's self as 'human' subject, that is, as well as object of the gaze of another. This genesis therefore precedes the phenomenological apprehension (I am black or white). Of course, the game of colours is not chosen here by chance. Lacan's claim is essentially that every particular determination – ethnic, racial, sexual – obeys the same law of the prior logical and anthropological gaze, without which any particular factual recognition would be impossible.

At the same time, this law is in no way 'natural', but is rather an act of power. The recognition of the humanity of the other, prior to any particular recognition, is never given, but is a product of a struggle and a rivalry. Thus Lacan writes: 'the "*I*" in question here defines itself through a subjectification of

Impossible recognition: Lacan, Butler, Žižek

competition with the other, in the function of logical time' (Lacan, 2006: 170).

This scene from the *Écrits* is one of mutual recognition, where one must infer identity from colour. This experience is based on a phenomenological given: one sees. However, this vision eludes the subject for it takes place behind their back. Moreover, the subjects are all seen from behind by the warden, the incarnation of the law, who sees them caught in the same confines, the same structure, that of humanity, which is given in advance, but from which, at the same time, it is very easy to be excluded. This is to say that in a sense recognition is impossible insofar as it is never a decision of a subject, but always an effect of their subjection to the law.

Butler also insists on this impossibility. The prison warden is effectively the authority which interpolates the subject and towards which the subject must turn without necessarily seeing this authority. She refers on this point to the Althusserian theory of interpellation. Being recognised implies needing, first of all, to *take responsibility* for one's human condition, a condition which marks us behind our backs and in relation to which we must always prove our innocence, even if we are guilty, as the prisoners are supposed to be. Butler writes:

> 'Submission' to the rules of the dominant ideology might then be understood as a submission to the necessity to prove innocence in the face of accusation, a submission to the demand for proof, an execution of that proof, an acquisition of the status of the subject in and through compliance with the terms of the interrogative law. To become a 'subject' is thus to have been presumed guilty, then tried and declared innocent. Because this declaration is not a single act but a status incessantly *reproduced*, to become a 'subject' is to be continuously in the process of acquitting oneself of the accusation of guilt. It is to have become an emblem of lawfulness, a citizen in good standing, but one for whom that status is tenuous, indeed, one who has known – somehow, somewhere – what it is *not* to have that standing and hence to have been cast out as guilty. Yet because this guilt conditions the subject, it constitutes the prehistory of the subjection to the law by which the subject is produced. (Butler, 1997: 118)

Butler thus radicalises the Lacanian *mise en scène* by showing that the normative and logical framework of belonging to humanity corresponds to a structure of originary guilt. For Butler, the prisoners interminably turn around to the warden...

Butler thinks through this difficulty with recourse to the Hegelian categories of the master and the slave, in this way leading Foucault's thought to revive the dialectic, in a completely unexpected way. The enemy, in the life or death struggle, she asserts, is not somebody who stands before me, but something interior – Hegel, as we know, specifies that the master and the slave are inverted figures of the same consciousness. Reread by way of the master – slave relation, the Foucauldian problematic of subjectivation becomes a logic of what Butler calls 'self-incarceration' or 'self-slavery'. By way of support for her position, she cites a passage from *Discipline and punish*:

> The man described for us, whom we are invited to free, is already in himself the effect of a subjection much more profound than himself. A 'soul' inhabits him and brings him to existence, which is itself a factor in the mastery that power exercises over the body. The soul is the effect and instrument of a political anatomy; the soul is the prison of the body. (Foucault, 1991: 30)

As a consequence, Butler sets out to interpret the master – slave dialectic on the basis of what has, to my knowledge, never before been invoked in this context: the body.

The slave, she claims, is the body of the master, as that which allows the master to exist. Firstly, the slave ensures the material conditions of the master's survival. Secondly, the slave is also the master's symbolic representative, attesting, by his presence alone, to the effectiveness of the master's domination. The slave is therefore indeed a subject body, a subjected body. The body of the slave, insofar as it is the master's body, is produced by the master. But the master, who does not work and who in this way lives in denial of any relation to the body, denies this production, or as Butler puts it, this 'projection': 'You be my body for me, but do not let me know that the body you are is my body' (Butler, 1997: 35). At stake in this relation is the very connection between sex and gender. From the beginning, gender is only a slave of sex, which says to gender: embody me but conceal this embodiment, make it banal, be a man or a woman just like everyone else.

The master's first denial immediately calls for a second. By denying the fact that the slave is his body, the master sets up his own body as being other than what it is. This, the slave, is not my body. This means: my body is the other. This capacity for denial is what will in the end make possible the liberation of the slave. The slave only becomes autonomous because, from the beginning, the master denies his own body, constituting it, in an extremely paradoxical manner, as something autonomous. For Butler, it is a question of 'disavow[ing] one's body, to render it "Other" and then to establish the "Other" as an effect of autonomy' (Butler, 1997: 35). The autonomy of gender with respect to sex appears in fact to be a heteronomy, insofar as it is commanded from the beginning by the master. Because sex has no body, it can dominate, and dominate to the point of ruining the slave's work, which Hegel presents as the slave's salvation. Hegel says: the slave makes his mark on what he makes, and this is how he himself is made (*bildet*). In reality, Butler says, this is not entirely true, for each time the master consumes what is made, he effaces the mark of the slave in order to impose his own. Once again, the slave is condemned to write on the written. What thus emerges, Butler declares, 'is less a palimpsestic object – like Kafka's topographies – than a mark of ownership produced through a set of consequential erasures' (Butler, 1997: 39).

Impossible recognition: Lacan, Butler, Žižek

The master and the slave: it is subjectivation which discovers itself, which experiences the force of the link which unites its double signification, the chain which destines the subject to itself. The body and the soul alike must try to exceed the incarceration which gives birth to them. If the master is sex, and the slave gender, it is clear that – provided that this distribution of roles is not conceptualised in a rigid fashion – gender is not a fallow field, lacking any formative cultivation. It is a product of the master, that is, of the law, which is hidden as such but which is law. Gender is, from the beginning, a slave, and if the slave is not a form – if, as Aristotle says, the slave does not stand with a straight back, he is not without form either. A slave has an essence, since it is for this essence that the slave fears during combat. In this sense, a sexual identity is never created by being liberated from the subjectivation or domination of the master, sex, as if this identity could escape its control, its power to make its mark. A sexual identity is created – for there is an irreducible share of creation and possible subversion in sexual identity, sexuality, or gender – by agreeing to efface or disseminate its own signature through the repeated imposition of the signature of the master.

This interpretation obviously displaces the Hegelian concept of formation (*Bildung*). A gender is not fabricated, as we might believe, through the repetition of a formative activity which concludes when the servile consciousness is provided access to the form of the mind, by the elaboration of a matter or a material in a reflexive or speculative surface. We have just seen that the slave never works but for their own erasure.

This passionate reading 'Foucaultises' Hegel, if I can be permitted this expression. In return, the Foucauldian analysis sees itself dialectised. This is so in the first instance because the passage by which Hegel assigns rights to the psyche: there are psychic mechanisms by which the subject is formed in submission, mechanisms that Foucault, according to Butler, does not sufficiently take into account. In the second instance, this is because this formation, in order to be an erasure of the self, nevertheless remains a form, since an identity, in the end, emerges from it.

Subjectivation is constituted through a *return* or *turn* of the subject back upon itself, a troping of the subject. In Nietzsche, for example, as Butler explains in her second chapter, the will is said to be capable of turning back upon itself (Butler, 1997: 63). The paradigm of this troping of subjectivity is provided by the Althusserian theory of interpellation. In 'Ideology and ideological state apparatuses' (1971: 127–87), Althusser takes the celebrated example of a member of the police who hails a passer-by in the street: 'Hey, you there!' The passer-by turns around, having felt immediately and personally called. Althusser infers from this that all subjectivity is constituted through such a turning around, a movement which recognises the voice, which is the voice of the law. 'The subject is the modality of power that turns on itself' (Butler, 1997: 6).

Agonistic identity construction

What kind of breathing room does an individual have at one's disposal, then, to construct one's gender, formulate one's sexual, political and social identity? What breathing room does an individual have to look in front of itself? Subjectivation is far from being a condemnation, as Butler affirms on many occasions: the construction of gender is performative. It always proceeds, that is, from a certain power of creation. Furthermore, while agreeing at root with Althusser's analysis, Butler recognises that there can be 'bad subjects', individuals who are not exhaustively identified or completely identifiable by the voice of the law. If the desire to contest power as if it was an exterior instance is in vain (as Foucault has shown, there is no 'locus of great Refusal' (Foucault, 1990: 96)), it remains the case that active resistance is possible. Insofar as every process of identification in the final analysis succeeds through failure, no identity is ever definitive. As Butler writes, 'interpellation works by failing, that is, it institutes its subject as an agent precisely to the extent that it fails to determine such a subject exhaustively in time' (Butler, 1997: 197).

The only way of bringing to an end, or at least of circumventing, the structure of infinite regression which definitively subordinates phenomenology to normative logic is the narrative, the possibility of constructing the story of one's own subjectivation, what Butler expresses with the phrase 'giving an account of oneself'.

Recognition is definitively impossible without the symbolic supplement of the account of the self. Even so, is this account itself not always determined by that from which it would like to be liberated: guilt, the 'human norm'?

> If I try to give an account of myself, if I try to make myself recognisable and understandable, then I might begin with a narrative account of my life. But this narrative will be disoriented by what is not mine, or not mine alone. And I will, to some degree, have to make myself substitutable in order to make myself recognisable. The narrative authority of the 'I' must give way to the perspective and temporality of a set of norms that contest the singularity of my story. (Butler, 2005: 37)

Here, it is less a question of producing a rational argument, as in Lacan, than of writing a kind of justification of the self in narrative form, as if a narrative would free us from the prison. In delivering my story, will I not end up being recognised, seen as I am?

Far from it. A point of view, there again, guides my pen: a series of norms, a logic, an ideology. We constantly turn back towards ourselves without being able to see it. The originary invisibility of the self thus grounds subjectivation. Under these conditions, how can we be recognised? How can we make ourselves be seen or heard?

Žižek concurs in a sense with these conclusions concerning the impossibility of recognition, but his line of reasoning is deployed in an inverse sense to

Impossible recognition: Lacan, Butler, Žižek

Butler's. For Žižek, it is the very sense of the parallax. The logical framework enters into the visual framework which it also conditions. This is why every visual phenomenon is divided into two: on one side, its empirical content, on the other, its logical structure. If we return for a moment to our prisoners, the determination of colour and of the predicate 'human' will be presented to sight together, within a split unity. If I see the table, Žižek will say, I am also in the table. The subject enters into the images, producing a stain, a blind point. Invisibility is due to this excessive presence of vision in the visible. The subject sees itself seeing by not seeing itself. I include myself in the image that I have formed, thereby producing a deformation, which is precisely the definition of the parallax. The subject is not an external observer but is itself an element in the scene. This is also true of our prisoners: they look at each other looking at each other, with nowhere to hide and no exterior vantage point:

> The paradox here is a very precise one: it is at the very point at which a pure difference emerges – a difference which is no longer a difference between two positively existing objects, but a minimal difference which divides one and the same object from itself – that this difference 'as such' immediately coincides with an unfathomable object: in contrast to a mere difference between objects, *the pure difference is itself an object*. Another name for the parallax gap is therefore *minimal difference*, a 'pure' difference which cannot be grounded in substantial properties. (Žižek, 2006: 18)

In our context, this 'pure' difference would be that between the phenomenological and the logical, between colour and the norm of belonging to humanity.

Logic is not external to phenomenology, but is a result of a division internal to the latter. This is why Žižek will add: 'the true task of thought ... is to think the self-division of the One, to think the One itself as a split within itself, as involving an inherent gap' (Žižek, 2006: 183–4). This thought of the self-division of the One corresponds to a materialist position.

This position implies that neither the ideological framework nor the logical context which govern the phenomenological scene enjoy any transcendence. If we fail to recognise, and to be recognised by, the other, it is because of this difference internal to vision which distorts perspectives and obliges me to see the other as disfigured, deformed, other than what he or she is. The impossibility of recognition is due therefore to a dialectics of vision, and not to something which happens behind the back of the visible.

The danger for thought consists in fetishising this split, in attempting to turn the parallaxical difference into an object, when this difference is nothing but a *trompe l'oeil*. According to Žižek, traditional theories of recognition do not escape such a danger, insofar as they all fetishise this difference by calling it the norm or law of subjectivation.

Many twentieth-century philosophers, reading Hegel, have insisted on the end of the system, on its closure and on absolute knowledge. They have reproached Hegel for the brutality of his rationality, the presumed suspension of the aleatory and of alterity. The twentieth century, at its close, thought it had freed itself from logical and historical negativity, and saw in this freedom its victory. Contradictions, solutions, sublated negativity, the Stalinism of the concept: finally at an end. With the fall of Hegelianism, the fall of the Wall, the fall of communism, the reign of difference and of the Other could finally begin. Democratic morality, republicanism, the revindication of the rights of man, revisited versions of messianism, anti-anti-Semitism have come to replace the critique of capitalism.

With Žižek, the necessity of the dialectic is at last affirmed: a new Hegelianism sees the day, revived and updated.

He declares, first of all, that to criticise a system from the point of view of its closure brings closure itself into existence. To contest the systematic nature of a system amounts to locking oneself into this very system, never to recover, never to escape, caught in contradiction. The desire to go beyond the bounds of the system is meaningless, even if we assert that meaning, or hermeneutics, is always situated beyond the closure.

He shows, secondly, that the thought of an absolute other, Other or other-to-come – a figure of pure transcendence, a gap through which meaning can breach the system – is always revealed, unfortunately and fatally, as the expression of a fundamental allergy to the other. Since the Other is supposed to be found beyond the closure – and since such a thought must exist within it – the Other is always situated beyond a partition, whatever we might say about it. This separation is a metaphysical limit, wall, frontier, or threshold of tolerance. The Other is never the response to the system. It is not even the question.

The violence of the system must nonetheless be denounced, since violence is always that of the system, but this cannot be done in the name of the Other. A critique of the system where there exists no outside of the system, such is Žižek's profoundly Hegelian gesture, the way in which he writes *Violence* (2009) and asks us to think it.

What exactly does 'thinking' mean, if we must renounce hermeneutics and consequently also the deeper meaning of violence – a violence supposed to exist *deep down*, that is, once again, outside of the system?

Žižek proposes that we distinguish between three modalities of violence: objective, subjective and symbolic violence (Žižek, 2009: 10). Objective, or 'abstract', violence, whose concept is drawn from Marx, is the violence of capitalism, insofar as it functions automatically, mechanically. This is the 'systemic violence of capital' (Žižek, 2009: 11). This violence could be assimilated into the Lacanian category of the Real: without lack, absence, or division. There exists finally the symbolic dimension of violence, which real or 'objective' violence resists, that is, the domain of the signification of violence. This domain of the Symbolic is what Lacan considered as dimension of the Wholly Other. But Žižek introduces a distinction between the Lacanian Wholly Other and the Wholly Other of the thinkers of difference.

In our globalised society, the first two types of violence, subjective and objective, are just the inverse of one another, two faces of the same reality. There exists, on one hand,

> 'the ultra-objective' or systemic violence that is inherent in the social conditions of global capitalism, which involve the 'automatic' creation of excluded and dispensable individuals from the homeless to the unemployed, and [on the other] the 'ultra-subjective' violence of newly emerging ethnic and/or religious, in short racist, 'fundamentalisms'. (Žižek, 2009: 12)

The mistake committed by most philosophers or theoreticians today is to accord an autonomy to this subjective violence (conducted by particular subjects or groups), by thinking that it is a result of a deep sense of anger or resentment: anger on the part of Muslims against the Western way of life, anger against the rich or the police expressed during explosions of social discontent. Hence, a subjective response is presented to subjective violence: more tolerance, along with a call for reason, education, enlightenment.

Such an illusion, according to which one can produce the meaning of violence from subjectivity, corresponds to blindness to objective or systemic violence, and leads to nothing if not to the masking of this violence (by authorising it): 'to chastise violence outright, to condemn it as "bad", is an ideological operation *par excellence*, a mystification which collaborates [with the system] in rendering invisible the fundamental forms of social violence' (Žižek, 2009: 174).

We must denounce, then, in a radical manner: 'the hypocrisy of those who, while combating *subjective violence*, commit *systemic violence* that generates the very phenomena they abhor' (Žižek, 2009: 174). To illustrate this hypocrisy, Žižek takes the example of those that call themselves 'liberal communists' – that is, ultra-capitalists, like George Soros or Bill Gates: calling themselves humanists, they do good, try to reduce subjective violence, while nourishing objective violence as much as they can. Of the group formed by these liberal communists, he writes that 'their ideology has become all but indistinguishable from the new breed of anti-globalist leftist radicals'. He later adds that,

> above all, liberal communists are the true citizens of the world. They are good people who worry. They worry about populist fundamentalists *and* irresponsible, greedy capitalist corporations. They see the "deeper causes: of today's problems: it is mass poverty and helplessness which breed fundamentalist terror. So their goal is not to earn money, but to change the world, though if this makes them more money as a by-product, who's to complain! Bill Gates is already the single greatest benefactor in the history of humanity, displaying his love for neighbours with hundreds of millions freely given to education, and the battles against hunger and malaria. (Žižek, 2009: 17)

Obviously, though, such a 'humanism' is accompanied by massive redundancies, unprecedented acts of violence inflicted on those that one claims to render non-violent. Supported by the obscurity of objective violence, subjective non-violence appears insensitive to what it considers itself open to: the lives of the poor and traumatised. This is why the violence of the liberal communist, who fights violence, and the violence of

> the blind fundamentalist exploding in rage are two sides of the same coin. While they fight subjective violence, liberal communists are the very agents of the structural violence which creates the conditions for the explosions of subjective violence. The same philanthropists who give millions for AIDS or education in tolerance have ruined the lives of thousands through financial speculation and thus created the conditions for the rise of the very intolerance that is being fought. (Žižek, 2009: 31)

This mask that the subjective and violent face-off represents (rich and responsible subjects against poor and fanatical subjects) hides behind the thought of the Other and the idea of tolerance. According to this analysis, the Other is the one who comes from elsewhere, who has no relation to the system, whose transcendence makes good sense and who is irreducible to a banal presence. Sense, the Symbolic, are confused with this outside of alterity. Why are liberal communists, or left elitists (if there is a difference) always suspicious of the Other? Why do they keep their distance, protecting themselves from the Other, by positioning it, precisely, as Other?

> Today's liberal tolerance towards others, the respect of otherness and openness towards it, is counterpointed by an obsessive fear of harassment. In short, the Other is just fine, but only insofar as not really other ... tolerance coincides with its opposite ... What increasingly emerges as the central human right in late-capitalist society is *the right not to be harassed*, which is a right to remain at a safe distance from others. (Žižek, 2009: 35)

In reality, the 'subjects' of social violence lay claim to nothing, least of all good sense. Žižek offers a striking reading of the riots of autumn 2005 in the suburbs of Paris: 'There was no particular demand made by the protesters in the Paris suburbs. There was only an insistence on *recognition*, based on a vague, unarticulated *ressentiment [feeling]*' (Žižek, 2009: 63).

It is necessary, now more than ever, to resist the 'hermeneutic temptation' (Žižek, 2009: 65), that is, to resist this obscenity that consists in finding meaning in misery, in the explosions of rage which are caused by it, and in wounds and trauma. The symbolic must not be confused with 'profound meaning'. The system must indeed be criticised, and we must affirm, again, the necessity of social struggle, *jouissance* and desire, now more than ever, while denouncing the false generosity and provocative hypocrisy of the neo-capitalists. Nevertheless, thinking does not amount to transcending the system, but consists in discovering a space for play, within the system's component parts. The aggregate needs disassembling, which does not mean opening but deforming. There is always a way to dislodge, to disconnect the machinery or the joints of the system. Sense, if there is any, is found in this torsion. The system is superimposed upon itself, as in Hegel.

For Žižek, emancipation – that is, the achievement of mutual recognition between all subjects – does not unfold by way of theories of recognition, but by way of a renewed return to revolutionary thought of a Marxist kind, which consists in refusing the reification of the parallax, in refusing, at all costs, to turn back to the 'condition of possibility'. This involves unmasking the fetishisation of difference. In this way, 'every normative determination of the "human" is only against an impenetrable ground of "inhuman"' (Žižek, 2006: 111). The inhuman here is the impossible condition of possibility for the recognition of the human, which unfolds by way of the parallaxical division, which is not human or white or black, because it is, in fact, *nothing*.

Are the three prisoners from our opening scene imprisoned, then, by the law of the symbolic, by their originary guilt, both of which determine the logical genesis of their humanity, or are they victims of an optical error, a parallax view which distorts what they see? In both cases, recognition seems impossible. Could we not say, with Lacan, that the struggle for recognition, contrary to its promise, inevitably results in subjects being '*desubjectified to the utmost*' (Lacan, 2006: 172)?

Note

* Translated by Jon Roffe and Miriam Bankovsky.

4

The politics of suffering and recognition: Foucault contra Honneth

Lois McNay

THE relationship between Foucauldian thought and the philosophy of recognition has never been straightforward. Foucault and many of his contemporaries were explicitly hostile to the existential reinterpretations of Hegel's struggle for recognition that dominated the post-war intellectual scene in France in the work of thinkers such as Kojeve, Hippolyte, Sartre and de Beauvoir. In reaction to the centrality of the idea of recognition to Marxist thought, Foucault and his generation developed ways of thinking about power, self-hood and identity that explicitly resisted incorporation into any kind of notion of a dialectical intersubjective encounter. Since the 1990s, the idea of the struggle for recognition has acquired renewed prominence in contemporary thought through the publication of two influential works, Axel Honneth's *The struggle for recognition* (1995a) and Charles Taylor's *Multiculturalism and the politics of recognition* (1992).

Both these works have had a significant impact on the understanding of political conflict as driven not just by rational and strategic interests but also by feelings of shame and suffering that arise from misrecognition, that is, society's failure to meaningfully acknowledge certain individuals and groups as worthy of respect and esteem. The stress placed on psychological injury and suffering, as well as its transcendence through the realisation and public acknowledgment of 'authentic' identities does little to allay the hostility of Foucauldian thinkers to the idea of recognition. Indeed, Foucault's work on disciplinary normalisation has formed one of the primary sources for a powerful critique of the politics of recognition as a type of 'suffer-mongering' (Brown and Halley, 2002: 33) which binds individuals into a perpetual assertion of victim-hood resulting in a moralistic and dead-end politics of pity.

On the face of it, Axel Honneth's work on recognition struggles and his 'phenomenology of injustice' seems to perfectly encapsulate the troubling tendencies of this politics of the wound that attributes an incontestable moral legitimacy to the experience of suffering. However, in staging an encounter between Honneth and Foucauldians, I argue here that the latter fail to appreciate the analytical centrality of a phenomenological perspective on suffering for understanding crucial aspects of domination. In their overhasty elision of the experience of suffering with an uncritical subjectivism, Foucauldians ignore how an interpretative perspective on the experience of suffering is crucial for disclosing certain submerged or 'invisible' types of oppression that fall below the threshold of public attention. Furthermore, Honneth's work on social suffering alerts us to how the internalisation of domination – symbolic violence – prevents individuals from becoming effective political agents capable of acting in their own interests. Foucauldians tend to conceptualise agency and freedom as non-identity, that is, as an exploration of the submerged ethical potential for otherness within the actual. They do not sufficiently consider how the incorporated effects of symbolic violence as feelings of powerlessness, despair, or resignation may undermine the capacity of individuals to act in such a contestatory fashion. In short, Foucauldians, along with other post-foundational political thinkers, too easily presume the existence of ready-made political subjects and disregard the social conditions necessary for the emergence of effective agency. By taking hurt feelings seriously, Honneth's phenomenology throws this presumption into question and more generally queries the relevance of normative models of emancipation that are not sufficiently attentive to the specific experience of domination. I conclude, however, by claiming that the potential of Honneth's phenomenology of social suffering is seriously undercut by being developed in the overarching framework of an ontology of recognition. The normative exigencies set up by this ontology limit Honneth's understanding of the normalising effects of recognition to a simplistic dualism of ideological and genuine forms. While Foucault's idea of agency might lack phenomenological depth, his general theory of power offers a more nuanced and compelling account of the regulatory effects of individualising governmentality upon its subjects.

Recognition as suffer-mongering

There has long been a well-established critique by leftist and other radical thinkers of the politics of identity and recognition on the grounds that its inevitably particularist nature is in tension with or even destructive of a more universal and radical democratic politics. This critique, which can be traced back to Marx, has taken many forms but since the late 1990s a particularly prominent version has arisen, influenced primarily by Nietzsche and Foucault, that denounces identity politics as a type of 'suffer-mongering' (Brown and Halley, 2002: 33). This critique takes its cue from Foucault's assertion that disciplinary power subjugates individuals by tying them to their own identities and to a 'law of truth' that has profoundly normalising effects and obscures more radical notions of political practice and freedom (Foucault, 1994: 331). A politics of suffering focuses individuals inwards upon the hidden causes of their pain and, in this solipsistic turn towards the 'truth', blinds them to possibilities for more radical, world-oriented rather than self-oriented modes of action. Following Foucault, Wendy Brown (1995) has formulated one of the most devastating critiques of recognition as suffer-mongering where individuals are bound into a moralistic and politically regressive assertion of victimhood, articulating demands for reparation. An incontestable moral legitimacy is accorded to the idea of personal suffering which is taken as irrefutable evidence of oppression and injustice. However, not only is suffering far from being an automatic guarantor of social injustice but the continual focus upon injury sets up a negative psychic dynamic that attaches individuals compulsively to their own subjugation and, ultimately, stymies the political imagination. This view of recognition struggles as mobilising a moralistic politics of victimhood and ressentiment, where, in Lauren Berlant's words, 'trauma stands as truth', has been echoed by numerous other political thinkers (Berlant, 2000: 41) As Elizabeth Badinter puts it, 'the new heroic figure is no longer the warrior who lifts mountains, it is the defenceless victim ... Any kind of suffering calls for denunciation and reparation. The general cult of victimhood in society has meant a proliferation of tribunals. There is talk only of penalties and sanctions' (Badinter, 2006: 4).

At first sight, the work of Axel Honneth on recognition struggles and, in particular, his idea that 'social suffering' forms the 'moral' core of political conflict seems to exemplify many of the troubling features of this politics of the wound. Honneth locates the origins of all social and political conflict in the experience of three fundamental types of disrespect visited on marginal and oppressed groups. Driving even the most fully organised and strategic forms of collective action is a submerged layer of 'social' suffering that arises from society's failure to recognise groups of individuals as worthy of esteem and respect. All political conflict, even the most redistributive, can, in Honneth's view, be typified as a struggle for recognition. By emphasising the catalysing force of suffering, Honneth is attempting, among other things, to broaden the narrowly strategic and rational accounts of agency that prevail in the social and political sciences. In so far as hurt feelings can be interpreted as typical for an entire group, they can become the motivational grounds for political resistance and change (Honneth, 1995a: 138). The idea of social suffering is also intended to expand our understanding of oppression and is central to the strong claim made by Honneth about the nature of social justice: 'If the adjective "social" is to mean anything more than "typically found in society", social suffering and discontent possess a normative core ... such feelings of discontent and suffering

Suffering and recognition: Foucault contra Honneth

... coincide with the experience that society is doing something unjust, something unjustifiable' (Fraser and Honneth, 2001: 129). The suffering that arises from misrecognition has an intrinsically normative core because misrecognition violates the fundamental conditions necessary for healthy self-realisation. To support this ontological claim that self-development is optimally fulfilled through recognition Honneth relies heavily on theories of infant development put forward by object relations thinkers such as Donald Winnicott and Jessica Benjamin.

Honneth's strong claim that suffering is intrinsically normative and an incontestable indicator of something socially amiss – i.e. social injustice – does indeed seem to confirm the Foucauldian alarm about the moralisation of hurt feelings which is apparently such an entrenched feature of recognition claims. The construal of political demands in the language of the wound operates around a 'moral reproach' which sets up a zero sum power dynamic where the powerless victim demands reparations from the dominator. As Brown puts it: 'truth is always on the side of the damned and the excluded: hence Truth is always clean of power, but therefore always positioned to reproach power' (Brown, 1995: 46). Suffering itself is normalised as an authentic experience whose apodictic truth cannot be challenged thus making it difficult to adjudicate between genuine and imaginary claims of injustice. The depoliticising effects of the language of the wound seem to be compounded by Honneth's description of his methodology of recognition as a 'phenomenology of injustice' that further connotes an uncritical subjectivism where psychological injury is reified as the *sine qua non* of politics. Not only are many social injustices not accompanied by suffering but also, in an era of the commodification of suffering by the media, the experience itself can hardly be said to be authentic. Honneth pays little attention to the complex effects of the discursive mediation of suffering, to what Luc Boltanski calls 'suffering at a distance' where popular culture routinely appropriates and commodifies human misery with arguably distorting and 'banalising' effects on both those who observe and those who experience this misery (Boltanski, 1990b). Nor does Honneth engage sufficiently with the type of argument made by Berlant and others that a 'vicious yet sentimental' discourse of suffering pervades social and political life in neoliberal democracies resulting in a trivialisation of oppression in so far as injustice is conflated with manufactured hysteria. From a Foucauldian perspective, the recognition – suffering couplet is a way of inserting individuals into a regulatory regime that operates through the manipulation of the type of relation they have with themselves and a depoliticisation of the relation they have with the state. It is a form of misrecognition or, in Patchen Markell's words, 'liberal wish fulfilment' to describe a bourgeois property relation between individual and state as a progressive type of legal recognition (Markell, 2003: 187).

Phenomenology of suffering

The Foucauldian critique of recognition as suffer-mongering undoubtedly has much force but there is something troubling, nonetheless, about its rather overemphatic rejection of the discourse of suffering as an impediment to wider democratic aims. For a start, there is an uncomfortably dismissive and aristocratic connotation to the Nietzschean construal of recognition claims as *ressentiment*. As Susan Bickford puts it: 'to see identity claims as obsessed with suffering is to overlook the fact that it is the perspective of the dominant culture that marks them out that way' (Bickford, 1997: 117). The very vehemence of the critique precludes an acknowledgement that the tendency to masochistic suffer-mongering is not an inevitable feature of identity politics but a contingent effect sporadically generated by the specific, often hostile, context of any given struggle for recognition (Medearis, 2004). Perhaps more problematic, however, is the way that ideas of *ressentiment* and suffer-mongering foreclose an analysis of how the experience of suffering may reveal important aspects to oppression. Manufactured as it may be, the language of suffering attests, at least in part, to the way in which oppression and inequality is internalised by individuals as symbolic violence and lived within the body as feelings of shame, anguish, hopelessness and so forth. In other words, suffering may tell us something significant about the nature of social inequality and domination, but the Foucauldian critique marginalises this type of analysis in its too hasty eschewal of the category. The failure to explore more fully the connection between the experience of suffering and social inequality arises, in part, because the Foucauldian critique is oriented primarily to a general analysis of the intra-subjective effects of disciplinary subjugation – the government of individualisation. As valuable as this general theory of normalisation has been, it lacks a specific focus on the significance of certain generalised experiences of suffering in relation to inequality and domination. After all, what the Foucauldian critique of suffer-mongering significantly underplays is the fact that suffering is not evenly distributed around society but is closely correlated to class inequality, deprivation and social exclusion. Indeed, the reason why Honneth, following Bourdieu and others, uses the term 'social suffering' is precisely to highlight these collective, systemic aspects to the experience of suffering and to explore what this may tell us about the nature of domination. Social suffering is a collective not an individual category, it does not refer to the singular experiences of individual biographies but rather to generic types of subjective experience that are generated by unequal social relations. As Bourdieu puts it, 'the most personal is the most impersonal ... many of the most intimate dramas, the deepest malaises, the most singular suffering that women and men can experience find their roots in the objective contradictions, constraints and double binds inscribed in the structures of the labour and housing markets' (Bourdieu and Wacquant, 1992: 201; see also Renault, 2008b).

Suffering and recognition: Foucault contra Honneth

Of course, the critics of 'suffer-mongering' do not deny the pain that arises from oppression, rather they object to a subjectivist, psychologically reductive mode of analysis which attributes an apodictic truth status to the experiential aspects of suffering. In other words, a methodological objection to subjectivism underpins the political critique of suffer-mongering. To avoid this subjectivism, some critics have argued that there are more objective indices against which claims of unwarranted suffering and unjust treatment can be measured. To escape the vagueness of the 'free floating' model of psychological injury, Nancy Fraser, for example, famously redefines misrecognition in non-subjective, 'non-identitarian' terms as various types of institutional and, hence measureable, status subordination (Fraser and Honneth, 2001; see also Williams, 1998: 178–202). Brown also speaks of the need to distinguish between genuine and false forms of suffering although, unlike Fraser, she does not indicate specific criteria upon which such adjudication could rest. Moreover, the overall thrust of her critique is towards transcending any kind of subjectivist focus on suffering given its potentially regressive political effects. Ultimately, even those whose suffering has a legitimate basis are exhorted to move beyond the balkanising language of recognition claims and to embrace a more solidaristic and universal politics oriented towards 'diversity and the common, toward world rather than self, and involving conversion of one's knowledge of the world from a situated (subject) position into a public idiom' (Brown 1995: 51).

The theoretical cost of this overhasty association of the experiential with a politically and methodologically dangerous subjectivism is that Foucauldians fail to sufficiently appreciate that a focus on subjective experience may be analytically crucial for explaining the nature of domination. One feature of domination that Foucauldians recognise only too well is that the inscription of hierarchies of power onto the body naturalises certain types of oppression thus rendering them socially invisible, in a doxic sense. The orientation of Foucauldians to explaining processes of incorporation in the top-heavy terms of the operations of discourse means, however, that they neglect how the subject's own experience of suffering can be a crucial indicator of certain invisible or unthematised forms of inequality. Indeed, the phenomenon of power cannot be dealt with from a purely external, discursive point of view, because the subjective experience of exclusion, marginalization and domination is crucial to understanding its operations. As Hans Herbert Kogler puts it: 'subjects may not have the adequate conceptual tools to thematise how power relations actually function, yet, to be evaluated by the interpreter as oppression, the subjects' assessment and experience of them as oppressive is indispensable' (Kogler, 1996: 262).

In this light, Honneth's phenomenology of injustice can be understood not as a type of suffer-mongering but rather as 'disclosing social critique' that attempts, in its focus on suffering, to make 'something visible that would otherwise remain hidden in the horizon of accepted meanings' (Honneth, 2007a: 60). There are types of invisible social suffering that fall below the threshold of political mobilisation and public attention and are, for a large part, unarticulated as part of any political agency. Such experiences often only come to the fore through an interpretative perspective that attempts to go beyond the agendas of publically articulated forms of social injustice to uncover hidden forms of oppression. Bourdieu makes a such a point in his discussion, in *The weight of the world* (Bourdieu et al., 1999) of *grandes* and *petites misères*; the latter, everyday forms of suffering are 'malaises' that are often 'unexpressed and often inexpressible', often only visible through a phenomenological perspective, which focuses on the 'diffuse expectations and hopes which, because they often touch on the ideas that people have about their own identity and self-respect, seem to be a private affair and therefore legitimately excluded from public debate' (Bourdieu et al., 1999: 627). Like Bourdieu, Honneth's phenomenology aims to expose such socially generalised and often mundane experiences associated with immiseration and deprivation, which remain below the level of public perception, precisely because they are diffuse and do not take the form of explicit struggles. Such experiences such as the feminisation of poverty, long-term unemployment, the deskilling and 'precarisation' of the workforce have a dimension which pertains more to 'structures of feeling' and expectations rather than the distribution of material goods. The most vulnerable and deprived groups in society do not have the material and symbolic resources to push their suffering onto the political agenda but there are also subjective factors pertaining to the specificity of the experience itself which compound this invisibility. A common characteristic of the lived reality of domination is that it is often experienced in a fragmented, episodic manner, as 'senseless', as that which eludes coherent expression. The apparent senselessness of lived oppression does not, of course, mean that such experiences permanently defy coherent expression, but the unspeakable nature of suffering may be deepened by the individualised nature of the experience. Many individuals are often reluctant to articulate, or even acknowledge their suffering, because it is often experienced as personal failure, shame of inability to cope and so forth. Thus suffering is intensified because its unsayability means that, at the level of the individual, it is taken into the structure of consciousness itself as a form of personal denial and may result in depression and anxiety.

At a more general level, a widespread denial or disregard of everyday forms of social suffering may result in pathological social effects such as the destruction of communal bonds and political solidarity leaving individuals feeling further isolated and powerless to change their conditions of existence. As Jean-Philippe Deranty explains, 'the inability to say the suffering, even to oneself, contributes directly to the emergence and increase in pathologies' (Deranty, 2008: 460). In Honneth's view, for example, the 'organised self-realisation' characteristic of neoliberal democratic regimes, far from representing an increase in individual autonomy and freedom, in fact places an intolerable burden on individuals. Individuals are increasingly compelled to assume responsibility for states of affairs which, in fact, they are not responsible for, and this paradoxical situation manifests itself in elevated levels of mental illness and a loss of normative bearings (Hartmann and Honneth, 2006).

Although Foucault's account of the restructuring of the self as an 'enterprise' that takes place under neoliberal democracies strikingly resembles Honneth's account of organised self-realisation, it lacks any analysis of the emotional and psychic costs of this reorganisation and how they might intersect with existing and emergent inequalities (Foucault, 2008; see also McNay, 2009). For Honneth, it is, in particular, the changing nature of labour and its increased 'precarisation' under neoliberalism that renders the workplace one of the primary loci for this new diffuse but widespread type of suffering. The increasing precariousness of work under neoliberalism transcends established class lines creating new forms of inequality as it pulls workers from across all strata into its short-term, unprotected and unpredictable conditions, exposing them to greater uncertainty about their future (LaVaque-Manty, 2008: 107–8). At the same time, such precariousness deepens existing inequalities of class, gender and race, and intensifies feelings of vulnerability and despair (Griffin-Cohen and Brodie, 2007; LaVaque-Manty, 2008). Thus, despite increases in the standard of living, class deprivation persists due to lasting inequality in the distribution of classes for social recognition and, precisely because of its immaterial or symbolic nature, such inequality in recognition can be best revealed through a phenomenological approach which takes the experience of social disrespect seriously.

A phenomenological perspective discloses the existential significance of work for self-esteem and for the process of healthy identity-formation in general. Work is not simply instrumental activity but has central psychological and affective significance both for an individual's sense of being a valued member of society and also for their core ability to deal with the fears of living in an increasingly uncertain world. In the most fundamental sense, disrespect in the workplace weakens the individual's capacity to hope (Deranty, 2008: 456; see also Bourdieu, 2000a: 207–34). By failing to situate the experience of suffering more securely in the context of social inequality, the Foucauldian critique of recognition disregards emerging lines of oppression associated with the precarisation of labour and other types of oppression and, above all, their lived reality as a social pathology of hopelessness.

Agonistic identity construction

Presumption of agency

The political hostility of Foucauldians towards the language of suffering and the attendant methodological aversion to an essentialising subjectivism is, of course, deeply informed by a notion of critical knowledge as a break with the given, a deconstruction of the experiential in order to explore aspects of freedom that transcend present actuality. Ideas of freedom as non-identity are central to much post-foundational political thought and Foucault provides us with a paradigmatic formulation in his notion of a critical ontology of the present. This involves a scrutiny of modes of being intended to 'separate out, from the contingency that has made us what we are, the possibility of no longer being, doing, or thinking what we are, do, or think' (Foucault, 1984a: 46). Ethics of the self encapsulate this 'limit attitude' where a critical relation to self is established that explores the possibility of going beyond what seems natural, authentic, or inevitable in identities and behaviours: 'the critique of what we are is at one and the same time an historical analysis of the limits that are imposed on us and an experiment with the possibility of going beyond them' (Foucault, 1984a: 50). Critique, then, as a practice of freedom is, in some fundamental sense, anti-experiential and anti-subjectivist; it is a 'possible transgression' that undoes phenomenological certainties (Foucault, 1984a: 45). It is a refusal of the given: 'the art of voluntary insubordination' whose aim is 'the desubjugation of the subject in the context of ... the politics of truth' (Foucault, 2002: 194).

There is indisputably much political value in Foucault's formulation of a progressive ethical practice based on a deconstruction of prevailing norms and an openness to other potential ways of being. What often gets lost, however, in this critique of the experiential in the name of non-identity is an alternative, socio-centric mode of analysis which explores not so much the potential for alterity in the actual but on what the experience of the actual might tell us about domination and social inequality. To be sure, Foucault's ontology of the actual does not rule out *a priori* such systematic social critique and indeed, Foucault is, in many respects, the theorist of domination *par excellence*. While the idea of docile subjects is tremendously important in a general account of normalising subjugation, it has never been all that attentive to established social hierarchies of class and gender. Moreover, the way in which Foucauldians, and indeed many other post-foundational political thinkers, have overwhelmingly chosen to elaborate the idea of an historical ontology of our selves involves focusing not so much on specific dynamics of inequality but more on non-identity in the present, that is, the possible (McNay, 2010). As Judith Butler puts it, critique takes place beyond 'any received understanding of intention and deliberation' and involves 'risking the subject at the limits of its ordering' (Butler, 2002: 225). In the light of this orientation towards potentiality and non-identity, a focus on the actual often becomes tantamount to a reductive and potentially essentialising focus on the given. Existing social and political processes are tacitly endowed with the negative aura of 'being merely positivist, sociologist, empiricist, or ontic' (Bosteels, 2009: 246). As Bruno Bosteels puts it 'there is ... something intrinsically uncanny, not to say oxymoronic ... about an ontology of actuality, if we take into account the dominant orientations of post-foundational thinking. Foucault's provocation ... also consisted in enabling an historical ontology of ourselves that would not have to shy away from speaking about the present situation in the name of some knee-jerk aversion to the metaphysics of presence' (Bosteels, 2009: 244).

A consequence of this orientation to the idea of freedom as non-identity is that questions pertaining to the social conditions that facilitate or hinder effective political agency are too easily disregarded or displaced as second-order issues. In their accounts of radical action, Foucauldians tend to presume the existence of ready-made political agents rather than exploring in more detail how existing inequalities and forms of domination prevent individuals from acting in the interests of their own freedom. Consider, for example, what kind of capacities must necessarily be attributed to citizens for them to be able to implement the perpetual self-critique that is such a crucial part of ethical self-formation. As a way of expressing an ideal of democratic openness, the interrogation of the limits of identity is, of course, desirable. But, from the perspective of embodied individuals, it is unclear what this configuration of agency in terms of a process of 'voluntary insubordination' means, exactly, as a pragmatic strategy for action. At the very least, the elevation of the limits of intelligibility as a cipher for the openness of the democratic ethos assumes a certain level of political virtuosity and articulacy that, arguably, in the context of the unequal distribution of resources is not evenly distributed among democratic citizens. There is a mismatch between the abstract notion of non-identity as transgression that lies at the heart of Foucault's idea of progressive ethical practice and the social experience of non-identity as the senselessness and isolation that characterises the sometimes crushing emotional reality of domination (Charlesworth, 2000). The first notion speaks to positions of relative power and privilege *vis-à-vis* social norms where subjects can afford to run the risk of testing the limits of identity, the second notion speaks to positions of profound powerlessness where subjects struggle and often fail to make much sense of their experiences within a matrix of established social norms.

Ultimately, then, Honneth's idea of the invisibility of social suffering provokes us to consider fundamental underlying questions about political agency and the social conditions necessary for its emergence. Social suffering highlights the depoliticising effects of symbolic violence, where inequalities are taken into the body, naturalised and lived as profound physical and emotional dispositions. The internalisation of domination in this manner means that individuals often feel that their suffering is inevitable or unavoidable and that little or nothing can be done to change it. In other words, suffering undermines the ability of individuals to become effective political agents. Inequalities of class and gender can be lived as deep-seated, dispositional reluctances to participate in political processes or even perceive one's problems as politically articulable and redressable in the first place (Nielson, 2000). Even when individuals possess a critical understanding of their situation, their willingness to participate in corrective political action is far from assured. There is a huge difference between recognising injustice, identifying systemic domination and common interests, devising strategies for action and finally feeling able to act (Mansbridge and Morris, 2001: 238). Ultimately, even the most radical accounts of political action must reckon with this 'resistance of "reality"' if they are to have critical purchase (Bourdieu, 2000a).

But Foucault has surprisingly little to say about how social antagonisms that are incorporated into the body and lived as seemingly natural dispositions might be converted into a productive agonistic ethos, or a contestatory aesthetics of existence. Domination as the internalisation of inequalities means that many individuals do not experience their lives as amenable to reflection, experimentation and change, in the mode of a Foucauldian critique, but as crushing, overwhelming and unchangeable. What is not sufficiently acknowledged in the Foucauldian mode of critique is that the ability to take an ethical stance *vis-à-vis* established norms-of-being already involves being in a position of relative privilege and power (Oliver, 2001: 29). Any interrogation of the possibility of political agency must therefore address the individual's embodied experience and understanding of their situation and hence their reasons for acting or not acting in the way they do. Thus, to return to Brown, her exhortation of individuals and groups to abandon the divisive and self-referential discourse of suffering in the name of a more universal post-identity politics represents, at some level, a failure to engage sufficiently with the pathologies of identity wrought by social inequalities that are taken into the body and lived as deep-seated physical and psychological dispositions. It is not enough to simply urge individuals to lay aside a politics of personal injustice without inquiring first into how the experience of inequality and suffering might impose deeply felt constraints upon individuals' willingness to act as agents of their own interests.

The presumption of ready-made political agents is not confined to Foucault's work, but is arguably a widespread tendency in the work of other post-foundational political thinkers, where agency is often thought of as an abstract potential rather than as a capacity of embodied individuals living in conditions of inequality (McNay, 2010). Too often, equality is assumed as an 'unthematised condition of possibility' for political debate and action, rather than being thought more exhaustively in terms of what Deranty and Renault describe as the effort required to 'realise equality in conditions of social inequality' (Deranty and Renault, 2009: 43–4). This presumption of agency results in what Honneth has described as a growing discrepancy between the propositions of progressive normative theory and the social experience of those subjects on whose behalf it is supposed to speak. He explores this discrepancy primarily through his critique of the formalism of Habermas' theory of communicative ethics which derives from a profound inattentiveness to the lived experience of inequality. The overall viability of the deliberative model is thrown into question because it seriously underestimates how the emotional, episodic and fragmented nature of the experience of misrecognition may escape rational articulation as 'systematic normative demands' and thus undermines the ability of individuals to operate as effective moral and political agents (Honneth, 2007a: 85). What can be said of Habermas can also be said, *ceteris paribus*, of other types of post-foundational political thought, namely, that there is often an incongruity between theories of radical political agency and the experience of domination (McNay, 2010). Indeed, the tendency of contemporary post-foundational thinking towards investigations of the political in abstract terms such as indeterminacy, undecidability, spectrality, agonism and so forth speaks, as Bosteels has observed, to an 'eschatological even catastrophic desire for radicalization' (Bosteels 2009: 242). By disregarding underlying issues of the social conditions of possibility for effective agency, the important arguments of Foucauldians and other post-foundational thinkers remain vague exhortations that do not connect to the embodied experience of the very subjects they wish to mobilise. The risk entailed in this turning away from the actual is that 'the gesture of radicalization may very well have disabled in advance the pursuit of truly emancipatory actions in so far as the latter will necessarily appear far less radical' (Bosteels, 2009: 247). By taking hurt feelings seriously as an indicator of something amiss socially, Honneth's phenomenology is oriented less towards an abstract account of potential transcendence and more towards what the experience of suffering tells us about the actuality of political agency emerging in conditions of social inequality.

Ontology of recognition

Despite the insights of Honneth's phenomenology of suffering into the effects of domination on agency, their potential is significantly undercut by being developed within the context of an overextended theory of recognition, or what I call elsewhere, an ontology of recognition (McNay, 2008). The necessity of sustaining the normative primacy of recognition relations in his social theory limits Honneth's conceptualisation of the dynamics of power and subject-formation to a rather simplistic dualism of genuine and ideological modes of recognition. Thus, although his account of agency might lack phenomenological depth, Foucault's overall theory of power offers a more complex account of the ambivalent effects of individualising governmentality upon its subjects. For Foucauldians, it is not a question of having to distinguish genuine from ideological modes of recognition as if a clear line could ever be drawn between the positive effects of one and the distorting effects of the other. Rather it involves exploring how modes of recognition create subject positions that may be simultaneously enabling and constraining such that, in the very moment in which they create individuals as agents of change, they also redraft social hierarchies. Indeed, ultimately, the more complex Foucauldian model of power would require a complete relinquishment of the explanatory and normative primacy accorded by Honneth to the idea of recognition in favour of a more differentiated, multilayered account of the nature of oppression and inequality and of their potential political remedy (Fraser and Honneth, 2001; Bader, 2007).

Honneth makes the strong normative claim that modern societies can be understood as recognition orders, that is, recognition is constitutive of the basic intersubjective structure of social relations, and it also refers to the overall normative direction of social development. Modern societies are imperfect realisations of a recognition order which, if it were to be fully realised, would represent the maximal conditions for positive self-realisation and personal integrity. Relations of recognition are accorded this universal status and a normative pre-eminence over other types of social interaction on the basis that they are constitutive of human development and, as mentioned earlier, Honneth's primary source for this strong claim is the work of object relations theorists such as Winnicott and J. Benjamin (Honneth, 1995a: 96–107; Honneth, 1999). Multiple problems arise for Honneth's sociology of recognition by grounding it in such a strong ontogenetic claim, many of them stemming from the problematic effects that the ontology of recognition has on his account of power relations (McNay, 2008: 132–8). A major difficulty is that the normative and analytical senses of the idea of recognition blur into each other, with the effect that the positive valuation given to recognition as an ideal constrains its adequacy as a description of social relations. To put this in other terms, the monological dynamic of recognition cannot really capture the multidimensional and complex nature of social power relations without simplifying them, misrepresenting them, or even sentimentalising them (Bader, 2007). It results, *inter alia*, in a psychologically reductive social theory where social relations are persistently viewed as extrapolations from the primary dyad of recognition. The ontologisation of power in this manner resembles nothing so much as, in the words of Jonathan Lear, 'a secularised version of the fall' (Lear, 2008: 131). As a result, Honneth has rightly been taken to task by numerous commentators for his misrepresentation of oppressive social hierarchies of gender, class and race as imperfectly realised relations of recognition (Owen and Van Den Brink, 2007). The paradigmatic example of this normative sanitisation is Honneth's depiction of relations within the family as relations of care which mystifies women's domestic labour as affective recognition and also underplays the extent to which familial dynamics are contingent and historically shaped by forces of money, social control and often domestic violence (Donzelot, 1979; Fraser and Honneth, 2001: 219–20; Shapiro, 2001: 58–66; Thistle, 2000).

A consequence of Honneth's reliance on an ontology of recognition that views social relations as imperfect instantiations of a primal dyad is that he does not sufficiently acknowledge how recognition can itself be distorted and normalising. To sustain the normative pre-eminence of recognition, Honneth must overlook, for example, how the internalisation of harmful norms might pervert prevailing standards of recognition such that, in conforming to them, individuals are subjected rather than empowered. For Foucault, the quest for recognition shares the same structure as the confessional – the paradigm of individualising pastoral power – where individuals seek self-legitimation through being acknowledged within the normalising discourses of authority. From this perspective, what Honneth regards as the spontaneous and innate nature of the desire for recognition is an example of how, in late modernity, disciplinary structures have been so thoroughly internalised by individuals that they have become self-policing subjects. In his more recent work, Honneth addresses this problem of normalisation through recognition and, indeed, in the interview in this volume, he claims that it is Foucault's work on the productivity of power that allows him to develop a more nuanced understanding of the potentially 'regulative patterns' of certain dynamics of reciprocal recognition (Honneth, Chapter 2 of this volume; see also Honneth 2007b: 323–4). In fact, his response to this dilemma of normalising interpellation is decidedly un-Foucauldian in that he breaks down the monolithic concept of recognition into a simplistic dualism of 'morally justified' and ideological forms. He acknowledges that it is not easy to distinguish between the two sorts of recognition because they are often intertwined and also, like genuine types of recognition, ideological variants are not crudely negative but may have a positive appearance in that they are freely assumed and have a productive, evaluative content in terms of subject identification. Given these apparent similarities that make it difficult to definitively separate genuine from unjustified content from within 'the unbroken flow of a many layered struggle for recognition', Honneth goes on to stipulate that it is only the former that will be reinforced by corresponding progressive changes in the material circumstances of society, for instance, expansion of legal and political rights or economic redistribution (2007b: 342). Ideological forms of recognition are not underpinned by correlative changes in the concrete social world and, in so far as they lack material content and are illusory, an irrational core lies beneath their rational appearance. He writes, 'the deficiency by which we might recognise such ideologies could consist in the structural inability to ensure the material prerequisites for realizing new evaluative qualities' (2007b: 346). Thus, along with consumer advertising, Honneth identifies the neoliberal discourse that positions individuals as entrepreneurs *vis-à-vis* the world of work as ideological forms of recognition in so far as an 'abyss opens up' between their evaluative promise and material fulfilment.

An immediate difficulty with this distinction between genuine and ideological forms of recognition is its apparent resurrection of a reductive and untenable distinction between illusion and reality, the symbolic and the material which Foucault, among others, decisively deconstructed in his work on discourse and power (Foucault, 1980). A neoliberal discourse of entrepreneurship has many pernicious effects, but Honneth's idea that these are somehow ideological or illusory in that they are less instantiated in material institutions and practices is not really a satisfactory or convincing approach. In contrast, Foucault's analysis of neoliberal governmentality offers a more complex explanation of its effects than Honneth's zero sum model of genuine or ideological recognition. Like Honneth's idea of organised self-realisation, Foucault observes that the idea of the individual as an entrepreneur is a key feature of living within neoliberal regimes. In his view, the individual's life is lodged not within the framework of the state but within a multiplicity of interrelated, small-scale organisations or networks which 'are in some way ready to hand for the individual, sufficiently limited in their scale for the individuals actions, decisions, and choices to have meaningful and perceptible effects, and numerous enough for him not to be dependent on one alone' (Foucault, 2008: 241). The autonomous citizen is one who manages these diverse networks – work, household, pension, insurance, private property – in the most responsible and prudent fashion *vis-à-vis* the avoidance of risk and the maximisation of their own happiness. The self, as he puts it, is remade into 'a sort of permanent and multiple enterprise' (Foucault, 2008: 241). This neoliberal restructuring of the self as enterprise has ambivalent social and political effects. On the one hand, it strengthens individual freedom in that it involves the shaping of individual lives in a way that does not violate their 'formally autonomous' character (Miller and Rose, 2008: 39). It operates not through the delimitation of individual freedoms but through their multiplication in the context of a notion of responsible self-management. But, on the other hand, it has profoundly pernicious effects in that it depoliticises the state's relation to the individual, attenuating its duties and responsibilities towards vulnerable groups such as the poor and the ill who are seen as responsible for their own conditions (McNay, 2009: 10–11).

In such a vein, Judith Butler (2000) unpicks the ambivalent effects of a certain liberalising move on the part of the state towards family life and sexuality. The very moment at which the state progressively extends kinship and family rights to gays and lesbians is also the moment at which a more punitive, neoliberal response is shown to those who chose to live outside a two-parent family unit. A similar 'double entanglement' is described by Angela McRobbie (2008) where globalising capital 'brings forward women as individualised subjects [and] agents of change', in so far as it creates a new feminised workforce at the same time as it reworks gender hierarchies where women remain the most vulnerable and exploited of subjects. In these cases, the effects of neoliberal modes of recognition can hardly be termed 'ideological' in Honneth's usage but form part of a material reshaping of the social realm which controls individuals, not through explicit forms of domination, but through rationalised techniques and devices which orient action to certain socially useful ends – the conduct of conduct.

An implication of such Foucauldian analyses is that neoliberal governance forces us to rethink issues of subjectivity and identity politics beyond the formula, suggested in Honneth's dualism of genuine and ideological modes of recognition, that regimes of power necessarily acknowledge or distort human subjectivity. Rather these styles of government produce new modes of subjectification, ways of being and acting that 'make up subjects as free persons' in a manner that is neither authentic or inauthentic, genuine or ideological (Rose, 1999: 95). This mode of government of the self ultimately leads away from the recognition formulation of freedom as the realisation of authentic identities towards the idea of freedom as a form of power, as a capacity for liberty that is drawn out of individuals through the government of social practices. Freedom is not the obverse of domination or order or control, it is not genuine as opposed to ideological forms of recognition, rather it is 'the name we give to a kind of power one brings to bear upon oneself and a mode of bringing power to bear on others' (Rose, 1999: 95–6). Honneth claims that his idea of recognition is capable of accommodating these complexities because it is not a straightforward ontology in that it is never fully independent from specific cultural and social contexts. Although the need for recognition is pre-social, it is only ever manifested in variable and socially specific forms (Fraser and Honneth, 2001: 131–2). Yet, at the same time, recognition is not entirely a contingent construct: the psychological need for recognition is not relative to a given culture but is the fundamental pre-requisite of healthy human self-development. Through this equivocation, Honneth appears to want to have it both ways: recognition is both a universal and a contingent structure. It is hard to see, however, how this circular logic is anything but self-cancelling. The claim to historical specificity – that forms of recognition are entirely shaped by social forces – is surely undermined by the positing of a self-same dynamic of the desire for recognition that is the unvarying psychological cause behind social conflict and transformation. The normative centrality of the idea of recognition ultimately traps Honneth's thought in a circular and ahistorical logic of eternal recurrence. Moreover, it constrains the more promising form of enquiry opened up by his idea of disclosing social critique which highlights the importance of a phenomenology of suffering and explores what this might tell us about emerging forms of oppression and mobilising resistance to them.

5

Sartre and Honneth on conflict and recognition

Alice Le Goff

How might Jean-Paul Sartre's social philosophy contribute to contemporary debates on recognition? We will try to answer this question in this chapter. Axel Honneth, primarily responsible for the contemporary renewal of recognition theory, has claimed to draw inspiration from Sartre, identifying the latter as the most important of the French, post-Second World War writers (Honneth, Chapter 2 of this volume). However, while insisting that his own approach to social theory continues in the tradition of Karl Marx, Georges Sorel and Sartre, he also professes to overcome this tradition's limitations. Where Sartre presents only a partial sketch of the concept of recognition, Honneth believes that his own theory is more comprehensive. This chapter will use Sartre's work to critique both Honneth's interpretation of Sartre and Honneth's general perspective offering, more broadly, a critique of the way contemporary debates on recognition are structured.

The chapter will begin with an account of Honneth's reading of Sartre, so as to emphasise the way in which this interpretation intersects with and differs from the approaches to ethics that Sartre derives from his existential ontology. We will then show that a Sartrean perspective can bring to light certain blind spots in Honneth's theory, focusing on the problem of reification and the question of identity. We do not intend to provide an exhaustive account of the pros and cons of revitalising a Sartrean approach to struggles for recognition. Our aim is rather to show that our own interpretation of Sartre's philosophy can pave the way to the exploration of ideas which could enhance current debates on recognition. In particular, we will argue that Sartre's attention to the conflictual nature of recognition relations can contribute to the further development of approaches which are critical of the fixation on identity, instead focusing attention on the agonistic dimension of recognition, and defending an approach to struggles for recognition which is more pluralistic and differentiated than the one Honneth suggests.

Sartre, Honneth: conflict and recognition

Honneth's reading of Sartre

Honneth's recognition theory is informed by the idea that historical development can be construed in the light of a process of struggles for recognition. In developing this idea, Honneth revisits the history of post-Hegelian thought, focusing on Marx, Sorel and Sartre. Although Honneth believes these thinkers share the view that social conflict may be analysed in terms of demands for recognition, he claims that neither manages to throw light on 'the moral grammar' of such conflicts. With regard to Sartre (Honneth, 1995a: 141–60; and Honneth, 1995b: 158–68), Honneth argues that although Sartre would agree that social conflicts are to be understood as disruptions in relationships of recognition between collective actors (1995a: 156), he cannot provide more than a mere sketch of its nature due to inherent flaws in his existentialist reading of Hegel. As Honneth explains, in Sartre's early theory of intersubjectivity, the 'struggle for recognition' is an existential fact of human *Dasein*, where the ontological dualism of the 'in-itself' (unconscious being) and the 'for-itself' (conscious being) is applied to the transcendental problem of the existence of others (Honneth, 1995a: 156). As a being-for-itself, each human subject permanently transcends his or her projects, asking him- or her-self questions and being questioned by others. To achieve consciousness of self, the subject needs to be looked at and defined by somebody else, but also questions that look, experiencing the other's look as objectification. The subject can only escape such objectification by objectifying the other in return.

This negative dynamic of reciprocal reification indicates that in Sartre's conception of intersubjectivity, mutual recognition is impossible. As Honneth explains, Sartre himself soon became aware of the limits of his initial project, granting increasing importance to the concept of historical progress. Sartre's study of the reasons for anti-Semitism reorients his theory toward the possibility of mutual recognition, by describing anti-Semitism as a form of social disrespect, rooted in the historical and class-specific experiences of the Jewish 'petty bourgeoisie' in French society (Honneth, 1995a: 156). Concerned, here, with the possibility of transforming social conflict, Sartre no longer views the struggle for recognition as an inescapable feature of human subjectivity but rather considers it to be a phenomenon which can be overcome, caused by a non-symmetrical relationship between social groups (Honneth, 1995a: 157). This idea also lies at the heart of Sartre's analysis of anti-colonial struggle (Sartre, 2006). Honneth believes that in his political writings, Sartre introduces the idea that the 'negative account of recognition presented in the earlier work *can* be resolved, to some extent, in positive forms of non-conflictual, mutual recognition' (Honneth, Chapter 2 of this volume).

However, while acknowledging the increasing attention Sartre accords to the theme of struggles for recognition between social groups, Honneth also wants to remind us that a gap remains between Sartre's philosophy of intersubjectivity and his political writings. This gap prevents Sartre from providing any normative basis for an approach to social conflict, which Honneth believes lies in the moral ideal of mutual recognition. Sartre's later philosophical texts imply such an account without systematically developing or justifying it, and this means that Sartre could not use the notion of a struggle for recognition as a tool to analyse contemporary social pathologies (Honneth, 1995a: 158). The opaque nature of his idea of social recognition also explains why Sartre could not carefully distinguish between the different forms or levels of recognition, leading to a failure to acknowledge the moral significance of the formalism of bourgeois law, which Sartre rejects as 'a perfect justification for pillage' (Honneth, 1995a: 158).

It is worth mentioning that Honneth has since modified the reading of Sartrean philosophy offered in *The struggle for recognition*, and now believes that *Being and nothingness* 'provides one of the most convincing presentations of the socio-ontological and existential meaning of recognition' (Honneth, Chapter 2 of this volume). For Honneth, Sartre successfully draws attention to the need to distinguish between recognition as a cognitive state and recognition as an existential, socio-ontological stance towards others which conditions our capacity for practical action. Sartre's analyses in *Being and nothingness* (1993a) clearly show that recognition does not simply relate to the other person as an object of knowledge. Instead, recognition, in Honneth's account of Sartre, is part of a 'deeper sphere of our being-in-the-world', and can be understood as an existential stance towards others which affects our being-in-the-world. Honneth now believes that his own approach to recognition as the condition of self-realisation intersects with the Sartrean view that recognition relations play a constitutive role with respect to one's capacity to situate oneself existentially and practically in the world (Honneth, Chapter 2 of this volume).

Although Honneth has now qualified his reading, he still insists that Sartre's conception of recognition overlooks the possible resolution of conflict into stable and positive forms of mutual recognition. In this sense, he still distinguishes Sartre's philosophical texts from his political writings, maintaining his original view that Sartre could not reconcile the existential negativism of *Being and nothingness* with the positive forms of mutual recognition promised by his political writings. Consequently, although Honneth believes that his own theory intersects with Sartre's account of recognition as an existential stance in *Being and nothingness* and his tentative account of positive recognition among groups in *Anti-Semite and Jew* (1995), he still argues that Sartre overlooks the normative basis of intersubjective experience which should ground an approach to social conflict.

Sartre, Honneth: conflict and recognition

Sartre: two conceptions of ethics

Honneth's appraisal of Sartre's inability to account for the normative basis of intersubjectivity both intersects with and differs from the interpretations that tend to prevail in the field of Sartrean studies. Like Honneth's, most interpretations emphasise, in particular, the evolution of Sartre's thought from an individualistic to a historical perspective and the related evolution of Sartrean ethics from an ethics of authenticity to an ethics of integral humanity.

Sartrean ethics was initially defined as an ethics of authenticity due to the ontology introduced in *Being and nothingness*. This ontology hinges on the dualism between the unconscious being-in-itself, on the one hand, and conscious being-for-itself, on the other. For Sartre, the in-itself is self-identical and passive; it is simply what it is and, in this sense, avoids the 'negativity' of the for-itself. In contrast, the for-itself, as consciousness of an object, is consciousness of itself and, as such, equates to consciousness of itself as not-itself. In this sense, the for-itself is 'negativity' because it is non-identical with itself. This duality of the self as both non-negative in-itself and negative for-itself matches that of facticity and transcendence. As a conscious individual, one can transcend one's facticity, which implies transcending all that is 'given' in one's 'situation'. Existing designates the for-itself's basic choice of its mode of being, a choice which is possible only insofar as its 'given' can be transcended. The ontological foundation of our freedom lies in this transcendence. As a for-itself, one can always tear oneself away from one's facticity, withdrawing from the world, which means that consciousness is specified as the locus of both possibility and negativity. Freedom therefore constitutes one's very being: 'the *existence* of freedom and of consciousness precedes and conditions their *essence*' (Sartre, 1993a: 363), by which Sartre means that we can only define our essence by our 'project', that is, by the way we transcend our facticity so as to 'choose' ourselves. Admittedly, there remains an additional complexity in that Sartre also insists that the facticity of human existence cannot always be chosen, in that nobody can choose the brute-fact of one's birth. All human existence is defined in 'situation' (Sartre, 1993a: 428, 432, 447, 495, 510) so that it may seem that we cannot choose ourselves: we cannot escape our social position, our familial or political belonging and so on. However, 'situation' is not an argument against freedom because situation has meaning 'only in and through the free choice which human-reality *is*' (1993a: 629). The situations we are confronted with only make sense against the background of a life-orienting original project, which is why Sartre continually insists that we are 'condemned to be free', implying that our freedom is unlimited in that we cannot decide to stop being free.

In *Being and nothingness*, Sartre does not deal with the ethical implications of this ontology. He focuses instead on analysing the different ways in which human beings can attempt to flee from their own nothingness, by attempting to disregard their nature as for-itself and adopt the in-itself as a mode of being. He dwells in particular on behaviours related to 'bad faith' or self-deception, by which one denies either one's transcendence as a for-itself or one's facticity as an in-itself. Sartre nonetheless accords pride of place to the way in which consciousness can structure itself as a synthesis of the in-itself and the for-itself, which he sees as the 'fundamental structure of human-reality' (1993a: 614) whereby the for-itself sets itself the task of creating its self-identity. Sartre presents this task as a universal desire (1993a: 721) aiming to transform the for-itself into an in-itself but also relating to the for-itself's affirmation of freedom by which it distinguishes itself from the in-itself. This desire leads the for-itself to seek to become its own foundation, that is to say, to become God. Sartre hereby introduces an other mode of being, the for-itself-in-itself which the for-itself aims to become. Nevertheless no dialectic can enable such synthesis, which means that all human beings are marked by a 'useless passion' (1993a: 615). And yet this 'useless passion' bears upon the development of interpersonal relations whose conflictual dimension Sartre continually emphasises, in that they imply inescapable relations of mutual reification. In fact, Sartre describes concrete interpersonal relations in terms of transcendence, where the other being is a transcendence that the for-itself transcends (1993a: 408):

> If there is an Other, whatever or whoever he may be, whatever may be his relation with me, and without his acting upon me except by the pure upsurge of his being – then I have an outside, I have a *nature*. My original fall is the existence of the Other'. (1993a: 238–9)

If each interaction with the other implies that the for-itself experiences his degradation as a subject, we can understand why otherness is viewed as such a threat and why the only solution to counteract it seems to lie in an attempt to dominate the other.

The ethical views deriving from this Sartrean ontology thus seem quite bleak in that any kind of mutual recognition appears impossible, and inauthenticity inescapable. Nevertheless, Sartre attempts to show that a strongly humanist ethics, centred on the concept of responsibility, can be derived from this theoretical framework. Unlimited freedom goes hand in hand with coextensive responsibility: 'When we say that man chooses himself, we do mean that every one of us must choose himself; but by that we also mean that in choosing for himself he chooses for all men' (1948: 29–30). To choose this or that is to affirm the value of what is chosen, while both fashioning our image and creating an image of man as we would have him to be. Self-responsibility thus concerns mankind as a whole because 'in fashioning myself I fashion man' (1948: 30) without receiving any values or commands to allow me to legitimise my behaviour (1948: 30). Freedom, then, is the ultimate value of Sartrean ethics of authenticity in that it is the source of all values: a person must refuse behaviour which avoids his own nothingness, authenticity implying that the for-itself lives with a clear awareness both of its contingency and responsibility. Whereas interpersonal relations were initially described as inescapably conflictual, Sartre insists, in his ethical reflections, on the equal worth of each individual freedom, pointing out that the choice of freedom as an ultimate value means that the freedom of others is also an objective. He thereby suggests that, for the sake of coherence, living with a clear awareness of one's freedom implies both acknowledging and desiring the freedom of others.

Having dealt with the main ideas of Sartre's early ethics, we can now identify a discrepancy between these ideas, and the ontology, developed in *Being and nothingness*, on which the ethics is based. Authenticity can only be achieved by a radical conversion – driven by an existential ontology and existential psychoanalysis [1] which Sartre later discards as too idealistic and abstract. At first, inauthenticity is defined in such a radical way – as inescapable – that one could well ask how the radical conversion demanded by authenticity is even possible. Sartre must therefore address the following dilemma: either his initial description of the ontological structure of consciousness is incorrect or inauthenticity is not the effect of these structures alone (Baugh, 1991). Sartre favours the second option, as becomes clear in *Notebooks for an ethics* (1992). Although *Notebooks* continues to fall within the framework of Sartre's early ethics, he nonetheless deals with authenticity as a *social* problem, requiring a social solution. Whereas inauthenticity is at first introduced as resulting from an individual free choice, Sartre now insists in the *Notebooks* that it originates in specific social conditions which are determined by what he refers to as an 'original choice' on the part of humanity, to begin with oppression. In this way, authenticity is no longer viewed solely as the effect of a moral conversion but rather as the fulfilment of possibilities which belong to human existence in specific social contexts. This means that Sartre can now develop the theme of effective and necessary recognition. Baugh writes: 'Achieving authenticity implies understanding oneself as a freedom in situation and living with a lucid and true awareness of the situation, which is only made possible by an action that can be confirmed by an other' (Baugh, 1991: 102, author's translation). In view of an oppressive context, a 'purifying reflection' is not enough to guarantee a conversion because inauthenticity does not only originate in an individual's decision to flee their anguish, but also depends on the choice of humanity to 'reify' the other. Thus, morality cannot exist without an attempt to transform social structures, such that moral conversion is inscribed in a collective dynamic. This means that Sartre now analyses the dialectical relation between liberty and situation in a more balanced way, acknowledging that oppressive relations can restrain individual freedom, and granting more weight to social determining factors and to the way in which all transcendence remains somewhat 'coloured' by the given which it transcends.

Although *Notebooks for an ethics* and *Anti-Semite and Jew* question the individualist perspective that marks the initial formulation of Sartrean ethics and although they can be read as transitional texts between Sartre's earlier ethics and his later ethics of integral humanity, they still fall within the framework of the initial ethics of authenticity. Both texts express an awareness of the limits of the ethics implied by *Being and nothingness* but without proposing an alternative. It is only in *Critique of dialectical reason* (2004) that Sartre sketches the basis of a revised ethics. Here, Sartre introduces a social theory hinged on the notion of dialectical praxis defined either as a movement of totalisation which exceeds the contradiction between organic and inorganic or as the attempt on the part of an individual or group to alter the material environment so as to respond to a threat against organic integrity. Praxis is deeply rooted in the need to preserve one's life. On this basis, Sartre focuses in particular on the relation between freedom and collective action, and on analysing the way in which collective praxis constructs itself in opposition to the obstacle of the 'series' (Sartre, 2004). By the 'series', Sartre means a passive set of humans marked by a shared helplessness in the face of a realm which Sartre refers to as the 'practico-inert' in which praxis, which would normally aim to transform the environment, becomes fixed and inert. In contrast, the 'group' is an active set of humans characterised by a common praxis, which originates in response to a threat. A group can only construct itself in opposition to the collective inertia of seriality (notably through taking an oath or through institutionalisation). The Sartrean approach does not break, as such, with the theoretical framework of *Being and nothingness* in that praxis shares similar features with the 'for-itself', but it does emphasise more decisively those determining factors, both material and social, which weigh upon freedom, clarifying the way in which the practico-inert assigns each of us a particular 'class-being'.

Using the social theory developed in *Critique of dialectical reason*, Sartre attempts, in the 1961 Rome Conference, to create an ethics centred on the notion of 'integral humanity', rooted in a notion of needs associated with animality. Defining the objective of praxis as the satisfaction of human needs, Sartre introduces a concrete ethics focused on the development of the human organism in all its dimensions. In so doing, he constructs this ethics upon a wide range of needs, including basic bodily needs, affective needs (for love or esteem), and more complex needs including the need to have access to culture or the more general need for freedom. Integral humanity presents itself as the ultimate goal of praxis, its justification being derived from those given needs demanding satisfaction (Sartre, 1993b). The attempt to reformulate his ethics is synonymous with the increasing importance in Sartre's work of the explicit theme of a need for esteem in the constitution of individuality. This theme lies at the heart of Sartre's reflections on the work of Gustave Flaubert. In *The family idiot* (1981), Sartre emphasises the importance of social and familial conditioning on the development of personality, insisting on the significant impact on

Flaubert of his lack of a true maternal love which, combined with the indifference of his father whose had always preferred his brother, resulted in Flaubert's lack of self-esteem and passivity. Flaubert lacked the 'mandate' to live which each parent grants to his or her children (Sartre, 1981: 133).

In this way, Sartre insists on the impact of internalising social structures on the development of individual personality, in line with an ethics which presents persons as radically dependent on others. He explains this development using the notion of 'constitution' which refers to an individual's internalisation of social and familial structures and of the ideologies they generate, particularly during the events of early childhood. Sartre articulates the notion of constitution with that of personalisation, explaining that Flaubert made of himself what others made of him, such that his passivity as well as his creative writing were the product of a certain kind of choice. We find here a rephrasing of the connection between transcendence and facticity, but the fact remains that Sartre's analyses now clearly differ with his initial formulations of ontology. *Saint Genet* (Sartre, 1963) likewise emphasises the other's influence on the self-awareness of each individual. Sartre thus appears to have distanced himself from the idea of a self-transparent consciousness, which previously marked his early analyses. Moreover, Sartre pays close attention to the effects of recognition and of low self-esteem for both Jean Genet and Flaubert alike, throwing light on the manner in which agents need to be valued in the eyes of another to be able to assume their freedom and lead a life which fully satisfies their needs.

This reconstruction of the passage from an ethics of authenticity to one of 'integral humanity' – which draws on the work of Thomas Anderson (1993) – converges with and adds weight to Honneth's interpretation of Sartre. It confirms that Sartre's ontology creates a number of difficulties which impede the formulation of a concrete ethics. It also emphasises the way that the theme of recognition becomes more explicit in Sartre's work when he qualifies and corrects his initial account of ontology. However, this reconstruction also differs from Honneth's analyses in one important respect. Honneth presents the *Critique of dialectical reason* as a disappointing addition to Sartre's *Being and nothingness* (Honneth, Chapter 2 of this volume) and, in so doing, he overlooks, in our view, the interest of the social theory which emerges from a careful reading of the *Critique*. As our own reconstruction has shown, the social theory of the *Critique* serves to ground the mature Sartrean ethics of 'integral humanity' which provides a stronger sense of the social conditions of human flourishing accompanied by a revised conception of intersubjectivity which is far from being unilateral and exclusively negative. This much is clear from a careful reading of *The family idiot* and *Saint Genet*. On this basis, and having somewhat qualified Honneth's reading of Sartre, we would like to consider, now, whether Sartre's approach might, in fact, provide a useful contribution to a critical reading of Honneth's theory.

Agonistic identity construction

Towards a critique of contemporary debates on recognition

In presenting our reflections on how a Sartrean approach might throw light on certain blind spots in Honneth's theory, we will focus, first, on the concept of reification and, secondly, on the question of identity. Our aim is to show that a revival of a Sartrean approach to the social can support a critical perspective on both Honneth's framework and on the way in which contemporary debates on recognition are framed. In so doing, we do not wish to present an alternative to the existing theories of recognition but rather intend to amend them, so as to support the development of a more pluralistic approach to struggles for recognition.

A phenomenology of 'ordinary' or 'everyday' reification

The Sartrean analysis of the ontological structure of the 'for-itself' presents interpersonal relations as reifying. Explaining the experience of shame, Sartre shows how the other mediates between my being-as-object and myself as a free object. The other makes me aware of myself as an object in the encounter with another consciousness (1993a: 290). In this sense, Sartre continually insists on the alienating dimension of the look (1993a: 269). The fact of being surprised in an embarrassing situation makes us experience ourselves, in the other's look, as a fixed object in the middle of the world (1993a: 277). The relation between two consciousnesses is cloaked with the shame 'of having my being outside, engaged in another being and as such without defence, illuminated by the absolute light which emanates from a pure subject', of 'being an object, that is, of recognizing myself in this degraded, fixed, and dependent being which I am for the other' (1993a: 288 and 289).

Such an analysis relies on the rejection of any kind of ontological monism. Against Hegel and Heidegger, Sartre insists on the separation between two consciousnesses, internal negation being the only possible connection between them. The Other is 'the one who excludes me by being himself, the one whom I exclude by being myself' (Sartre, 1993a: 236). What does such an account imply? First, I can only react to my being objectified by the Other by trying to objectify him or her in return. Hence, either I feel objectified by the Other and I thus cannot know him or her; or I try to know the Other but can only seize him or her as an object. Relations between self and other are thus circular. However, given that the Other is the foundation of my being-in-itself, I can also try to absorb his freedom so as to become my own foundation. When I try to free myself from the Other, he or she does likewise and if I try to subjugate the Other, he or she tries to subjugate me in return. Love is thus utterly agonistic: it is linked to the attempt to reappropriate oneself by incorporating the Other's freedom (Sartre, 1993a: 364–79). Love seeks to assimilate the Other's freedom but it seeks in vain because the lover wants the beloved to remain free while also seeking to master the beloved. The lover wants the beloved to freely consent to be captured by himself 'so as to will its own captivity' (Sartre 1993a: 367). Seeking to 'infect' the Other with his or her own facticity, the lover must captivate the Other (Sartre, 1993a: 372). As an attempt to cancel the negation that characterises relations between two consciousnesses without abolishing the internal negation, love is contradictory: 'If the Other loves me, he radically deceives me by his very love. I demanded of him that he should found my being as a privileged object by maintaining himself as pure subjectivity confronting me; and as soon as he loves me he experiences me as subject and is swallowed up in his objectivity confronting my subjectivity' (1993a: 376). Such failure can lead to the reverse attempt to avoid incorporating the Other while maintaining his Otherness so as to be incorporated by the Other, leading to a whole range of masochistic relationships by which one aims at being a being-in-itself founded on the Other's freedom. Masochism is as vain as love in that the masochist can never seize his or her own being as an object. On the whole, Sartre insists that such reiterated failures lead not to the pursuit of an assimilation with the Other's consciousness but rather to the attempt to confront it so as to appropriate the Other's freedom. This attempt is also doomed to failure because I can only seize the Other as an object. Again, the seizure of the Other as object is the principle of a whole range of attitudes such as indifference towards the Other, sexual desire (by which I attempt to capture the Other's free subjectivity by making him or her an object for me 'in order to impel the Other to realise for herself and for me her own flesh' (1993a: 391), and sadism or hatred (by which I try to destroy the Other's consciousness). But even hatred is a contradictory attitude because the attempt to destroy the Other's consciousness always implies an acknowledgement of the Other's existence.

We have already pointed to the limits of such an analysis, namely, that it provides an abstract account of interpersonal relations, precluding the possibility of achieving any kind of mutual recognition. We could nevertheless argue that such analyses sustain a critical point of view towards the Honnethian frame. Honneth emphasises the role of diverse forms of recognition in the intersubjective constitution of subjectivities without providing a precise and concrete account of ordinary, everyday processes of recognition and without throwing light on the obstacles such processes can come up against. A Sartrean approach promises to identify such obstacles.

Although Honneth does not deal with this question in *The struggle for recognition*, he nevertheless considers the processes of recognition in later writings, within the framework of a reflection devoted to social ontology, in 'Invisibility' (2001) and *Reification* (2008). The objective of these writings is to understand the way in which recognition precedes cognition, insofar as any kind of cognitive identification presupposes the ability to perceive qualities which are valued by interaction partners. In *Reification*, Honneth argues that we cannot understand anything without an active concern for others. Consequently, reification can be defined as a 'forgetfulness of recognition' (Honneth, 2008: 155). Honneth's goal is to revitalise the category of reification for contemporary problems. In attempting to define an account of reification which would be effective on a practical level, Honneth holds to the literal and ontological sense of the idea, according to which reification involves treating a human being as a thing, instituted by the objectivising stance of others, the world or the self. Honneth's central motivation is to question the connection established by Georg Lukács between reification and an indifferent or contemplative attitude, in contrast with the idea of an 'existential engagement'. Honneth thus insists that Lukács' approach converges with Martin Heidegger's account of care and John Dewey's concept of practical involvement, in that a kind of sympathy always precedes the observation of persons (Honneth, 2008: 38 and 150). Honneth thus emphasises the genetic priority of recognition over cognition and the Honnethian frame integrates a form of recognition which is more elementary than those previously distinguished. This more basic form of recognition can be defined as 'affective participation' or even 'elementary recognition' (Honneth, 2008: 152). Such recognition precedes and conditions all forms of attachment, whether in the form of love, respect, or esteem. Such recognition is neither a rational act nor an understanding of the other's motives but rather a pre-cognitive stance by which we acknowledge in the other person an intentionality similar to ours or by which we feel an existential concern for the other person (Honneth, 2008: 152). On such a basis, reification is defined as the process by which we lose awareness of this original recognition, forgetting our elementary affective participation.

Honneth relies on two models to explain this process. According to the first, an objective or goal becomes autonomous of a context such that 'we stop paying attention to the other' (Honneth, 2008: 59). On the second model, the prevalence of thought schemas and interactive patterns lead participants to approach others as mere objects to be manipulated for self-interested motives, which is incompatible with the priority of intersubjective recognition over cognition. We notice, here, that Honneth only applies the category of reification to extreme forms of objectivation, disregarding the recognitive structure of intersubjective interactions. He himself acknowledges that his analysis demonstrates the improbability of true cases of reification in everyday social life so that it is only in exceptional circumstances, when sociability takes on its darkest character, that we can speak of an abolition of recognition (Honneth, 2008: 157). Consequently, Honneth restricts the use of reification uniquely to describe massive slaughters of totalitarian regimes and modern forms of slavery, such as the sex trade (Honneth, 2008: 158), paying little attention to other possible forms of reification, where persons are treated *as if* they are things and not *as* things, forms which he prefers to describe as 'fictive reification' (Honneth, 2008: 157).

Sartre, Honneth: conflict and recognition

We are now in a position to understand the potential contributions which a Sartrean account of the dynamic of mutual reification governing interpersonal relations could bring to Honneth's explanation of reification. Sartre offers a way of thinking through the limits of Honneth's analysis, by providing concrete analyses of the processes which inform the diverse types of 'fictive reification'. Although Honneth's concern to hold to the literal meaning of reification is commendable in that it avoids diluting the concept, it unfortunately leads him to focus attention almost exclusively on only those extreme forms of reification, even while admitting that they are far rarer than the 'fictive' cases. In contrast, the Sartrean analyses throw light on those ordinary forms of reification (which Honneth would define as 'fictive'), forms which are frequently encountered in the day-to-day interaction of social life. These everyday forms of reification effectively deny the Other's unlimited freedom and attempt to reduce him to a fixed definition of himself. Admittedly, Sartre initially and rather excessively reduced all recognition relations to relations of mutual reification, however we have seen that his later analyses are more qualified such that it allows space for more positive forms of mutual recognition. Moreover, the analyses developed in *Being and nothingness* also appear to be relevant in that they throw light on the obstacles to recognition relations, which are far more concrete and ordinary than the forms of reification Honneth emphasises. Where Honneth maintains a clear opposition between recognition and reification, the Sartrean analyses provide resources for developing a more realistic account of recognition relations which would point to the fragility of such relations threatened by ordinary forms of 'reification'. Instead of opposing Sartre's approach as a merely negative account of recognition which prevents mutual recognition, the Honnethian approach could benefit from focusing on its strengths. We would now like to consider how a framework of recognition might present a more balanced account, where Sartre constitutes a remedy to Honneth's excessive optimism and where Honneth remedies Sartre's excessive pessimism. Sartre's approach need not be interpreted as opposed to Honneth's framework but rather provides resources to help us qualify Honneth's analyses by emphasising the inescapable fragility and ambivalence of recognition, even in its more positive forms.

Recognition and freedom: the critical dimension of recognition
We would now like to deepen this critical reflection on Honneth's understanding of reification by considering Sartre's account of anti-colonial struggle. Honneth argues that Sartre's approach to this question demonstrates an evolution of his initially negative account of recognition in that Sartre implies that anti-colonial struggle seeks to redress colonialism, which he takes to be a social state that distorts intersubjective relations of recognition so that groups follow a quasi-neurotic pattern of behaviour (Honneth, 1995a: 157). The notion of neurosis allows Sartre to account for relations between colonist and colonised as

deriving from a dynamic of 'denial-maintenance' of mutual recognition, a 'historically relativized model of conflict' thus prevailing in the texts devoted to the anti-colonial movement of *négritude* (Honneth, 1995a: 157). Drawing on Frantz Fanon's analyses, Sartre refers to the concept of neurosis, continuing to define the 'colonial system' as a reciprocal relation of 'fabrication' between colonised and coloniser. He thus draws attention to the contradictory situation in which the colonist can exploit only by dehumanising, which requires desiring both the death *and* the multiplication of the colonised, Sartre therefore insisting on the structure of reciprocity between colonists and colonised:

> A petrified ideology applies itself to considering men as animals that talk. In vain: in order to give them orders, even the harshest, the most insulting, you have to begin by acknowledging them; and as they cannot be watched over constantly, you have to resolve to trust them. Nobody can treat a man 'like a dog' if he does not first consider him as a man. (Sartre, 2001: 52–3)

This passage is of crucial importance. The colonised condition is presented as a neurosis which both lays claim to and denies a certain human condition whereas the colonist must both despise and recognise the colonised. Honneth is not wrong when he points out the interest of such an analysis, which exhibits the link between structures of colonial domination and pathological forms of recognition, and he also underlines its problematic ambiguity regarding the normative status of the claim to human rights, because Sartre himself refers to the discourse of human rights to throw light on the disrespect suffered by the colonised while also denouncing that discourse as a guise for exploitation.

However, Sartre's analysis invites us to deepen the critical reading of Honneth's approach to reification. Honneth's restriction of the scope of reification to those extreme forms of objectification is challenged by Sartre's insistence that even radical forms of colonial exploitation require acknowledging those individuals as human beings. Even when the colonisers dehumanise the colonised, they do not treat them like mere things. The colonisers aim to instrumentalise the colonised by treating them like animals, but instrumentalisation and humiliation are inseparable and humiliation presupposes the humanity of the colonised. If victims of this radical form of exploitation are not treated merely as things, as Honneth believes, this raises the question as to whether his account of reification is in fact appropriate. Sartre's analysis invites us to consider the importance of those forms of reification that Honneth refers to as 'fictive' and to which he devotes little attention.

Recognition and identity

Moreover, Sartre's perspective promises to be fruitful not simply with respect to reification, but also with respect to Honneth's account of the connection between recognition and identity, and between recognition and reconciliation.

Sartre's account of anti-colonial struggles leads us to question the model of a 'unified identity' which recognition theory assumes. Sartre's *Anti-Semite and Jew* (1995) and Fanon's *Black skin, white masks* (2008) both present a psycho-existential account of recognition relations which is undeniably a major source for the concept of identity politics, but it also helps us to identify this concept's limits (Kruks, 1996). *Anti-Semite and Jew* presents anti-Semitism as both passion and a worldview, that is, on the basis of a deep-seated fear of freedom, the anti-Semite chooses mediocrity and, out of pride, makes of this mediocrity a rigid aristocracy, choosing a 'scale of petrified values' (Sartre, 1995: 27–8). This analysis also involves a critical reflection not just on the anti-Semite but also on the good democrat who assimilates the Jew, leaving nothing but the man, the subject of the universal rights of man. Where the anti-Semite wishes to destroy the Jew as a person and leave nothing in him or her but the pariah-Jew, the 'good liberal' wishes to annihilate the Jew as a Jew but defend him or her as a person (1995: 56). Consequently, defining the Jewish person as a function of the ways in which others relate to and label the Jew, Sartre argues that what constitutes Jewish community is not a shared identity but a 'condition' (1995: 67 and 85) such that a decision to assimilate on the part of Jewish people corresponds to inauthentic behaviour (1995: 92). Sartre describes the 'authentic' Jew as one who affirms himself as a Jew 'in the face of all and against all' (1995: 137). However, this attitude is not sufficient. On the one hand, anti-Semitism is a passionate effort to realise a national union *against* the division of society into classes. Anti-Semitism is therefore a bourgeois representation of class struggle and it could not exist in a classless society (1995: 149). On the other hand, Sartre explains that authenticity does not imply making sense of an identity defined in cultural or ethnic terms, or even in terms of shared ethical values. Authenticity lies in the true awareness of a situation and of the responsibilities it implies.

The question of authenticity is also the starting point for Fanon's work that describes the psycho-existential neurosis to which black men and women are subjected and which prevents them from reaching authenticity. This neurosis derives from the internalisation of racist stereotypes and Fanon shows that Afro-Caribbeans subjected since childhood to the values of a white culture end up identifying with it and experiencing utter alienation within it. The internalisation of a worldview which casts whites as superior causes inauthenticity, leading either to a kind of self-objectification which comes with the desire to be recognised as white or to an adherence to rationalistic universal values. The only path to authenticity appears to lie, as in Sartre, in the affirmation of difference. Nevertheless, Fanon identifies the movement of *négritude* as a mainly reactive process, where the very concept of *négritude* is built on the inversion of racist stereotypes. Here again, Fanon concurs with Sartre on the affirmation of both the necessary *and* unbearable character of *négritude*, even as he criticises Sartre for having clarified its transitional dimension – thus undermining its vitality.

And, like Sartre, Fanon appears to implicitly outline a form of recognition focused not on 'identity' but on the transcending freedom of each individual (Fanon, 2008: 201–2). While Fanon and Sartre's analyses have been criticised for failing to consider the way that institutions mediate between particular existential experiences and more general historical processes (Kruks, 1996), Sartre nevertheless addresses this problem explicitly in the *Critique of dialectical reason*, as does Fanon, in *The wretched of the Earth* (2005), when he reflects on the fact that freedom cannot be sought within the realm of recognition alone. Although Fanon's defence of armed struggle for national liberation is grounded in the context of decolonisation, it nonetheless signals the insufficiency of any claim to identity, and it is this point which we would like to emphasise here. The claim to identity can admittedly be a source of empowerment on the psychological level, but it cannot liberate in the absence of deep institutional transformation.

Recognition and reconciliation

With their critical account of recognition focused on freedom, Fanon and Sartre identify some of the limits of a model of recognition which focuses on identity while also defending a pessimistic view of recognition relations as constitutively related with appropriation and assimilation (Yar, 2001: 62).[2] For Fanon, recognition presents us with a dilemma, requiring that we choose either between indifference, or affirmation of an identity which is reductive (Schaap, 2004: 537). In this way, Sartre and Fanon appear to question the link established by Charles Taylor and Axel Honneth between recognition and reconciliation. In the frame of his reflection on the possible connection between a politics of equal respect and politics of recognition, Taylor relies on a dialogical approach of individual identity, an ethical ideal of authenticity, whose tensions we have already reflected on, in that the ideal combines the claim of fidelity to an original identity with the insistence on the fact that identities are social constructions (Taylor, 1992). Taylor also associates recognition with the promise of 'a fusion of horizons' (1992: 67, 70–3 and 92) and overlooks the fact that every kind of recognition has an anti-political dimension in that its logic risks the reduction and violent appropriation of the other and thus the denial of possibilities for self-creation – notably when the logic of recognition is considered as aiming to secure a common identity (Schaap, 2004: 533). In a similar manner, Honneth associates struggle for recognition with the idea of moral progress in a reflection which includes teleological assumptions which he does not attempt to justify. This commitment to 'a fusion of horizons' appears excessively optimistic about the possibility of struggles for recognition allowing both social transformation and reconciliation which, as Andrew Schaap suggests, is concerned with dealing with the legacy of grave wrongs perpetrated by a former regime (2004: 10).

Sartre, Honneth: conflict and recognition

Schaap attempts to theoretically combine the recognition of the Other's identity with the affirmation of the Other's non-identity to that identity, through a kind of agonistic recognition (Schaap, 2004: 538). Affirmation of non-identity is a mode of recognition which leaves open the possibility of questioning the terms of recognition themselves. This recognition – reconciliation relation would be agonistic and would not aim to salvage a common identity but rather to 'make available a space for politics within which citizens divided by the memories of past wrongs could debate and contest the terms of their political association' (Schaap, 2004: 538). This agonistic form recognition becomes clearer when we reflect on the legal politics of reconciliation in divided postcolonial societies, like Australia. Schaap thus concurs with James Tully (2004) who insists on the necessity to break away from monological perspectives on recognition, focused on an interactionist and dyadic model of social conflict (master versus slave, bourgeois versus worker), so as to consider the relational and multilateral aspects of struggles. Hence, both prefer to speak of struggles *about* recognition (see David Owen's contribution in Chapter 6 of this volume).

Tully understands struggles of recognition to be 'struggles over recognition', that is, struggles over the prevailing intersubjective norms of mutual recognition, by which members are recognised and governed (Tully, 2004: 86–7). By highlighting the way in which such norms are relations of meaning and power relations, constituting the behaviour and expectations of the partners in varying degrees (Tully, 2004: 88), Tully demonstrates that norms play a central role in the subjectivation and normalisation processes. This means, for Tully, that they must remain open to contestation: the idea of struggle over norms of recognition implies the idea of struggles over the relations of communication and power by which we are governed (2004: 90). Struggles over recognition concern freedom and not exclusively justice or identity and, in this sense, struggle over norms of recognition conflicts with the very meaning of recognition.

Consequently, Tully is also concerned to question the 'finality presumption' (Tully, 2004: 81, 95–8; Tully, 2008: 306), which he believes characterises theories of recognition in that they wrongly assume that there are definitive solutions to struggles over recognition. Tully thus rejects the idea that a perfectly achieved form of recognition would be possible in so far as every norm of recognition is complicit in a normalising process which should therefore arouse resistance. No matter what motivates processes of recognition and how reciprocal these norms might be, their effects should not be immune to contestation. The horizon of struggles for recognition cannot be the settlement of procedures and definite solutions but the institutionalisation of a specific type of democratic freedom that Tully defines as civic freedom, that is to say, the freedom to oppose oppressive, exclusive, or assimilative norms of mutual recognition (Tully, 2004: 98–102).

The renewal of Sartre's perspective would concur with such approaches.

However, at this point, we would like to point out that we do not think that Sartre's perspective should aim to provide an alternative to Honneth's theory which would somehow be independent of that framework. Our aims are more modest. We think that Sartre could help to make critical sense of the way in which contemporary debates on recognition have been framed. As Nikolas Kompridis (2007) points out, these debates are fairly confined, and deal with the question as to whether recognition should be construed as a matter of identity, on the one hand, or a matter of justice, on the other. The debate between Honneth and Nancy Fraser tends to eclipse the more central question of the very meaning itself of the struggle for recognition, as if this question had already been resolved (Fraser and Honneth, 2001). However, the meaning of struggling for recognition has not been settled, and we should resist the temptation to try to fix it in advance of those struggles themselves, which inevitably involves privileging one specific normative ideal over another. In this sense, we should rather focus on developing a pluralistic and contextual approach to struggles for recognition. This orientation, suggested by Kompridis, would take seriously the heteronomous nature of praxis and expectations at stake in struggles for recognition, pointing out that these are far less rigid and stable than recognition theorists like Honneth and Fraser make out. The interest of a Sartrean approach lies in the manner in which it outlines a critical account of recognition which would be utterly agonistic and, like Tully's and Schaap's versions, focused on freedom. It would sustain a reflection on agonistic forms of recognition and attempt to overcome the opposition between construing recognition as a question of identity or a question of justice. Drawing on Sartre, we can develop an account of freedom which does not attempt to substitute itself for a model of recognition focused on identity but rather intends to nourish it with a critical counterpoint. An agonistic account of the practice of freedom should be part of an understanding of struggles of recognition, in addition to considerations about identity and justice.

Conclusion

Our aim in this chapter has not been to provide a comprehensive neo-Sartrean alternative approach to recognition but rather to point out why renewing the Sartrean perspective could be productive. Consequently, our reflections have attempted to identify the main drivers in Sartre's thought which could bring a more critical approach to Honneth's theory, while also questioning the narrow manner in which debates about recognition's nature have been framed. We began by qualifying Honneth's interpretation of Sartre's work, showing how the theme of recognition becomes more central to Sartre's reflections, producing a revised concept of intersubjectivity which is not exclusively negative, as per Honneth's description. We then showed how the Sartrean approach provides a useful contribution to a critical reading of Honneth's theory.

Sartre, Honneth: conflict and recognition

A first contribution is its capacity to draw attention to the importance of those ordinary forms of reification to which Honneth devotes insufficient attention. In so doing, Sartre helps us develop a more realistic account of the way in which even positive forms of recognition relations are inseparable from the threat of objectification. Our point has not been to deny the possibility of positive recognition relations but to suggest that instead of presenting Sartre's and Honneth's approach as opposing accounts of recognition (the first, negative and the second, positive), we should rather acknowledge that each thinker balances the emphasis of the other. In this sense, Sartre promises to remedy the limits of Honneth's overly optimistic account of recognition. A dialogue between Sartre and Honneth could help us avoid the pitfalls of a binary opposition between authentic and inauthentic recognition, instead acknowledging the fragility and ambivalence of every form of recognition – even authentic and positive ones.

A second contribution lies in the capacity of Sartre's and Fanon's work to help us question both the fixation on identity which marks Honneth's recognition theory and the articulation between recognition and reconciliation that prevails in Taylor's and Honneth's work. Such reflections allow us to challenge the limited treatment of the meaning of recognition which prevails in contemporary debates on recognition, which tend to construe recognition either as a matter of identity or as a matter of justice. Sartre's legacy supports a concept of democratic freedom to oppose oppressive, exclusive, or assimilative norms of mutual recognition.

Of course, Sartre's work has its own problems. We could argue, for example, that, despite the way it eventually considers collective recognition, it offers insufficient consideration of the importance of the mediation of social institutions. The social and institutional framework of objectifying behaviours is insufficiently emphasised.[3] However, although Sartre's approach cannot provide a comprehensive ethical and political theory of recognition, Sartre's insights can certainly contribute resources for a pluralistic approach to struggles of recognition, as we hope to have demonstrated in this chapter.

Notes

1 Existential psychoanalysis is a method of inquiry that interprets an individual's behaviour in the light of his fundamental project in the world (Sartre, 1993a: 557–74).
2 Reciprocal recognition, to which Fanon refers, is recognition of a 'contradictory activity' (2008: 193).
3 In this sense, Pierre Bourdieu's sociology promises to throw light on institutional constraints, questions that Sartre did not consider. See the contributions of Christian Lazzeri and Robin Celikates to this volume (Chapters 9 and 10).

6

Tully, Foucault and agonistic struggles over recognition

*David Owen**

IN contrast to the work of Charles Taylor, Axel Honneth and Nancy Fraser, the critical practice of Michel Foucault is not usually related to discussions of recognition or the politics of recognition. This is ironic since an integral feature of Foucault's work concerns the way in which struggles over intersubjective norms take place, norms in terms of which participants in a practice of government structure their interactions and see each other as subjects of this practice. This is to say, as James Tully points out, that Foucault is directly concerned with struggles over recognition (Tully, 2008: 293).

Tully's own work from *An approach to political philosophy* (1993) to *Strange multiplicity* (1995) to, most recently, the two volumes of *Public philosophy in a new key* (2008 and 2009) offers us both a reading of Foucault that makes perspicuous his contribution to contemporary debates concerning recognition and an original elaboration and extension of that contribution. My concern in this chapter is, consequently, two-fold: to consider Tully's relationship to Foucault and to show how Tully's use of Foucault within his own work provides a distinctive approach to questions of recognition. I shall take up this task attending to two aspects of Tully's use of Foucault, first, as a critical mode of historical philosophy for approaching the topic of recognition and, second, as a basis for an agonistic account of struggles over recognition.

Tully, Foucault and public philosophy

We can distinguish three steps in Tully's approach that comprise what he refers to as the critical activity of public philosophy.

The first is that, following Ludwig Wittgenstein, Quentin Skinner and Foucault, it grants a primacy to practice, that is, it focuses on the practices of governance and the exercise of freedom within and over the norms of these practices that shape the forms of thought, conduct and subjectivity characteristic of the present (Tully, 2008: 16). From Wittgenstein, Tully draws out the point that Hannah Arendt's understanding of the practice of freedom – of speaking and acting differently in the course of a language game and so modifying or transforming the game – is not a special feature of politics or a form of freedom restricted to certain modes of human interaction but, rather, is a general feature of human practices and relationships (Tully, 2008: 139–41). Tully takes Skinner and Foucault to be the primary inheritors of this outlook. In the case of Skinner, this involves tracing the intersubjective conventions that govern political reflection in a given context in order to show how political actors in that context have exercised their freedom in modifying those conventions (Tully, 2008: 141). In the case of Foucault, it involves providing a genealogy of the problematisations in terms of which we understand ourselves as bound by certain limits; a genealogy which is, at the same time, a redescription of those limits. Foucault's approach shares both Arendt's understanding of the activity of freedom as modification or transformation of games of governance and the view of Wittgenstein and Skinner that such freedom is a feature of any and all human practices, even the most rule-governed, but Foucault also develops Nietzsche's point that this activity of freedom is an *agonistic* relationship. He writes: 'Rather than speaking of an essential freedom, it would be better to speak of an "*agonism*" – of a relationship which is at the same time reciprocal incitation and struggle; less of a face-to-face confrontation which paralyses both sides than a permanent provocation' (Foucault, 1982: 222–3). As Tully points out:

> Foucault's unique contribution to this reorientation in the twentieth century is to link together the following elements: the practice of freedom, the modification of the rules governing the relationships among players in the course of a game and agonistic activity. He sees the modification of the rules of any game as itself an agonistic activity of freedom: precisely the freedom of speaking and acting differently. He asks us to regard human activities as games with rules and techniques of governance to be sure, and these are often agonistic games, but also, and more importantly, to look on the ways the players modify the rules by what they say and do as they carry on, and, in so doing, modify their identities as players: that is, the games of freedom within and against the rules of the games of governance. (2008: 143)

Public philosophy in Tully's sense begins with the calling into question and concern to modify a game of government on the part of those subject to it. In this respect, it is best construed as an expression and enabling of the agonistic activity of freedom.

The second step is that, following Foucault, Tully does not attempt to develop a normative theory as a way of adjudicating or evaluating the calling into question of the game of government. Rather public philosophy engages in what might be termed 'redescription with critical intent'. First, public philosophy focuses on disclosing the historically contingent conditions of possibility for the practices of governance in question and the form of problematisation that it exhibits before, second, offering a redescription that alters the self-understanding of those subject to it, and struggling within it, in ways that enable them to perceive 'in what is given to us as universal, necessary, obligatory, what place is occupied by whatever is singular, contingent, and the product of arbitrary constraints' (Foucault, 1984a: 45). Public philosophy achieves this objective through two elements.

The first of these, which we may call the archaeological, is a critical survey of the languages and practices of governance within which the struggles in question arise and the ways in which these struggles, the range of possible responses and the solutions to them are articulated. The second element, which we may call the genealogical, is historical in character. Here Tully draws on a thought given expression by Skinner: 'it is remarkably difficult to avoid falling under the spell of our own intellectual heritage.' Skinner continues: 'As we analyse and reflect on our normative concepts, it is easy to become bewitched into believing that the ways of thinking about them bequeathed to us by the mainstream of our intellectual traditions must be the ways of thinking about them' (Skinner, 1998: 116). Thus, as Skinner stresses, one reason for engaging in this type of historical reflection is that:

> [t]he history of philosophy, and perhaps especially of moral, social and political philosophy, is there to prevent us from becoming too readily bewitched. The intellectual historian can help us to appreciate how far the values embodied in our present way of life, and our present ways of thinking about those values, reflect a series of choices made at different times between different possible worlds. This awareness can help to liberate us from the grip of any one hegemonic account of those values and how they should be interpreted and understood. Equipped with a broader sense of possibility, we can stand back from the intellectual commitments that we have inherited and ask ourselves in a new spirit of enquiry what we should think of them. (Skinner, 1998: 116–17)

What distinguishes Tully from Skinner, however, is that he also follows Foucault's practice in which the task of criticism is not simply to generate reflective distance but also that of analysing and reflecting on limits:

> But if the Kantian question was that of knowing what limits knowledge has to renounce transgressing, it seems to me that the critical question today has to be turned back into a positive one: in what is given to us as universal, necessary, obligatory, what place is occupied by whatever is singular, contingent, and the product of arbitrary constraints? The point, in brief, is to transform the critique conducted in the form of necessary limitation into a practical critique that takes the form of a possible transgression. (Foucault, 1984a: 45)

Tully, Foucault: agonistic struggles over recognition

This mode of analysing and reflecting on limits is presented by Foucault as 'work carried out by ourselves upon ourselves as free beings' (Foucault, 1984a: 47) which seeks to 'give new impetus, as far and wide as possible, to the undefined work of freedom' (Foucault, 1984a: 46). There are two points to notice with respect to these remarks of Foucault's which have become increasingly central to Tully's understanding of his own work. The first is that the practice of public philosophy is not distinct in kind from the reflections of citizens, rather, it involves the methodical extension of the self-reflective character of historically situated practices of practical reasoning oriented to the reflective elucidation and negotiation of the content and bounds of practical reason. The second is that this activity is a practice of freedom itself.

The final step in Tully's critical activity is that this 'hard-won historical and critical relation to the present does not stop at calling a limit into question and engaging in a dialogue over its possible transformation' but also 'seeks to establish an on-going mutual relation with the concrete struggles, negotiations and implementations of citizens who experiment with modifying the practices on the ground' (Tully, 2008: 17). Public philosophy does not aim to speak for those subject to government, but rather aims to provide them with resources for speaking for themselves.

The debt of Tully's conception of public philosophy as critical activity to the work of Foucault is clear and Tully acknowledges this by presenting the following remarks by Foucault as a précis of his approach: 'The critical ontology of ourselves must be considered not, certainly, as a theory or a doctrine; rather it must be conceived as an attitude, an ethos, a philosophical life in which the critique of what we are is at one and the same time the historical analysis of the limits imposed on us and an experiment with the possibility of going beyond them' (Foucault, 1984a: 50, cited in Tully, 2008: 19).

What bearing does this conception of political philosophy have for the question of recognition? We can discern two stages in Tully's work here. The first is given in *Strange multiplicity*, in which Tully draws on Foucault's genealogical approach to focus on struggles of cultural recognition. The second is articulated in *Public philosophy in a new key* (2008) in which a more deeply Foucauldian position leads Tully to widen the focus to struggles of recognition in their generality. I shall conclude by drawing attention to a final feature of Foucault's influence on Tully that has become integral to his understanding of his work.

Tully's Foucauldian approach to recognition

The first phase: a critical mode of historical philosophy (**Strange multiplicity**)[1]
The question addressed in *Strange multiplicity* is this: 'Can a modern constitution recognise and accommodate cultural diversity? ... The question is not whether one should be for or against cultural diversity. Rather it is the prior

question of what is the critical attitude or spirit in which justice can be rendered to demands for cultural recognition' (Tully, 1995: 1). It is the Foucauldian concern with the critical attitude or ethos which motivates Tully's first step in responding to this question, namely, a consideration of whether the language in which such enquiries proceed is capable of giving each speaker his or her due. Consequently, Tully's strategy is to adopt a historical approach to the question at hand which combines archaeological and genealogical dimensions identified by Foucault in a normatively inflected way. This historical approach intends to achieve the following:

1. To provide a perspicuous representation of the character of demands for cultural recognition by 'surveying the range of political struggles which have rendered cultural diversity problematic, causing it to become a locus of political action and philosophical reflection' (Tully, 1995: 1). This is the first archaeological moment.
2. To elucidate the nature and significance of claims for the constitutional recognition of cultural diversity and to outline a set of conventions that would allow speakers their due.
3. To survey the hegemonic language of modern constitutionalism in order to lay open to view those conventions which obstruct our understanding of claims for cultural recognition and, thereby, prevent us from rendering what is due to the advocates of such claims. This is the second archaeological moment. And to offer an historical account of how the language of modern constitutionalism has become hegemonic within the language of contemporary constitutionalism, marginalising and excluding what Tully refers to as the language of common constitutionalism. This is the first genealogical moment.
4. To free us from the grip of the picture given expression in the hegemonic language of modern constitutionalism by way of a historical survey of the language and practices of common constitutionalism which shows how this 'modern' picture causes us to overlook distinctions and uses of concepts in the language of contemporary constitutionalism which enable us to do justice to demands for cultural recognition. This is the second genealogical moment.
5. To show that once we are freed from captivity to the conventions of the language of modern constitutionalism, we can see the justice of the constitutional conventions that Tully recovers and reconstructs from historical examples of the practice of common constitutionalism for addressing contemporary struggles.

Tully, Foucault: agonistic struggles over recognition

In this section, and at the risk of overschematising Tully's argument, I shall sketch each of these stages of the argument in turn.

Stage 1
In what we may call the 'archaeological' dimension of his project, Tully uses the phrase 'the politics of cultural recognition' to gather together 'the broad and various political activities which jointly call cultural diversity into question as a characteristic constitutional problem of our time' (1995: 1–2). Despite the bewildering diversity of these struggles,[2] Tully argues that we can identity three salient similarities between them. First of all, demands for cultural recognition aspire to self-government: 'What they share is a longing for self-rule: to rule themselves in accord with their customs and ways' (Tully, 1995: 4). Secondly, and as a consequence of the first characteristic, struggles unite around the 'claim that the basic laws and institutions of modern societies, and their authoritative traditions of interpretation, are unjust in so far as they thwart the forms of self-government appropriate to the recognition of cultural diversity' (Tully, 1995: 5). The third and final characteristic of these diverse struggles grounds the two prior characteristics, namely, these struggles share 'the assumption that culture is an irreducible and constitutive aspect of politics'. Tully continues: 'The diverse ways in which citizens think about, speak, act and relate to others in participating in a constitutional association (both the abilities they exercise and the practices in which they exercise them) … are always to some extent the expression of their different cultures' (Tully, 1995: 5–6).

In respect of these similarities, the plurality of examples of struggles for cultural recognition 'share a traditional political motif: the injustice of an alien form of rule and the aspiration to self-rule in accord with one's own customs and ways' (Tully, 1995: 6). Since the struggles of indigenous peoples are contemporary with the emergence and development of contemporary constitutionalism, Tully takes these struggles as exemplary for considering the politics of cultural recognition.

Stage 2
The significance of this account of the politics of cultural recognition for Tully's question is spelt by reference to two further arguments. First, Tully argues that there is 'a certain priority' with respect to cultural recognition in comparison with the many other questions of justice that a constitution must address: 'Since other questions must be discussed and agreements reached by the citizens, the first step is to establish a just form of constitutional discussion in which each speaker is given her or his due, and this is exactly the initial question raised by the politics of cultural recognition' (1995: 6). It is for this reason that Tully argues that the crucial question is whether – and, if so, how – 'a constitution can give recognition to the legitimate demands of the members of diverse

cultures in a manner that renders everyone their due, so that all would freely consent to this form of constitutional association' (1995: 7).

Now it may seem that there has been something of a leap in Tully's argument insofar as we have moved from the recognition that the normative dimension of 'struggles for cultural recognition' is predicated on the assumption that 'culture is an irreducible and constitutive aspect of politics' to granting 'a certain priority' to cultural recognition with respect to a just form of constitutional association. What grounds this assumption and legitimates this priority? To draw out the relevant ground, consider these related remarks which Stanley Cavell directs critically at John Rawls' *A theory of justice* (1971):

> That liberty is limited by the conditions necessary for institution and preservation of the social order ... is no doubt true. But what the content of that order is to be is something into which my voice is to enter. The issue of consent becomes the issue of whether the voice I lend in recognising a society as mine, as speaking for me, is my voice, my own. (Cavell, 1990: 27)

The point to which Cavell directs our attention is the significance of experiencing one's political voice as one's own voice. This aspect of the issue of consent – which is repressed by comprehensive conceptions of consent predicated on 'the voice of no one' (e.g. Rawls' original position) – marks out the sense in which one can be estranged from one's political voice, experiencing it as alien, precisely insofar as the language of self-government in and through which one is constrained to speak – if one is to speak politically at all – is not one's own (Cavell, 1990: 27–8). Indeed, Tully argues that it is precisely this position which characterises the contemporary impasse between struggles for cultural recognition and the language of modern constitutionalism:

> How can the proponents of [cultural] recognition bring forth their claims in a public forum in which their cultures have been excluded or demeaned for centuries? They can accept the authoritative language and institutions, in which case their claims are rejected by conservatives or comprehended by progressives within the very languages and institutions whose sovereignty and impartiality they question. Or they can refuse to play the game, in which case they become marginal and reluctant conscripts or they take up arms. (1995: 56)

So the ground of the assumption that culture is an irreducible aspect of politics is simply the recognition that being able to speak in one's own voice requires that one is able to speak in one's own ways. It is on precisely this ground that cultural recognition has 'a certain priority' with respect to a just form of constitutional association because, since such an association is one to which each member can consent, it must begin by rendering each member their due such that each can consent with respect to matters of constitutional justice in his or her own voice.

Second, Tully argues that the first step in rendering members their due with respect to their own voicing of consent is 'mutual recognition' (1995: 7), but spelling out what this entails requires a consideration of the concept of culture. In other words, while the argument so far points to the limitations of political approaches which are culture-blind ('Esperanto constitutionalism'), it does not yet specify anything about the sort of recognition that cultural diversity requires. If, for example, cultural recognition is conceptualised in terms of the 'billiard ball' model of culture which has been largely dominant since the late eighteenth century (i.e. the view of cultures as internally homogenous and externally discrete), then the appropriate sort of recognition is deemed to be national statehood. An implication of this mode of cultural recognition is that 'when forms of multilateral federalism are advanced as solutions to some of the demands for cultural recognition, they appear ad hoc, even as a threat to democracy, equality and liberty' (Tully, 1995: 9), precisely because they appear as (unfortunate but necessary) compromises between the normative ideal and conditions of practicability. However, while it is still prevalent in political philosophy, the 'billiard ball' model of culture has been effectively criticised in contemporary anthropological literature and replaced by 'the view of cultures as overlapping, interactive and internally negotiated' (Tully, 1995: 10). As Tully explains:

> The identity, and so the meaning, of any culture is thus aspectival rather than essential: ... Cultural diversity is a tangled labyrinth of intertwining cultural differences and similarities, not a panopticon of fixed, independent and incommensurable worldviews in which we are either prisoners or cosmopolitan spectators in the central tower. (1995: 11)

A crucial implication of this anthropological revision of the concept of culture is that as 'a consequence of the overlap, interaction and negotiation of cultures, the experience of cultural difference is internal to a culture':

> On the older, essentialist view, the 'other' and the experience of otherness were by definition associated with another culture. One's own culture provided an identity in the form of a seamless background or horizon against which one determined where one stood on fundamental questions ... Having an identity consisted in being oriented in this essential space, whereas the loss of such a fixed horizon was equated with an 'identity crisis'; with the loss of all horizons. On the aspectival view, cultural horizons change as one moves about, just like natural horizons. The experience of otherness is internal to one's own identity. (Tully, 1995: 13)

This implication is crucial because it entails that we find ourselves in a situation that is negotiated, intercultural and aspectival (Tully, 1995: 14). Consequently, there is no one appropriate form of constitutional recognition of cultural diversity; rather mutual recognition involves a commitment to the activity of intercultural dialogue as a working through of similarities and differences oriented to finding an appropriate form of constitutional recognition.

On the basis of this discussion, Tully proposes that a contemporary constitution must be reconceived as a 'form of accommodation' of cultural diversity, in accordance with three conventions; mutual recognition, cultural continuity and consent. 'A constitution should be seen as a form of activity, an intercultural dialogue in which the culturally diverse sovereign citizens of contemporary societies negotiate agreements on their forms of association over time in accordance with the three conventions' (Tully, 1995: 30). However, recognition of this 'simple and somewhat obvious answer' is obstructed within the language of contemporary constitutionalism. To begin the task of clarifying and dissolving this obstruction, Tully draws a distinction within the language of contemporary constitutionalism between 'a dominant "modern" language and a subordinate, "common-law" or simply "common" language' (Tully, 1995: 31). The purpose of this distinction is to allow him to survey, by reference to the exemplary struggles of indigenous peoples, these two dissimilar languages in order to show how the former 'has been developed by leading theorists since the seventeenth century to exclude and assimilate cultural diversity in the name of uniformity', whereas the latter has 'been open to the recognition and accommodation of different cultures' (Tully, 1995: 31).

Stage 3
In giving a genealogical account of the language of modern constitutionalism with respect to the politics of cultural recognition, Tully identifies seven features of this language that serve to exclude or assimilate cultural diversity. These are the following:

a Concepts of popular sovereignty 'which eliminate cultural diversity as a constitutive aspect of politics. The people are sovereign and culturally homogeneous in the sense that culture is irrelevant, capable of being transcended, or uniform' (Tully, 1995: 63).

b A stages view of history: an understanding of a modern constitution as imperial, defined in contrast to an ancient or historically earlier constitution, be it a pre-modern European constitution, or the customs of non-European societies who are reportedly at an 'earlier' or 'lower' stage of development (Tully, 1995: 64).

c A commitment to uniformity: 'An ancient constitution is multiform, an "assemblage" as Bolingbroke puts it, whereas a modern constitution is uniform. Because it is the incorporation of varied local customs, an ancient constitution is a motley of overlapping legal and political jurisdictions, as in the Roman republic or the common law of England ... The sovereign people in modern societies, in contrast, establish a constitution that is legally and politically uniform: a constitution of equal citizens who are treated identically rather than equitably, of one national system of institutionalised legal and political authority rather than many, and a constitutional nation equal in status to all others' (Tully, 1995: 66).

d The recognition of custom in a theory of progress: 'the unintended historical progress of economic and social conditions gradually undermines the ancient constitution of customs and ranks and creates a society of one "estate" or "state" of equal and legally undifferentiated individuals with similar "manners" ... A modern constitution thus merely recognises the transformed character of modern societies' (Tully, 1995: 67).

e A modern constitution 'is identified with a specific set of European institutions; what Kant calls a "republican constitution" ... These definitive constitutional institutions in turn compose a modern sovereign state ... marking it off from lower, stateless, irregular and ancient societies' (Tully, 1995: 67–8).

f A constitutional state is a nation: 'From Pufendorf onward, this corporate identity of nation and nationals in a state is seen as necessary to the unity of a modern constitutional association' (Tully, 1995: 68).

g A modern constitution 'comes into being at some founding moment and stands behind – and provides the rules for – democratic politics' (Tully, 1995: 69). This feature is reinforced 'by the popular images of the American and French revolutions as great founding acts performed by founding fathers at the threshold of modernity' and 'by the assumption that a modern constitution is universal' (Tully, 1995: 68).

Having delineated these features, Tully shows how they were forged and established by way of a series of historical examples. These range from Locke's provision of a justification 'for taking [American] land and establishing European sovereignty without requiring the consent to the native peoples' (Tully, 1995: 70–8) to Vattel's and Kant's related justifications for the denial of the claim that aboriginal peoples satisfied the criteria of sovereign nations under international law (79–82) – and from the justifications offered by Pudendorf and Sieyès for the unity of a modern state and, thereby, for policies designed 'to break down the anachronistic customs of backward citizens and immigrants and reform them so that they acquired the manners and policy of a civilised and enlightened age' (82–91) to Paine's arguments for 'the sovereignty of the Continental Congress over the states' as providing a justification not only for policies designed to forge institutional and customary uniformity but also for policies of empire oriented to 'the removal, assimilation and extermination of Aboriginal peoples' (91–6). The point of these examples is highlight different aspects of the hegemonic picture of constitutions in order to show that 'the language of modern constitutionalism that has been forged in constitutional theory and practice over the last three hundred years is a partial forgery':

While masquerading as universal it is imperial in three respects: in serving to justify European imperialism, imperial rule of former colonies over indigenous peoples, and cultural imperialism over the diverse citizens of contemporary societies. When members of the authoritative schools today write about constitutionalism, whether they claim to be universal, historical or transcendental, they do so with the conventions of universality, history and transcendence of this captivating map of mankind. They ... think that they are tracing the contours of humanity's constitutions, yet they are merely tracing round the 'splendorous' frame through which they look at them. (Tully, 1995: 96)

Precisely because the seven features demarcate a 'universal' view of modern constitutions as an agreement of free and equal citizens (who are identical in the relevant respects) which founds a democratic constitutional nation-state characterised by legal and political uniformity, the language of modern constitutionalism can only either exclude claims for cultural recognition or assimilate them by redescribing – and misdescribing – them as another type of claim (e.g. claims for special advantage on the basis of historical injustice). In this regard, Tully is concerned precisely with the question which, as we saw earlier, Foucault highlights: 'in what is given to us as universal, necessary, obligatory, what place is occupied by whatever is singular, contingent, and the product of arbitrary constraints?' (Foucault, 1984a: 45).

Stage 4
It is at this stage that Tully introduces a certain 'object of comparison' by drawing our attention to the ways in which the language of modern constitutionalism has, from its inception, been contested by advocates of common constitutionalism, and by providing examples of the plural practices of common constitutionalism that have been, and still are, part of contemporary constitutionalism. By briefly reviewing this second aspect of Tully's genealogy of constitutionalism, we can show how Tully recovers and reconstructs the three conventions which he advocates, namely, mutual recognition, cultural continuity and consent.

The first example that Tully offers is Chief Justice Matthew Hale's common-law arguments against Hobbes' constitutional theory, the latter being the foundation of modern constitutionalism. Hale argues that making and maintaining a constitution is not something that a solitary and clever person deduces from essential definition. Rather, it is a skill that is developed by 'use and exercise' through reading, study and observation as well as conversation. Without such practice, 'actions, and the application of remedyes [sic] to them' are 'so various', 'different' and 'diversified from another' that abstract rules are a hindrance rather than a help 'when it comes to particulars' (Hale, 1924: 500–18; Tully, 1995: 114). Hale's view, Tully argues, 'is typical of the Renaissance humanist culture against which Hobbes constructed his scientific alternative':

Tully, Foucault: agonistic struggles over recognition

> The reasons that Renaissance humanists give for the practical and dialogical character of moral and political philosophy are similar to Wittgenstein's. One should always, they argue, listen to the other side (audi alteram partem) because it is always possible to speak on either side of a case (in utramque partem). The reason why this is always possible is that the criteria for the application of moral and philosophical concepts are so various and circumstantial, rather than essential and universal, that any case is always open to more than one description and evaluation, by means of comparison with other cases (what they call paradiastole). Therefore, the correct attitude or worldview is a willingness to exchange and negotiate alternative descriptions. (Tully, 1995: 115)

The purpose of Tully's first example, then, is to distinguish the dialogical ethos of the language of common constitutionalism from the monological ethos of the language of a Hobbesian-style modern constitutionalism.

Tully then provides two extended examples of the practices of common constitutionalism. The first considers Chief Justice John Marshall's judgement on US – Aboriginal relations in the 1832 case of *Worcester* v. *The State of Georgia* (Tully, 1995: 117–29). Tully's second example looks at the arguments for, and instances of, 'compact' or 'diverse' federalism in Canada and the USA (1995: 140–57). With the first example, Tully shows how Marshall reconstructs and affirms the recognition and accommodation of the Aboriginal peoples of America as equal, self-governing nations by surveying the history of treaty-making between agents of the British Crown and Aboriginal peoples between the 1630s and 1832. Marshall's survey shows this history involved negotiating a form of mutual recognition which in this case took the form of the recognition of both parties as independent and self-governing nations.

This, in turn, meant that the convention of consent – which the Europeans drew from the Roman law maxim *quod omnes tangit ab omnibus comprobetur* (q.o.t.) – could not be finessed by arguing, as Locke, Vattel and Kant had, that Aboriginal peoples existed in a state of nature; consequently, 'the only just way that the Crown could acquire land and establish its sovereignty in North America was to gain the consent of the Aboriginal nations' (Tully, 1995: 122).

Further, the convention of consent entails the third convention of cultural continuity 'in opposition to the doctrine of discontinuity in, for example, Norman law' because to amend the constitutional association without the agreement of both of the parties to it is to breach the convention of consent. With the second example, Tully shows how the process of confederation which modern constitutionalism 'interprets as the subordination of the provinces to the sovereign federal government and the creation of uniform provinces' was viewed by the thinkers of common constitutionalism 'as the creation of a federal government by the delegation of some provincial powers and the continuity and co-ordinate sovereignty of the diverse provinces' (1995: 140–1). Thus Justice

Agonistic identity construction

Thomas-Jean-Jacques Loranger argues that the confederation of the provinces of Nova Scotia, New Brunswick, Lower Canada (Quebec) and Upper Canada (Ontario) to form Canada in 1867 was characterised by the following three features. First, 'the four provinces recognised each other as autonomous, self-governing constitutional associations under British rule' (Tully, 1995: 141). Second, 'the act of confederation consisted in reaching agreement, by the consent of the four colonial governments through three years of negotiations, on which powers they would delegate to constitute a federal government to govern their common affairs' (Tully, 1995: 141). As Loranger puts it, these governments delegated 'a portion only of their local powers to form a central power' (Loranger in Tully, 1995: 141). Third, once more from Loranger's perspective, the political and legal institutions of the provinces continued through the confederation, which meant that instead of a relation of subordination to federal government, there existed 'an equality between them or rather a similarity of powers, and that each of the two powers [was] sovereign within its respective spheres' (Loranger in Tully, 1995: 141–2). Thus, again, this example illustrates the conventions of mutual recognition, consent and cultural continuity.

Stage 5
These two substantive examples show how a non-imperial practice of common constitutionalism has sought to accommodate cultural diversity – and, thus, gives the lie to the identification of contemporary constitutionalism with the hegemonic language of modern constitutionalism and, thus, to the claimed 'universality' of modern constitutionalism. They illustrate how a constitution can be reconceived as a 'form of accommodation' of cultural diversity.

The point of Tully's genealogical survey is now clear: 'the politics of cultural recognition ... can now be seen as the extension of this common constitutionalism ... a third cluster of anti-imperial struggles against the seven features of modern constitutionalism and for the liberty to engage in self rule in accord with citizens' diverse cultural ways' (1995: 184). Once the three conventions of common constitutionalism are disentangled from the seven features of modern constitutionalism, we can see an amended form of contemporary constitutionalism that is just because it articulates a practice in which each speaker is rendered their due in and through a common orientation to the formation of a constitutional association to which each can consent in their own voice.

This raises the question, however, of whether the irregular crazy quilt character of such a form of constitutionalism will breed disunity. On Tully's account, the contrary is the case:

> The mutual recognition of the cultures of citizens engenders allegiance and unity for two reasons. Citizens have a sense of belonging to, and identification with, a constitutional association in so far as, first, they have a say in the

formation and governing of the association and, second, they see their own cultural ways publicly acknowledged and affirmed in the basic institutions of their society ... If these two conditions are not met, the association is experienced as an alien and imposed yoke that suppresses the members' liberty and cultural identities, causing resistance and disunity. (1995: 197–8)

The sheer persistence of the struggles of indigenous peoples provides significant support for this claim but we can also note that the position with which Tully concludes shares a fundamental commitment to Foucault's own reflections on dialogue (Foucault, 1984b: 381–2; see pp. 103–4).

The second phase: an agonistic account of struggles over recognition

Strange multiplicity demonstrates Tully's original appropriation of Foucault's genealogical approach. However, in his work since that book, Foucault's influence and its effect on Tully's approach to struggles of recognition has become more marked in two significant respects. First, Tully has come to see struggles of recognition as a far broader category than struggles of cultural recognition. Second, his contemporary survey and historical genealogy of some examples of this broader category has led him to foreground and contest two limits on our political reflection on struggles of recognition that he finds to be embedded in our theoretical responses to such struggles. I shall address each of these points in turn.

The first relates to the use of the term 'recognition' and emerges from Tully's reflection on Foucault's point that practices of governance are norm-governed activities in which the norms articulate the terms in which participants in the practice come to recognise each other as governors and governed, as standing in certain relationships, and form their practical identities on the basis of these practical relations of recognition. Moreover, as Tully notes, 'Norms of mutual recognition are a constitutive feature of any system of rule-governed cooperation, not just of formal political systems' (2008: 293). The crucial point being made here is that the scope of the notion of recognition is co-extensive with practices of governance. In this respect, it is not helpful to restrict the notion of recognition to a narrow sense in which it refers simply to identity-related differences concerning issues such as culture, ethnicity, race, gender and religion; a point brought home by noting that such struggles of recognition in the restricted sense are often contrasted with the liberal recognition of the individual as free and equal (Tully, 2008: 294).

The second point is that the approach taken here to struggles of recognition is not that of providing a theory of recognition. A key difference between theoretical and public philosophical approaches with respect to the working out of the form and content of recognition can be articulated as follows. For advocates of a theoretical approach, struggles by individuals or groups are seen as struggles for recognition in which the form and content of recognition is spelt out in terms of a theory of justice or, for critics of liberalism such as Taylor and Honneth, a theory of ethical life – and such theories will include some accounts of how the goods specified by the favoured metric of equality (e.g. primary and secondary goods, resources, opportunity for welfare, etc.) are to be distributed. By contrast, for proponents of a public philosophical approach, struggles by individuals or groups are seen as struggles over recognition in which the form and content of recognition is governed by the conditions of public reasoning (i.e. compatibility with acknowledging each other as free and equal members of the polity) and the actual processes of deliberation and contestation in which citizens engage. The point here is not to deny that struggles for recognition involve the contestation of intersubjective norms; it is rather to re-orient our perspective towards struggles of recognition from a conceptualisation of them as struggles for recognition to one as struggles over recognition. Theoretical approaches – i.e. approaches which conceptualise struggles of recognition as struggles for recognition – focus on a claim for recognition advanced by an agent and go on to evaluate it in abstraction from the field in which it is raised, whether the claim is advanced in terms of rights, identities, or culture (this is precisely why Honneth needs to appeal to the idea of a formal conception of ethical life). In contrast, Tully holds that we should focus on the field of interaction in which the conflict arises and needs to be resolved. A conflict is not a struggle of one minority for recognition in relation to other actors who are independent of, unaffected by and neutral with respect to the form of recognition that the minority seeks. Rather, a struggle for recognition of a 'minority' always calls into question and (if successful) modifies, often in complex ways, the existing forms of reciprocal recognition of the other members of the larger system of government of which the minority is a member. The most perspicuous way of putting this is to say that struggles over recognition are struggles over the intersubjective 'norms' (laws, rules, conventions, or customs) under which the members of any system of government recognise each other as members and coordinate their interaction. Hence, struggles over recognition are always struggles over the prevailing intersubjective norms of mutual recognition through which the members (individuals and groups under various descriptions) of any system of action coordination (or practice of governance) are recognised and governed – and are to be addressed not through appeal to, for example, a formal conception of ethical life, but rather through ongoing processes of public reasoning. It should be noted that in drawing on Foucault's account of power in making this argument, Tully is not only able to provide more nuanced reflections on what is involved in struggles of recognition but is also not limited to restricting what counts as 'struggle' on the basis of a theoretical standpoint such as Honneth's thin conception of ethical life.[3]

As Tully goes on to note, it is not simply that acting in accordance with the norms of mutual recognition leads members (individual or groups) to recognise each other as members who stand in particular relations to each other but also that these forms of subjectivity or practical identity can be analysed in terms of three axes:

(1) Their characteristic discursive forms of self-awareness or self-consciousness;
(2) Their characteristic non-discursive forms of conduct within the practice;
(3) Their degree of access to, or exclusion from, resources and power through those rights, duties and entitlements that are attached within the practice to the practical identities under which they are recognised. (Tully, 2008: 294)

A struggle over recognition may emerge in relation to the norms of a practice along any of these axes – and the dual quality of norms as both normalising and normative involves acknowledging not only that acting in accordance with a norm is normalising but that learning to follow a rule (to act in accordance with a norm) is also (and necessarily) learning how to challenge and modify it: 'Rule-following is interactive rather than passive obedience to a prescriptive norm' (Tully, 2008: 296).

With this understanding of the norm of mutual recognition and of struggles over recognition as practices of agonistic freedom, Tully rejects two features which his contemporary and historical surveys lead him to identify as characteristic of modern theoretical approaches to recognition, which he refers to as the monological and finality orientations. He instead favours a dialogical and processual orientation to struggles over recognition which begins with the view that an acceptable norm of mutual recognition should be worked out by those subject to it through the exchange of reasons in negotiation, deliberation, bargaining and other forms of dialogue. This feature is, of course, already apparent in *Strange multiplicity*, but it is now a more direct focus of Tully's argument.

There are four arguments for the dialogical inclusion of those subject to a norm in working out an acceptable norm. The first combines Foucault's reflections on the ethics of dialogue with Rawls' and Habermas' reflections on democratic constitutionalism. Foucault comments:

In the serious play of questions and answers, in the work of reciprocal elucidation, the rights of each person are in some sense immanent in the discussion. They depend only on the dialogue situation. The person asking the questions is merely exercising the right that has been given to him: to remain unconvinced, to perceive a contradiction, to require more information, to emphasise different postulates, to point out faulty reasoning, etc. As for the person answering the questions, he too exercises a right that does not go beyond the discussion itself; by the logic of his own discourse he is tied to what he has said earlier, and by the acceptance of the dialogue he is tied to the questioning of the other. Questions and answers depend on a game – a game that is at once pleasant and difficult – in which each of the two partners takes pains to use only the rights given him by the other and by the accepted form of the dialogue. (1984b: 381–2)

Tully applies this understanding of dialogue to contemporary constitutional democracies through recourse to the idea of the rule of law (constitutionalism) and popular sovereignty (democracy) as equiprimordial critical and abstract norms that are immanent to the dialogue of citizens. On constitutionalism and dialogue, Tully argues that constitutionalism (or the rule of law) requires that political power be exercised in accordance with and by means of a system of principles which also include procedures for amending these principles (Tully, 2008: 93). On democracy and dialogue, Tully suggests that the principle of democracy (or popular sovereignty) requires that, although subject to a constitutional system, the people or their entrusted representatives must also impose this system on themselves, thereby achieving sovereignty and legitimising this system. This self-imposition takes place by means of exchanging reasons in democratic practices of deliberation, either directly or indirectly through their representatives. In this sense, democratic practices of deliberation are themselves rule-governed but also open to democratic amendment if they are to be democratically and constitutionally legitimate (Tully, 2008: 93).

Our orientation to these critical and abstract norms specifies the shared mode of our problematisation of our political identity. We recognise that these norms are critical not because they are agreed to and applied directly in particular cases, but rather because there are a diverse plurality of ways of understanding these norms and the respective weightings of them in any given case. Their equiprimordiality points to the fact that democratic rule which is not constitutional is open to the populist tyranny of the majority, and constitutional rule which is not democratic is open to the juridical tyranny of alien rule.

Tully's second argument follows from this basic account of legitimate democratic constitutional rule as a 'multilogue' and concerns the conditions of the acceptability of a norm of mutual recognition. For Tully, the identities under which cooperating individuals and groups are reciprocally recognised are only their own if they can accept them from a first-person perspective: that is, acknowledge them as their own. Otherwise, they are experienced as imposed and alien. Consequently, individuals and groups must be involved, directly or via representatives, in the process of negotiating norms. Notice that this point applies not only to those who initiate a struggle over recognition but to all whose identities would be affected by an alteration of the norm of mutual recognition. Hence Tully concludes that 'to ensure that a new norm of mutual recognition is acceptable by all, it needs to pass through an inclusive dialogue or what we should call a "multilogue". If all affected are not included in the exchange of reasons they will not understand why the agreement was reached, what were the reasons for the demands of others that helped to shape the agreement, why their own negotiators seemed to moderate their demands, and so on. The agreed-upon norm of mutual recognition would thus seem like a sell-out or an unnecessary compromise, and thus as imposed and unacceptable' (2008: 302–3).

The third reason for rejecting the monological orientation relates to a significant characteristic of the identities recognised under any norm, namely, that our identities are not fixed but worked out in and through our relations with one another: 'our understanding of who we are, of the partners with whom we are constrained to cooperate, and hence the acceptable norms of mutual recognition change in the course of the dialogue. Accordingly, the members need to be in on the webs of interlocution of the struggle in order to go through these changes in self-understanding and other-understanding or they will literally not be able to identify with the norm of recognition that others, who have gone through the negotiations, find acceptable' (Tully, 2008: 303).

This final consideration is characterised by Tully as pragmatic, but I think this is a mistake. According to Tully, we each bring different perspectives to bear in such discussions and so the less diverse the community of interlocutors, the less able they are to recognise the limitations of their own perspectives. This, however, strikes me as a central point about the ethics of dialogue, one stressed by Arendt in her considerations on the constitution of the public realm, namely, that any dialogue that seeks to generate a common world – i.e. an agreement on norms of mutual recognition – must involve the widest diversity of perspectives to ensure that the public realm so constituted is one that its members can hold in common.

Having rejected the monological orientation, Tully turns to the other feature that he takes to limit the modern political imagination with respect to struggles over recognition, namely, the orientation to a just, definitive and final resolution of the struggle over recognition. Tully's rejection of the presumption of, and orientation to, finality is based on the claim that no matter what procedures for the exchange of reasons are applied to proposed norms of mutual recognition, in either theory or practice, an element of 'reasonable disagreement' or 'reasonable dissent' will remain (2008: 306).

Tully's first reason for the inevitability of reasonable disagreement appeals to Rawls' argument concerning the fact of pluralism and the burdens of judgement, noting that, first, this 'insight has brought about the profound reconceptualisation of the law as a field of norms over which there is always ongoing reasonable disagreement, and thus must be understood in terms of the norms of democracy and constitutionalism' (see also Walker, 2002) and, second, that 'in practice, reasonable disagreement may seem an obvious point to anyone familiar with negotiations' (Tully, 2008: 306). Practical features such as asymmetries in power and knowledge, limitations of time, disagreements over what the agreement entails, etc. are pervasive features of real-world deliberations and undermine the thought that we could be sufficiently confident in any agreement to judge it as legitimately final. His second reason notes that since our practical identities are not fixed but are altered in the course of the struggle, consensus and reasonable disagreement seems inevitable. Third, and crucially for Tully, a certain 'room for manoeuvre' is involved when interpreting and acting in accordance with the norm of mutual recognition, be it in dialogue or in implementation after negotiations. As Tully points out:

> Even in the most routine activity of acting in accord with a norm of mutual recognition, the members of an association subtly alter it in unpredictable ways through interpretation, application and negotiation. They can often appear to agree while thinking and acting differently. In other cases, overt agreement, or a manufactured consensus, can mask the vast terrain of hidden scripts and arts of resistance by which subjects act out their reasonable disagreement to oppressive norms in day-to-day life. (2008: 30)

Consequently, any 'agreement' on a norm is subject to the 'uncertainty, the suspense, the possibility of irreversible change, which surrounds all significant action, however "rule-guided"' (2008: 307). However, Tully notes that even those who agree with these claims have often retained the finality presumption with respect to 'a definitive theory of the just procedures of dialogue' (2008: 307), where the thought is that such a theory could be developed to serve as a transcendental standard to judge any actual dialogue. Yet, as Stuart Hampshire (2000) has argued, the procedures of dialogue cannot themselves be immune from revision in the course of the dialogue and are equally subject to reasonable disagreement. Consequently, Tully concludes that the orientation to finality should be dropped. Instead, we should endorse a commitment to a processual view of dialogic civic freedom in which, first, members have the ability to effectively contest the practices of government and the correlative norms of mutual recognition to which they are subject and, second, any resolution is recognised as open to revision.

If Tully's argument is cogent, what implications follow? The route to resolving conflicts over norms of mutual recognition lies in inclusive and dialogical practices of negotiation. If, even in the best of circumstances, there will be reasonable disagreement over imperfect procedures and particular resolutions, it follows that the primary orientation of reconciliation should not be the search for definitive procedures and solutions, but, rather, the institutionalisation and protection of a specific kind of democratic or civic freedom. This civic freedom, if effective, requires not only rights as the enabling conditions of its exercise but also a duty of responsiveness on the part of our political institutions and fellow citizens 'to enter into an open dialogue governed by *audi alteram partem*' (Tully, 2008: 310). Thus, the primary aim is to ensure that those subject to and affected by any system of governance are always free to question its prevailing norms of recognition and action coordination, to enter into dialogue with those who govern and who have a positive duty to listen and respond, to challenge prevailing procedures of negotiation in the course of the discussions, to reach or fail to reach an imperfect agreement regarding amending (or overthrowing) the norm in question, to implement the amendment and then to ensure that the implementation is open to review and possible renegotiation in the future. This is the fundamental democratic or civic freedom of citizens – having an effective say in a dialogue over the norms through which they are governed. Here Tully offers a contextualisation of Foucault's reflections on agonism and dialogue for the specific terrain of politics.

There is, however, a further and final twist in Tully's argument which recalls the Foucauldian point that acting in accordance with norms is normalising, that it leads to the formation of a practical identity. His point here is that insofar as we engage in these kinds of dialogues, we acquire a new kind of second-order citizen-identity and solidarity appropriate to free, open and pluralistic forms of association which provides, like the kind of identification that develops in games towards the game itself and not simply one's own team, a democratic source of stability and peace in complex and conflicted societies.

Conclusion

The work of James Tully offers a clear and, in my view, compelling account of struggles of recognition in which central Foucauldian insights concerning freedom as an agonistic practice and the role of historical reflection in freeing us from the grip of certain limits to our thinking and acting are taken up and extended. In conclusion, though, we should note one further point of relationship between Tully and Foucault, namely, that Tully's public philosophy is to be understood not only as a form of political practice oriented to enabling struggles over recognition but also as a form of ethical self-formation in Foucault's sense, as an exercise of freedom by freedom for freedom. Public philosophy is a way in which the philosopher as philosopher can take up that most difficult of tasks, namely, to become able to recognise him- or her- self as a citizen.

Notes

* This chapter was written while a Fellow at the Forschungskolleg Humanwissenschaften in Bad Homburg sponsored by the Exzellenzcluster 'The formation of normative orders' and I am very grateful to them for such ideal writing conditions. I also owe particular thanks to Jim Tully, Tony Laden, Paul Patton, Rainer Forst and Peter Niesen with whom I have discussed these issues over many years. Thanks, finally, to the editors of this volume for helpful comments on an earlier draft.
1 This section draws on my article, 'Political philosophy in a post-imperial voice' (Owen, 1999: 520–49).
2 These activities include, on the one hand, the struggles of nationalist movements for

statehood or autonomy within a multinational federation, the pressures on states to recognise and accommodate supra-national associations, the struggles (between these two levels) of long-standing linguistic and ethnic minorities for constitutional recognition and, on the other hand, the intercultural claims of citizens, immigrants, exiles and refugees for forms of recognition and protection of the cultures they bring to established nation-states, the demands of women's movements for the accommodations of their (multicultural and contested) ways of speaking and acting and the struggles of Aboriginal peoples for the recognition and accommodation of their customary ways.

3 It should further be noted that Honneth is faced with significant problems concerning the possibility of ideological forms of recognition in his theory. For constructively critical reflections, see 'Reification, ideology and power: expression and agency in Honneth's theory of recognition' (Owen, 2010).

PART III
EMBODIMENT AND VULNERABILITY

7

The theory of social action in Merleau-Ponty and Honneth

Jean-Philippe Deranty

ON a cursory glance, Merleau-Ponty's phenomenology and Honneth's theory of recognition do not appear to have much in common. In particular, the ontological ambitions of Merleau-Ponty, notably in his last period, seem to be squarely at odds with the 'post-metaphysical' character of the essentially normative social philosophy that the theory of recognition aims to develop.

This chapter intends to question this initial impression of an unbridgeable gap between the two projects. I attempt to show first of all that some of the key intuitions and intentions of the two projects resemble each other, particularly their shared aim of founding a theory of social action in a theory of embodied intersubjectivity. On the basis of this common ground, I will attempt to identify what recognition theory might have to gain, from a normative point of view, by making its proximity with Merleau-Ponty more explicit. I will suggest four fruitful avenues of engagement.

Two apparently incompatible projects

At first glance, this suggested rapprochement of Merleau-Ponty and Honneth might appear surprising. Honneth certainly, in contrast to Habermas, has always been interested in French philosophy and sociology. However, while devoting careful attention to the more celebrated French thinkers of the twentieth century (notably Sartre, Bourdieu, Foucault and Lévi-Strauss), Honneth's rich bibliography contains only two short texts on Merleau-Ponty: a few pages in the book published with Hans Joas in 1980, *Social action and human nature* (Honneth and Joas, 1980: 114–17); and a review, concluding on a rather sceptical note, of a number of German publications, including reissues and new translations of Merleau-Ponty's writings, a collection of essays documenting the traces of Merleau-Ponty's thought in contemporary philosophy, and applications of Merleau-Ponty to the problems of a critical theory of society, including that of the German expert on Merleau-Ponty, Bernhard Waldenfels (Honneth, 1995b: 150–7).

If we briefly consider the core projects of the two thinkers, the differences appear to exclude any extensive similarities between them. In general terms, the phenomenological enterprise is primarily ontological and epistemological. Through the characterisation of types of intentionality, opening onto diverse modes of access to ontological realms, phenomenology aims first and foremost to critically reground knowledge. Honneth's theoretical aims are more limited, and concern social philosophy from a normative viewpoint. His main philosophical approach is not to describe but to 'reconstruct' the normative presuppositions of social life, through critical interpretations of key classical and contemporary references in the social sciences.

At this point, one could note that Honneth's social philosophy, like that of Habermas, contains an important hermeneutic moment, which involves analysing social experience from the perspective of the participants, similar to a phenomenology of social life. However, Honneth's main aim, above all, is to reconstruct constitutive normative elements, and not to engage in ontological or epistemological inquiry. Moreover, the epistemological implications of Honneth's social philosophy are restricted to the social sciences, or rather the interaction between social philosophy and the social sciences (see also Deranty, 2009: Chapter 8).

One might also remark that Merleau-Ponty's phenomenology, at least in its early form, is existential, highly influenced by Heidegger and Sartre. This means that the social, the political and even the ethical, have an important place in it. But once again, Merleau-Ponty's approach here is strictly descriptive, 'ontological', and pays no obvious attention to normative issues. Moral and political action as well as social experience are addressed inasmuch as they are different ways in which the individual can 'be in the world'. In those passages which can be interpreted as developing something like a 'social ontology', Merleau-Ponty does not explicitly address questions relating to the precise structure and justification of the norms inherent in forms of action and experience. He does not deal head on with questions relating to principles of moral decision, procedures and foundations of democracy, nor does he explore claims arising from experiences of injustice.[1]

The distinction between a description with ontological ambitions and a normative reconstruction with more modest aims reflects the methodological rejection of the phenomenological method that defines a 'post-metaphysical' scene in which Honneth clearly situates himself (Honneth, 1995b: 156–7). From the point of view of Habermas' influential concerns, the pages in Merleau-Ponty's work dedicated to 'social ontology' can only appear as outdated and obsolete. From this 'post-metaphysical' perspective Merleau-Ponty appears to project himself directly in the structures of the social, without the mediation of

The theory of social action: Merleau-Ponty, Honneth

the sciences specifically dedicated to it. Worse still, even after his 'liberal turn' in the mid-1950s, the very language and conceptual framework which enable him to reformulate his social theory remain anchored in a discredited philosophy of history, namely a 'Western Marxist' interpretation of historical materialism revolving around the confused concept of 'praxis'. In his later writings, Merleau-Ponty even appears to attempt a re-founding of the phenomenological method returning, in Heideggerian style, to a deep ontology. By contrast, when Honneth underpins his normative analyses with descriptive arguments, he does so in full allegiance to the Habermasian method, by recourse to the tradition of social theory and empirical inquiry.

From the perspective of contemporary critical theory, a number of factors appear therefore to lead to a negative appraisal of Merleau-Ponty's work. I would like to show, however, that beyond these initial reservations there is in fact a profound similarity of intuition and intention between Merleau-Ponty and Honneth in their accounts of the social. My aim is not to identify every possible affinity between them, but to emphasise a shared fundamental inspiration, in the hope that my comparative analysis could serve a more useful purpose, namely, identifying the ways in which a return to Merleau-Ponty could enrich the contemporary theory of recognition.

Honneth's programme of social theory

The best way to uncover the broad overlaps between the phenomenological approach to the social and the critical social theory of Honneth is by articulating the key intuitions that originally motivate the latter. The theory of recognition grew out of frustration towards the theories of social action prevalent in the 1970s. Honneth explicitly took his distance from such theories, attempting instead to devise a programme of research that would give full weight to the creativity of social action. It is this latter characteristic that makes Honneth's research coincide with the social ontology implied by Merleau-Ponty's work.

An opposition to structuralist theories of social action

The first theoretical frustration guiding Honneth's initial steps in social philosophy is a response to conflicts in Marxist interpretation. Honneth's early texts are written when the Althusserian wave is at its peak, on the point of receding to make room for other versions of post-structuralism. Edward P. Thompson's revealing work on *The making of the English working class* (1963) played a crucial role in opposing the structuralist hegemony, documenting with great historical and sociological detail the importance of moral and cultural dimensions in experiences of social domination and revolt. Offering a powerful critique of structuralist approaches, Thompson's book reveals the usefulness, for theory and practice alike, of hermeneutic and sociological approaches to the study of class relations. It is precisely this methodological approach that the young Honneth develops in his early interventions into critical social theory, in the context of the larger debate in Germany at that time about the best way to interpret Marx.[2]

The conclusion Honneth draws from these debates is that a structuralist reading of Marx cannot offer a differentiated model of social action. Honneth believes, however, that such a model is indispensable for a fruitful development of historical materialism. In contrast with structuralism, then, a social theory should follow Thompson's historical sociology and give full weight to a rich concept of social action. The notion of social action operating in Honneth's early texts takes two distinct but interrelated senses. The first understanding expresses the social determination of individual action and, reciprocally, the coordination of individual actions in collective action. The link between these two dimensions is ensured by class experience, which unites individual destinies and gives a specific value to collective forms of experience and action. The second understanding of social action is more narrow and designates an active critique of social injustice, first in the lived experience of injustice, and subsequently in properly political forms of action which respond to experiences of injustice. Social action thus relates to the critique of social domination and the efforts of social transformation.

For the young Honneth, the structuralist readings of Marx and of the social more generally fail to account for the phenomenology of class experience and, consequently, ignore the potential creativity of social action. First of all, this criticism appears true in a 'synchronic' sense, from the perspective of the sociology of domination, which structuralist schemes can only address from an external, overbearing point of view. A theory of the social overly fixated on the systemic aspects of modern society overlooks the active nature of the participation of dominated classes in social life with their own symbolic productions which develop into counter cultures and in some cases provide cultural resources for articulating practical attempts to denounce and overthrow injustice. Structuralist schemes tend to defuse the explanatory role as well as the critical and transformative potentials of class struggle. Secondly, the lack of sensitivity of structuralist approaches for the creativity of social action also has a 'diachronic' dimension, treating the historical material with disdain, notably the rich historiography of the proletarian movement, including the diverse attempts by dominated populations to survive and struggle.

An anthropology of practical intersubjectivity
So as to give substance to an adequate (critical) theory of social action, Honneth notices at the outset that it is essential to base his theory on a model of social relations in all their weight, retrieving their significance from the point of view

The theory of social action: Merleau-Ponty, Honneth

of the agents involved in them. This is why the young Honneth attempts to provide a new foundation for historical materialism, namely, a theory of the radical intersubjective dependency of the human subject. The key concepts summing up this new approach in social theory are those of 'historical intersubjectivity' and 'practical intersubjectivity'. The first book, written with Hans Joas, provides Honneth with the opportunity to retrieve the anthropological, Feuerbachian strain in Marx's thinking, through the positive review of modern, anthropological readings of Marx, notably from the Budapest school (Heller and Markus) and from German philosophical anthropology. In this rich tradition, Honneth discovers the core idea of the social constitution of individual experience, which lies at the inner core of subjective life and includes the body itself (the '*corps propre*'). As early as 1980, it is Mead who allows Honneth to articulate with great theoretical force the central thesis of the radical intersubjective dependency of the human being.

Honneth's reconstruction of this substantial theoretical material leads to an 'intersubjective' conception of the social, wherein individual experiences and actions are essentially interrelated, not only through the sharing of common symbolic resources, but also through processes of reciprocal expectations and claims. Social life now appears to result from the interactions of individuals and groups, which do not consist merely of power relations or utilitarian calculations but are shot through with symbolic and normative dimensions. These interactions, however, are in principle conflictual. Indeed, the emphasis on the effective contribution of individuals and groups to their integration in social life, combined with the fundamental premise of an inherent tension between classes, allows Honneth to produce a rich account of class experience. Social action designates more specifically the modes of social reproduction which belong to each class, and which, via specific forms of 'cultural action', refract their place in the division of labour and in the symbolic and hierarchical structures of society (Honneth, 1993: Chapter 3). The intersubjective conception of the social also allows Honneth to analyse injustice in terms of social pathologies, interpreted as affronts to and breaches of the intersubjective expectations of socialised individuals, produced by social domination and exclusion (Honneth, 2007a: 3–48). The critique of class relations can then base itself on empirical data from critical sociology and clinical psychology, allowing, finally, a flexible theory of social and historical action which returns the political initiative to those groups suffering from the different forms of injustice.

Honneth's mature theory of recognition is the direct product of this early attempt at anchoring social action in anthropological arguments, that is, in an 'anthropology of practical intersubjectivity'. The notion of social action, in particular, retains its centrality and richness in Honneth's later writings.[3] This point is essential for the comparison with Merleau-Ponty. Ultimately, one would be entitled to say that Honneth's theory of recognition develops a 'philosophy of praxis' which explicitly endorses the different connotations of that term in Western Marxism, that is, as a form of intersubjective interaction forming the core of social life, and the springboard for emancipatory politics.

A critique of Habermasian logocentrism

The theory of recognition defines itself against a second major model, namely, Habermas' theory of communicative action. Honneth quickly recognised the importance of Habermas' attempts at a 'reconstruction of historical materialism'. It is worth noting, for instance, that it is Habermas himself who, in *Knowledge and human interests* (Habermas, 1971: 43–64; see also Habermas, 1973: 142–68), first proposes to return to Hegel's Jena model of recognition so as to conceptualise the normative dimensions of social interaction.

However, from the very outset, Honneth signals a reservation which continues to mark his writing. According to Honneth, Habermas' position gives rise to a number of difficulties which prevent him from satisfactorily accounting for social action. A first difficulty concerns Habermas' early adoption of arguments borrowed from systems theory, notably for the purpose of establishing an evolutionary theory of social models. Honneth, concerned with rescuing the praxeological moment of social action from functionalism, identifies an inherent functionalism in Habermas' social theory. The second and greater difficulty Honneth identifies in Habermas' work is a certain logocentrism, that is, a reformulation of the major problems of social and political theory on the basis of the exclusive primacy of language as the medium of interaction.[4] This privileging of language leads to a multidimensional concept of communicative action, which allows Habermas to apply his theory of norms inherent in dialogue not only to norms of moral action but also to the description of the structures of modern society, the diagnosis of social pathologies and the theory of democracy.

For Honneth, these two major problems (the importance of functionalism and logocentrism) prevent Habermas from developing a theory of social action that is both hermeneutically adequate and grounded in intersubjective interdependence. Honneth's objections are both theoretical and practical. For him, the combination of systemic argument and the interpretation of moral suffering as an injury to communicative expectations leads social analysis to become disconnected from the real experience of social suffering. A diagnosis of social suffering in terms of restrictions on communicative capacities is not adequate to the phenomenology of that suffering. In particular, it ignores the bodily aspect of social experience, not only from the immediate perspective of the phenomenology of social relations, but also from the perspective of processes of socialisation, through which the intersubjective vulnerability of individuals is instituted.[5] For Honneth, individuals who live with injustice suffer above all from injuries to the very conditions enabling them to establish their identity and develop their autonomy. These conditions are not limited, as Habermas

The theory of social action: Merleau-Ponty, Honneth

believes, to respecting the implicit rules of dialogue but instead concern multifarious forms of interaction, many of which are not primarily linguistic. Mead's theory of interaction makes this crystal clear, by linking his model of subjective formation to the internalisation of external forms of behaviour. From this perspective, Habermas' approach to the social is not only overly abstract, in limiting the scope of social relations to discursive exchange, but it is also dualistic, in rigidly separating the different social spheres. Consequently, the circle that was intended to define critical theory is ruptured: social experience no longer informs theory, and theory can no longer become practical so as to inform real social movements.

In stating that Honneth's theory of recognition is built, in large part, to correct these two problems in Habermas, I do not simply mean that Habermas' problems are the 'genetic' source of Honneth's mature theory. Rather, I intend to say something more substantial about the core project behind Honneth's writings in social theory. On the one hand, the concept of recognition is constructed with a view to inheriting the decisive progress that Habermas' theoretical innovations represent, notably his insistence upon the intersubjective constitution of the individual. On the other hand, the concept of recognition also intends to correct the abstractions of Habermas' model, allowing us to account for the full spectrum of possible social relations, not just the narrow domain of discursive exchange. Honneth also intends to maintain direct contact with the phenomenology of social experience, because its three main delineations (the three spheres) cover the different types of normative claims which individuals want their social context to include. Finally, when political theory is derived from a theory of recognition, its theoretical language is not disconnected from the language of social experience expressed by real political movements, which should, in fact, ground emancipatory politics.

The convergence between Honneth's and Merleau-Ponty's social theories

This summary sketch of Honneth's project is meant to highlight the fact that his recognition theory contributes substantially to the theory of social action. This claim is fully compatible with Honneth's concern to respect a number of significant methodological rules. The first such major methodological rule relates to the link between social theory and the findings of the social sciences, which must always be closely considered so that conceptual arguments are empirically verified. Most importantly, all normative discussions (about moral action, the conditions of social life, or the principles of democratic procedures), must uphold a number of assumed methodological requirements, notably the principle of value pluralism. However, these methodological reservations render more complex, but do not detract from, the attempt by recognition theory to renew the theory of 'praxis'. It is this concern with 'praxis' that produces a convergence

Embodiment and vulnerability

between Honneth's social theory and that of Merleau-Ponty. I will now attempt to justify this claim by summing up the main features of Merleau-Ponty's social theory, underlining their proximity with Honneth's.

Moving beyond Merleau-Ponty's most explicit objective, namely the critique of Galilean science, a close reading of his first books reveals that his phenomenology of perception is in fact framed by the broader frame of a philosophy of history. Not unlike the materialist conception of rationality that marks the first generation of critical theory, Merleau-Ponty maintains Hegel's account of reason's historical constitution (Merleau-Ponty, 1962: 448ff.). The analyses of perception, which describe the corporeal mediation by which the human being takes a place within his or her worlds (natural, symbolic, social, historical), are not conducted solely for the purpose of critiquing traditional epistemology, but aim also to define a new account of social action. The emphasis on the embodied nature of intentionality is not simply an afterthought to analyses of social life and collective action. Rather, the concluding chapter on political action in the *Phenomenology of perception*, and the bulk of Merleau-Ponty's post-war writings, suggest that Merleau-Ponty's philosophical project moves beyond a critique of rationalism and empiricism to re-think the nature of social action, by re-examining the very structures of interaction. Borrowing one of Honneth's early terms, it would be accurate to describe this project as an effort to define 'historical intersubjectivity'. In other words, we see in Merleau-Ponty, an effort, first, to account for the link between the production of social action and social transformation; second, to sketch the experience on which transformative social action is based; and, finally, to identify the goals of such action.

Phenomenological Marxism and materialist philosophical anthropology thereby converge in a more general project of renewing the theory of praxis (Merleau-Ponty, 1994: 125–36). In both cases, emphasis is placed on the intersubjective constitution of action, that is, the fact that individual experience is constituted by continual reference to an other person. The social is consequently understood in an interactionist manner, in terms of such concepts as 'co-existence' and 'communication'. As in Honneth, this interactionist perspective inscribes class struggle at its heart. Class struggle is the central mechanism organising social life and forms of social experience.[6] Similarly, interpreting the social in terms of reciprocal interaction entails a fundamental consequence for the analysis of supra-subjective 'structures', amounting to a strong alternative to the functionalist approaches. The intersubjective constitution of the self allows both thinkers to develop a dialectical relationship between individual experience and structure, avoiding a view of the subject as moulded from the outside in utter passivity.[7] When both poles are used to describe the fullness of social life, social action then takes on a strong, dynamic meaning, where structures are shown to require acting, living and breathing subjects to actualise and renew them.[8]

The most striking point of similarity between Honneth and Merleau-Ponty is, of course, the reference to the body as the foundation of social experience, which, concomitantly, leads both to a relative downplay of the importance of language. For Merleau-Ponty, the body is already 'expression' and 'signification' on account of the structure of its behaviour (Merleau-Ponty, 1962: 187). This means that the secondary modes of signification (the different types of language: natural, artistic, scientific) are themselves grounded in this 'general equivalent' which is the human being's inscription in the world via the body.[9] In other words, the subject's intersubjective constitution cannot be reduced to the acquisition of pragmatic rules of language-use, neither from a developmental nor a phenomenological perspective of interaction. There are certain forms of interaction which exist before or beyond language and are equally as meaningful and significant for subjects.

One might object at this point that while it is possible that some of the fundamental orientations between these two 'social ontologies' overlap, Merleau-Ponty's theory does not explicitly include social critique, neither in the form of a diagnosis of social pathologies nor in terms of a discussion of methodological issues involved in social critique. However, both aspects define Honneth's project. In response, we should recall that the evolution of Merleau-Ponty's post-war thinking appears to have been largely influenced by such concerns. At a very general level, the attempt to develop a theory of 'historical intersubjectivity' originates in a critique of the present largely determined by a Marxist analysis of the situation.[10] The necessity to re-think social action is, for Merleau-Ponty, both a practical and a theoretical necessity. Indeed, as in any project in the tradition of critical theory, a relation of reciprocity exists for Merleau-Ponty between practice and theory. In fact, it is in the name of such unity that Merleau-Ponty invests himself in the *Temps modernes* journal project, and it is precisely his desire to secure an appropriate link between theory and practice which leads him to break with Sartre (Stewart, 1998: 327–55; Deranty and Haber, 2009; Deranty, forthcoming).

It is also possible to claim that a further background concern informs the major shifts in Merleau-Ponty's post-war thinking, namely, the need to renew political thought after the failure of communism, so as to reorient militant action and revitalise theoretical inquiry. The middle period, centred on the analysis of expressive phenomena, attempts to ground historical intersubjectivity on the model of language and no longer within a classical materialist dialectic. Here, within symbolic resources, Merleau-Ponty tries to identify both the bonds uniting social agents and the source of political creativity. The ontological inquiries of his final period aim to formulate a radical form of intersubjectivity, no longer simply the classical Marxist 'recognition of man by man' as per *Humanism and terror* (2000), but the fundamental chiasm which links the human being to every dimension of the real, notably other organisms and nature as a whole. However, this fundamental bond between beings is now

Embodiment and vulnerability

also at the very origin of emancipatory praxis. In fact, the political and 'social-theoretical' background of the ontology of 'overlap' appears very clearly in the last lectures presented to the Collège de France in 1960 and 1961, dedicated to Hegel and the young Marx, where Merleau-Ponty unexpectedly returns to questions that were central for him immediately following the war, namely, the problem of a philosophical refoundation of praxis (Merleau-Ponty, 1997: see, in particular, 77–83). The notion of the human being's radical openness onto its environments entails a strong normative dimension, even though Merleau-Ponty himself never makes it fully explicit. The normative dimension implies that damaged forms of life cannot but affect beings who are constitutively dependent upon their environment for the very development of their capacities. All that is lacking is an explicit account of the moral and political conclusions which flow from this ontological description of the human being's chiasmatic openness.

Of course, this chapter's tentative defence of an underlying concern with the unity of theory and practice in Merleau-Ponty, and his implicit concern for normative questions, cannot by itself justify any substantial comparison with Honneth as concerns normative questions, where these latter are understood in the highly technical (and Kantian) sense which the term enjoys today. Rather, the chapter intends to identify the point where the theories of Merleau-Ponty and Honneth overlap as concerns the terms of an anthropological foundation of normativity. Beyond a merely historical or exegetical interest, this is also the point where the comparison might yield interesting results for the theory of recognition.

Implications for the theory of recognition

The main issue for a productive contrast between the theory of recognition and Merleau-Ponty's social theory concerns the place of the body in social theory. As we just remarked, the emphasis on embodied forms of interaction is one dimension which Honneth's project shares with Merleau-Ponty's phenomenology of the social. The incarnation of intentionality in Merleau-Ponty's phenomenology corresponds to the Meadian thesis on which Honneth draws so heavily: the capacity of human beings to coordinate their actions originates in the intersubjective constitution of the subject, which for the most part mobilises resources and processes which are non-linguistic (Rosenthal and Bourgeois, 1991). This genetic argument is also true of social action itself. The structure of human behaviour which 'opens' (Merleau-Ponty's fundamental metaphor) the human subject onto the human world – that is, the intersubjective world and the world of symbolic forms – must be explained through the specificity of human embodiment. From this significant point of agreement between Merleau-Ponty and Honneth regarding the fundamental mechanisms underpinning the possibility of social action, four important consequences can be drawn for critical social theory.

First consequence
The first such consequence concerns one of the most serious dangers in social theory, namely, intellectualism or the tendency to treat social interaction as though it were only mediated by representations – or, worse, 'reasons' – by means of which social agents provide justifications.

By contrast, there is an idea in Merleau-Ponty's work which is central to social theory, namely, the view that the individual enters the world and, in particular, the social world by internalising *habitus* and by shaping his or her body schema accordingly. The category of 'habitus' plays a central role in social theory.[11] In terms of intellectual lineage, we could say that Bourdieu's work in social theory mediates between Merleau-Ponty, who significantly influences Bourdieu's underlying vision of the subject, and Honneth, who borrows from Bourdieu the notion that social fields are structured by tensions between groups around the articulation of norms and values.

The claim that social action is primordially governed by a 'practical logic' which is, at the very outset, embodied, runs up against much of contemporary social philosophy, which tends to explain social action in terms of representations, beliefs and reasons alone. It would also fall foul of a Habermasian approach to the social. The dangers of an embodied conception are clear: pre-linguistic modes of interaction do not seem to allow room for normative *reflexivity*. This raises the question as to whether a justified critique of social relations, the basis for a progressive politics, could, in fact, be successfully anchored in a social theory which emphasises embodiment, especially if one insists, as does critical theory, that the very norms of critique are immanent.

However, although insisting on the pre-linguistic dimensions of social action makes it more difficult to link social theory with normative critique, this difficulty alone is not a good argument against embodiment. The imperative to rationally evaluate social realities should not be confused with a rationalistic description of social realities. Philosophers should avoid projecting their own normative concerns onto reality itself. Indeed, the complications which result from emphasising the embodied dimensions of social interaction reflect the messiness of social reality and the difficulty of extracting normative demands from the complexity of social relations.

This insight into the complexity of social reality corresponds to the intuition underpinning many of Honneth's critical interventions in social theory. Honneth constantly reminds us that there exists a whole continent of social pathologies with their associated forms of suffering, which cannot be adequately discussed using the terms of constructivist or proceduralist theories of justice. This basic insight lies at the heart of Honneth's alternative approach to normativity: non-recognition, or misrecognition, he argues, is a form of injustice, primarily because they harm deep subjective expectations that are the conditions of personal identity. Structures of non-recognition and social contempt violate the concrete conditions of autonomy, where autonomy is understood not simply as a capacity of rational conduct, but a much broader capacity for action, akin, we might say in reference to phenomenology, to a generalised 'I can'.

The extension of the concept of autonomy which results from emphasising the organic and psychological conditions of personal integrity produces a new definition of 'pathology' in the spirit of Canguilhem: a pathology designates the disturbance of 'normality' defined as the capacity to institute one's own norms of action in changing environments (Canguilhem, 1991). This opens fruitful perspectives for critical sociology and critical psychology alike, as well as for a political theory which intends to maintain a strong link to the latter. It provides the conceptual framework to discuss social pathologies in terms of the malformation, rigidification and atrophying of *habitus*, allowing the diagnosis of social conditions preventing the flourishing of subjective identities while also pinpointing conditions which prevent social agents from accessing the means to make political claims. Consequently, in a complex and roundabout manner, it opens the way to a realistic theory of de- and re-politicisation (Haber, 2008).

Second consequence

The second consequence, for critical theory, of the concern with embodiment entails more critical implications for Honneth as regards the place of sexuality and more generally of vital processes in social theory. The socialised subject is also a sexualised subject. The development of subjective autonomy via socialisation means first and foremost the control a subject has of his or her drives and, more basically, organic life. The subject's history is above all a gradual mastery of one's own body, the formation of a psychic structure whose primary aim is to control organic forces, which if left unchecked would overcome subjective identity (Dejours, 2003). This key aspect of subjective identity was already carefully analysed by Merleau-Ponty both in the chapter dedicated to sexuality in the *Phenomenology of perception*, and in subsequent texts on psychoanalysis where he emphasises the structuring role of sexuality, and more simply, of organic life, in the development of practical identity.[12]

It is important for the theory of recognition to keep the organic ground of individual life in view, because this expands the circle of vulnerability to which a critical theory must respond. By conceptualising socialisation as constructing an individual history aiming to reconcile the biological and the symbolic, a theory is forced to redefine autonomy as a series of defences against those threats, biological, psychic and social in origin, which constantly challenge it. It is clear that constitutive vulnerability lies at the heart of recognition theory's account of the subject and of its theory of normativity (Honneth and Anderson, 2005: 77–100). The structural link it establishes between vulnerability and normativity is its most original (and most controversial) feature. However, for Honneth constitutive vulnerability is mostly, if not exclusively, the result of the subject's affective dependence upon others. If the theory also considered the organic, and more specifically sexual, dimensions of intersubjective vulnerability, it would be able to expand its circle of vulnerability, providing insight into those psycho-social processes often overlooked by the current model of recognition. These psycho-social processes might involve defensive and rationalising mechanisms which often block the proper or full representation of pathologies, forms of injustice and possible avenues of redress, both for those suffering from injustice and for the others. Defining autonomy as a general defence against suffering could thereby play a key role in understanding powerful compensatory mechanisms which cloud suffering from view or make it appear more tolerable than it really is (Dejours, 1998; Renault, 2008a). Such considerations might appear to lack significance from the viewpoint of a purely philosophical normative theory, but they are of utmost importance for a theory of normativity which aims to ground itself in social reality, as does the theory of recognition. Such considerations not only enrich social diagnosis but also have an impact on political theory in that the absence of any motivation to participate in democratic life is itself one of the central problems of politics (Deranty and Renault, 2009: 43–56).

Third consequence
A return to Merleau-Ponty's implied social theory would also correct Honneth's reduction of the concept of interaction to interpersonal relations. Constitutive vulnerability, a consequence of the embodiment which radically 'opens' onto different worlds, makes the human being dependent not just upon relations with other human beings, but also on material reality, whether the latter is simply a mediation of inter-human relations, or if it determines and even creates specific forms of interaction. Once again, the expansion of the circle of vulnerability broadens the scope of the normative, with important effects on social criticism and political theory.

In a very general sense, the role of material worlds in the pathological effects of social formations is not just expressive. Whether in ostentatious consumption, in the expression of social positioning, or in the power relations within work structures, material organisations are not simply the reflections of asymmetrical recognition but rather complicate recognition relations, either by making asymmetries worse, through their own, inherent logic, or by making social inequality less visible or less overbearing. Conversely, attempts to remedy inadequate relations of recognition can be facilitated or impeded by material structures. Relations between things can also have a bearing on relations between people, not simply because relations between things express or reflect relations between people but because both express a similar general attitude towards the world. In this case, we would have a form of normative parallel between the lack of respect shown towards objects and machines, and the lack of respect shown towards humans.

Finally, whether in reference to the passages dedicated to sexuality in the *Phenomenology of perception* or to Merleau-Ponty's 1957 lectures on nature (Merleau-Ponty, 2003), his analyses allow us to enlarge Honnethian intersubjectivity so as to conceptualise the constitutive attachments of the subject in a more 'libidinal' sense, involving the '*corps propre*' in its full and deepest affectivity as 'flesh'.[13] A significant dimension of this perspective of the subject in interaction is the latter's capacity to project itself into the object of perception and reciprocally to reproduce the qualities of the external world within, through modifications of the body schema. These two mechanisms (projection and introjection) are specific to a human's manner of being in the world, and they grant a certain normative value to a human's relations with materiality (Merleau-Ponty, 2003: 225). This 'libidinal' relation to the world of objects and its normative significance are particularly clear in the case of workers' relation to the most important objects in their work. In such cases, however mistaken it might be on an epistemic level, anthropomorphism (the tendency to treat objects like persons) nevertheless represents an undeniable aspect of moral life. For instance, a worker is not indifferent to the situation in which his or her privileged objects are treated with care or without care (Dodier, 1995: 189–216). The idea, here, is an intuition at the heart of Adorno's ethics which appears to attract Honneth in his more recent writings: it is only by cultivating a kind of 'libidinal' (or affective) relation to the world (beyond mere respect for human beings as rationally autonomous beings) that a new form of moral life can be created, which would forgo the destructive anthropocentrism (and associated ecological crisis) produced by our current ethics.

Fourth consequence

Finally, a more specific consequence for critical theory follows from the aforementioned point about the relation of human beings to natural objects. As Merleau-Ponty writes in his *Nature* lectures, 'the human being is not animal + reason. That is why it is important to focus on the human being's body: before it is rationality, humanity is a kind of corporeity' (Merleau-Ponty, 2003: 208).

The essential vulnerability of the human being, the down side of its essential 'openness' to the world, is in fact shared by other organisms. Whatever differences separate human and animal bodily-being, it appears that the mechanisms of introjection and projection, the opportunities for attachment and empathy, are infinitely greater towards living organisms, and above all complex organisms, because many aspects of the bodily-being of complex animal organisms

The theory of social action: Merleau-Ponty, Honneth

trigger affective echoes in our own body schemas. Merleau-Ponty's conclusion, which he intends in an ontological sense, has a clear normative significance: 'the human being should be taken within the "*ineinander*" (being in the midst of) with animality and nature' (Merleau-Ponty, 2003: 208). It is an abstraction to talk of an interacting human without also speaking of the location of the human within the natural environment, alongside other non-human living beings, some of whom uncannily resemble us. We recall, at this point, that such considerations were already well established by the first generation of critical theory and were, in fact, already present in the early work of Marx. Whereas Habermas rejects the moral relevance of interactions with non-human living beings and the natural environment, it seems distinctly possible to retrieve such concerns by means of a certain interpretation of Honneth. This interpretation emphasises the idea that social emancipation cannot be thought in isolation of the 'liberation of nature' (see also Deranty, 2005 and Haber, 2006: Introduction).

Notes

1 The passages particularly relevant to this chapter's task of extracting a theory of social action from Merleau-Ponty's writings are: Part II, Chapter 4 and Part III, Chapter 3 of the *Phenomenology of perception* (1962); *Humanism and terror* (2000); Chapter 1 of *Adventures of the dialectic* (1973a); and the middle section of *The prose of the world* (1973b).
2 See in particular Honneth's very first article, reprinted as 'History and interaction' (Honneth, 1994).
3 The centrality and richness of social action is particularly obvious in Honneth's recent lectures on reification (2008a), where the old term of 'praxis' is explicitly embraced and recognition is articulated using genetic arguments of an undeniably anthropological import.
4 Honneth articulates his most direct criticism of the nefarious consequences of Habermas' logocentrism for social theory in 1980, reprinted in Honneth, 2007a: 80–96. Honneth expresses a similar concern in his contribution to this volume in Chapter 2.
5 For further consideration of the possible contributions of a phenomenology of the body and of social relations for a theory of recognition, using both Merleau-Ponty and Beauvoir, see Marie Garrau's contribution to this volume in Chapter 8.
6 See in particular the last pages of *Adventures of the dialectic* (1973a) where Merleau-Ponty is at pains to point out that his attempt to define a non-dogmatic Left position continues to be guided by the notion of class struggle.
7 The analyses in Merleau-Ponty's middle period (1973b) reflect on the way in which the phenomenology of speaking (*parole*) is not fully determined by the total structure of signs (*langue*) (thereby avoiding an account of a purely passive subject).
8 Merleau-Ponty expresses this intertwining of individual experience and structure at the end of the *Phenomenology of perception*: 'we confer upon history its significance, but not without its putting that significance forward itself' (Merleau-Ponty, 1962: 450).
9 Even after Merleau-Ponty's discovery of Saussure, and the increasing importance he

ascribes to symbolic forms of expression (language and arts), language continues to be conceptualised as 'retrieving and overflowing the shaping of the world that begins with perception' (1973b: 61). In an extraordinary footnote (1973b: 19), Merleau-Ponty declares that language is founded 'upon carnal generality', a type of reciprocal interaction between speakers which mobilises the whole body using processes which can only be analysed in terms of Freudian metapsychology: the spoken word is a medium of empathic projection – introjection.

10 Texts where Merleau-Ponty engages in a critique of the present include: the last section of the *Phenomenology of perception* (1962) which concludes with the destruction/realisation – *Aufhebung* – of philosophy within action; the conclusion of *Adventures of the dialectic* (1973a); as well as a number of shorter texts from the post-war period. The initial words of *Adventures of the dialectic* resonate strongly with the concerns of critical theory: 'In the crucible of events we become aware of what is not acceptable to us, and it is this experience as interpreted that becomes both thesis and philosophy' (1973a: 3). In the preface to *Signs* (1964: 13), Merleau-Ponty calls for a philosophical, non-dogmatic Marxism which would influence politics 'at a distance', describe the 'Being we inhabit' (historical, linguistic, communicative and temporal 'fields').

11 For further discussion of Bourdieu's concept of *habitus*, please consult Christian Lazzeri's and Robin Celikates' contributions to this volume in Chapters 9 and 10.

12 A particularly vivid passage on organic life in the *Phenomenology of perception* states that 'living (*leben*) is a primary process from which, as a starting point, it becomes possible to "live" (*erleben*) this or that world, and we must eat and breathe before perceiving and awakening to relational living … Thus sight, hearing, sexuality, the body are not only the routes, instruments or manifestation of personal existence: the latter takes up and absorbs into itself their existence as it is anonymously given' (Merleau-Ponty, 1962: 160).

13 Although Honneth's lectures on reification include a 'libidinal' interpretation of recognition following Adorno's thinking, he nonetheless maintains his intersubjectivist reading of affective attachments, which prevents him from given full weight to the organic nature of the subject.

8

Between gender and subjectivity: Iris Marion Young on the phenomenology of lived experience

Marie Garrau

IN her first book, *Justice and the politics of difference* (Young, 1990), Iris Marion Young develops a critique of recent theories of justice, showing that they tend to reduce social justice to distributive justice and calling into question the constructivist method that obscures the social and institutional context of justice. Following the critical method of the Frankfurt School, Young instead proposes to define justice by identifying concrete forms of injustice, focusing the analysis on the ways that injustice is experienced by people and defined by social movements. Her analysis leads her to reconceptualise injustice in terms of the categories of domination and oppression. Domination is defined as a set of institutional constraints that prevent people from freely determining their actions or the conditions of their actions. Domination frustrates self-determination. Oppression is defined as a set of systematic institutional processes which prevent self-development, thereby inhibiting the development and use of subjective capacities and limiting an individual's ability to interact with others and express their feelings and perspectives. Oppression frustrates self-realisation (Young, 1990: 38). Young distinguishes five types of oppression, namely, exploitation, marginalisation, powerlessness, cultural imperialism and violence (Young, 1990: 39–65). Clearly, the discovery of these five types of oppression uncovers a deep political problem for Young, who then has to figure out ways of overcoming these different forms. Moreover, the description of oppression also raises an anthropological and epistemological problem for the critical theorist. First, from the anthropological perspective, the analysis of oppression requires a conception of the subject which discloses the way in which oppression affects people's lives, illustrating the way in which social processes facilitate or limit the subject's identity and agency.

Second, from an epistemological point of view, the analysis must also explain how, exactly, oppression is to be accessed, described and diagnosed. This problem of epistemological access is derived from the fact that oppression typically deprives affected subjects of the very linguistic and symbolic resources necessary to describe, and attest to, their experience as, precisely, an experience of injustice (Young, 2000). To solve this problem, critical theorists like Nancy Fraser have traditionally focused analysis on the demands and claims expressed by social movements. However, as Axel Honneth points out, a critical theory which begins with the demands of social movements runs the risk of again overlooking those very processes which are responsible for oppression itself.[1] This is why Honneth, in *The struggle for recognition*, defends a rather different phenomenological method of accessing and describing experiences of oppression, which begins with and analyses the negative, subjective feelings which are produced by experiences of misrecognition and disrespect (Honneth, 1995a).

In this chapter, I aim to show that Iris Marion Young's book *On female body experience* (Young, 2005), which unites articles on the topic written over a span of more than two decades, provides a new way of responding to these anthropological and epistemological problems. As the title makes explicit, these articles focus on the bodily experience of women and aim to describe a way of being-in-the-world mediated by the specific potentialities of the body, including the potentiality of carrying children or of having periods. However, this way of being-in-the-world should also be understood as a relational position within a social space, that is, as a position which has been socially constructed as distinct from, and opposed to, the masculine position. This is the reason why the description of female bodily experience is combined, in Young's analysis, with a critical intent: the description also aims to convey a social situation of embodied oppression, which brings us back to the question of social justice and opposes the reduction of justice to redistribution alone.

In what follows, I will show that the reference to the phenomenological and existential theories of Merleau-Ponty and Beauvoir is central to the development of Young's position, and assists her in resolving the two problems (anthropological and epistemological) that we mentioned earlier. This reference serves a double purpose. First, it allows Young to lay the foundations for a social and concrete anthropology based on the concept of lived experience. Second, and consequently, the reference also allows her to anchor critical theory in subjective experience itself, supplementing the classical reference to the claims and demands of social movements. However, I will then reflect on the limits of phenomenology for Young's project. I will point out that it is not entirely clear that we can combine, as Young believes, the description of lived experience and the intention of social critique. I will focus my questions on this articulation and the epistemological and political interest which underlies it, drawing attention to the possible limits of Young's project. To what extent can the phenomenological description of female lived experience found a critique of the social oppression of women? What is the status of such description in her project? Can phenomenological description fulfil the function which Young ascribes to it and, if so, under what conditions?

Merleau-Ponty's contribution: from an anthropology of the embodied subject to the critical interest of phenomenology

Bodily experience and its significance

Young's first reason for turning to Merleau-Ponty's work can be found in the conception of the subject that emerges from the ontological argument which Merleau-Ponty defends in his *Phenomenology of perception* (Merleau-Ponty, 1962). Here, Merleau-Ponty develops a conception of the subject as both embodied and situated, whose relation to the world is first mediated by the body conceived as a lived-body. Opposing the dualistic implications of reductionist conceptions of the body developed, albeit in different ways, by behaviourist psychology and by the idealist tradition (Merleau-Ponty, 1962: 73–97), Merleau-Ponty redefines the body as a lived-body; the passive – active mediator between subject and world. The body equates to an ability 'to provide itself with one or several worlds' (Merleau-Ponty, 1962: 130). It is defined first by its practical unity or its ability to coordinate,[2] second by its openness to the world or its transcendence and third by its specific intentionality or its ability to signify and express. Hence, the embodied subject is always an 'I can' (Merleau-Ponty, 1962: 137) before being an 'I think', which means that thought itself finds its condition of possibility in an originary openness, deeply enrooted in the world, which characterises embodied existence (Merleau-Ponty, 1962: 383–92).

There are several aspects of this practical, embodied and situated subjectivity which attract Young's attention. First, she is interested in the intentionality of the lived-body (Merleau-Ponty, 1962: 137–41) by which she understands that our involvement in the world is always already meaningful and, consequently, that our world is always already tinged with value. The concept of bodily intentionality draws attention to the body's potentiality, to the fact that the body possesses a kind of practical sense, a pre-reflexive and non-conceptual knowledge of the world that is mobilised in action. It also highlights the relation of expression that unites the practical subject with a world which he or she has the power to project and which also includes the subject.

The second idea that interests Young is the idea of habit (Merleau-Ponty, 1962: 137). According to Merleau-Ponty, habits are the sedimentation of past actions that remain alive in our present way of being, radically shaping our relation to the world through a set of gestures, attitudes and activities. The sedimentation of habit indicates that our openness to the world can evolve, narrow, or widen through the process of learning, in the course of incorporating and appropriating objects, finding ourselves in different situations and responding to them in a significant and creative way (Merleau-Ponty, 1962: 137).

Finally, Young retains from Merleau-Ponty's work the concept of situation (Merleau-Ponty, 1962: 454–6) that refers to the intertwining of the body with the world, both natural and social, leading to a practical involvement that cannot be undone and that we do not initially choose. Being situated means that our perception of the world is always perspectival and partial and that the world presents itself as a horizon, partially opaque, necessarily unfinished.

Where Merleau-Ponty builds upon this conception of the embodied subject so as to throw light on new sources for a philosophy of knowledge, Young claims to discover the outline of a concrete social anthropology that would not only allow one to make sense of the structural relationship uniting subject and social-world but also to elaborate a conception of freedom which would not abstract from the subject's social situation. Indeed, for Young, the world of Merleau-Ponty's embodied subject has to be understood as an intersubjective and social world (Merleau-Ponty, 1962: 23; and 346–54), where every object indicates the imminent presence of another subject and is endowed with an already given meaning. The subject can act freely only by being situated in a social world that both precedes and includes him, which is why freedom is not conceptualised by Merleau-Ponty as sovereign. Freedom, for Merleau-Ponty, does not involve abstracting oneself from one's situation but is rather conceived as a power to respond to that situation in a creative way, to resignify it.[3] As Merleau-Ponty notes, concrete liberty 'comprises the general power of putting oneself into a situation' (Merleau-Ponty, 1962: 135). Defined in this way, freedom contrasts with both destiny and detachment. Such a conception seems sociologically plausible, in so far as it is compatible with the idea that social constraints weigh upon the social subject, shaping the subject's way of perceiving and acting, without the subject reflexively representing these constraints to him- or her-self, and with a concept of social change which includes the innovative and creative (though never entirely spontaneous) actions of agents in the world.

Having reminded ourselves of the relevant aspects of Merleau-Ponty's conception of the subject, we can now turn toward the use Young makes of it when describing women's oppression from the standpoint of the lived experience that such oppression implies. Young intends to return to women's ways of being-in-the-world, to what their bodies say and do. In this sense, she focuses attention on an object of analysis which runs deeper than mere discourse, namely, attitudes and practices where oppression is thought to be inscribed and reproduced.

Documenting the lived experience of women's oppression
In her book's introduction (Young, 2005: 3–11), Young reviews in detail the different tasks she assigns to phenomenology, explaining that she will use it

Between gender and subjectivity: lived experience

more as an approach than as a rigorous method. She underlines two main tasks. The first, which we could call 'expressive', aims at articulating experiences that are generally ignored in both public and intellectual spheres. She wishes to make these experiences visible and to create in her reader's mind the sense of recognition and solidarity that is necessary to stand up, speak out and take action. The second task, which we will call 'critical', consists in not only singling out within women's lived experience the types of constraints that have a negative impact on the development of capacities but also in discovering positive experiences where women, despite these constraints, act in creative ways, bearing norms of possible action and exhibiting something like an emancipatory interest. By starting from the lived experience of women as it reveals itself in women's bodily encounters, attitudes and activities, Young wants to shed light on the social situations that make this experience possible.

Young's well-known article 'Throwing like a girl: a phenomenology of feminine body comportment, motility and spatiality' (Young, 2005: 27–46), originally published in 1980, is typical of Young's theoretical project but also illustrates the problems that arise from the attempt to make her empirical descriptions coincide with her critical intent. Here, Young tries to show that women's oppression is manifest in the way they conduct themselves, in the way they move and in the space which their typical forms of movement produce. Young makes use of empirical studies conducted in the 1970s with little girls and boys, which suggest that girls and boys use their bodies in very different ways when confronted with the same task, in this case, throwing a ball. While boys spontaneously use their whole body, bending their knees, twisting from the waist and engaging their entire body in the movement, girls are more hesitant on the whole and tend to use their arm alone to throw the ball. On the basis of this example and others, Young puts forward her first hypothesis that girls have a distinct style of movement in space and she describes it by sorting out three of its modalities, which directly echo the work of Merleau-Ponty. This feminine style of movement is, in Young's view, characterised by an ambiguous transcendence, an inhibited intentionality and a discontinuous unity.

'Ambiguous transcendence' marks every living body in so far as the body that projects itself in the world is always rooted in a situation, characterised, as such, by a kind of immanence rather than transcendence. But, according to Young, women's embodied existence tends to remain in immanence. The fact that only a limited part of the body is involved in action reveals that women 'remain within', having difficulty projecting themselves and feeling their body as a burden.

'Inhibited intentionality' refers to the fact that, for women, the understanding of the world around them, which manifests itself as a power of doing and acting, is often contradicted by a lack of understanding, which demonstrates powerlessness, expressed in hesitation, suspension of movement, and retreat.

For Young, this means that a woman's bodily possibilities are not experienced as her own: they remain abstract, possibilities for a 'body in general' but not for hers.

Finally, 'discontinuous unity' refers to the fact that instead of expressing an intimate subjective connection with the body in the world, a woman's motility produces a kind of distance between subject and world and, moreover, between subject and self: her gestures are uncoordinated, her 'grip' on the world is loosened. Young concludes that women's motility, riddled with practical contradictions, produces a living-space which is enclosed, wherein women become positioned instead of positioning themselves. For Young, this deficient development is caused by women's particular situation within post-industrial and urban contemporary societies. Here, Young puts forward a second hypothesis, this time explanatory, which states that the contradictory dimension of women's lived experience is caused by the fact that women experience their body not as a power for acting but as an object for the masculine gaze, where activities tend to be defined and evaluated from this masculine viewpoint.

Although she certainly draws on Merleau-Ponty's conceptual vocabulary, Young's description of female motility appears to be quite removed from his perspective. For Merleau-Ponty, unity, intentionality and transcendence describe the fundamental structures of being-in-the-world. These structures may be altered in such cases as illness or deviance, but they are never explicitly understood with reference to specific social processes such as gendered oppression. Moreover, if Merleau-Ponty draws attention to the sexualised body, it is only to show that the body projects a world which is always affective and erotic, a world of sexual possibilities, so as to underline the fact that the body possesses an 'absolutely individual sexual schema' (Merleau-Ponty, 1962: 154–8). Here again, Merleau-Ponty's theory is situated at an ontological, rather than sociological, level. By contrast, Young's project has a very different purpose and character, on account of her specific objective as well as the sociological level on which the work is developed and the critical intent which drives it.

These differences raise at least two questions. First, from what source does Young derive those norms for critique which allow her to distinguish between a normal mode of being-in-the-world and the problematic if not pathological mode that Young believes is typical of women's mode of existence? Second, to what extent can it be said that the reference to this women's mode of being is, in fact, arbitrary? Or, to put it another way, what explanatory power is it possible to assign to gender and why should it be privileged over other factors in the description of lived experience? These questions bring us to the problem of the link between descriptions of lived experience and social critique.

Between gender and subjectivity: lived experience

From description of lived experience to social critique: from Merleau-Ponty to Beauvoir

Norms within the movement of existence: Merleau-Ponty's analysis of illness
In the *Phenomenology of perception*, when Merleau-Ponty presents illness as an alteration of a subject's mode of being-in-the-world, he suggests that norms inhere in the movement of existence. Studying the alterations produced by illness can indicate the character of the normality to which illness alludes (Merleau-Ponty, 1962: 107). If we look at Schneider, the case-study for the first part of the book, we can see that illness primarily alters the capacity to project oneself into the world, that is, the practical intentionality which allows the subject to respond to a situation, give it a new meaning and transcend it. Schneider is described as incapable of distancing himself from the present situation and of setting projects for himself. In contrast, he appears trapped within his situation, so that illness presents itself, from an existential point of view, as a closure of possibilities. The normal capacities that are defective in illness include creativity (the capacity to adapt in an imaginative way to a new situation), and expressivity (the capacity to give meaning to the situation so as to incorporate it into habitual existence). What is lacking in illness is a form of spontaneous, pre-reflexive and shared understanding of the world: the world resists appropriation and appears to be strange and unfamiliar. As Merleau-Ponty notes, illness entails a suspension of the world's familiarity (Merleau-Ponty, 1962: 132).

If we go back to the categories with which Young describes women's movement, we cannot but note the resemblance between, on the one hand, Merleau-Ponty's description of the effect of Schneider's illness, and, on the other hand, Young's description of a feminine movement which expresses and contributes to oppression. In each case, what is described is an inhibited way of being-in-the-world, and, in each case, the description evokes the loss of freedom conceived as the capacity of acting and giving worlds to oneself (Merleau-Ponty, 1962: 135). Oppression, as illness, alters the subject in her totality, by inhibiting her creativity and expressivity and preventing her from feeling 'at home' in the social world.

Nevertheless, the comparison between illness and oppression, based on the resemblance of their effects on the embodied subject, remains problematic, or at least inadequate. The problem does not so much arise, as one might initially expect, from the tendency for such comparison to justify a 'medicalisation' of social critique. It is clear that Merleau-Ponty is concerned with the existential rather than medical character of illness. Instead, the problem concerns the existence of a gap or hiatus between the descriptive aims of the phenomenological approach and the intention of social critique which characterises Young's approach. In contrast to Merleau-Ponty, Young does not merely intend to identify specific modes of being and diagnose them as abnormal so as to derive from these descriptions an account of normal human existence. Her project goes much deeper than this and concerns social critique. Young wants to show that women's mode of being-in-the-world is informed and constructed by an unjust social position which is specific to their subject-type. From this perspective of social critique, Merleau-Ponty's phenomenological descriptions lack the requisite analysis of the social processes which subtend oppressive experiences, thereby preventing us from identifying such experiences as injustices, as Young wishes to do. Consequently, this leaves phenomenological description unable to facilitate reflection on the ways in which the processes that cause injustice might be remedied and transformed.[4] This is precisely the reason why Young departs from Merleau-Ponty's standard phenomenological analysis, so as to use Simone de Beauvoir's work to qualify women's lived experience not only as a particular or even problematic way of being-in-the-world, but as the product of a specific social position.

The second sex: *between the phenomenology of sexual difference and the sociology of gender domination*

As Young notes, Merleau-Ponty's analysis of the lived-body should be valid for any human being whatever its sex, which is precisely why this analysis cannot explain the specificity and the negativity of women's bodily experience. Consequently, this specificity and negativity has to be understood in light of a new assumption. As mentioned earlier, this facilitating assumption is that women exist in a social situation specific to liberal, post-industrial societies, and that this existence produces a distinct type of bodily-experience. It is with a view to explaining this assumption that Young turns toward Simone de Beauvoir's *The second sex* (2010).

The second sex attracts Young's attention because it suggests a strong link between women's lived experience and the oppressive social structures which shape and define it, drawing on an original interpretation of the phenomenological concept of 'situation'. Beauvoir identifies certain practices, discourses and norms that produce femininity as a specific figure of a paradoxical subjectivity destined to remain man's Other (Beauvoir, 2010: 3–19). In so doing, Beauvoir attributes as much importance to the task of identifying these norms (for which Book 1 provides an immanent critique) as she does to the description of the way in which these practices, discourses and norms are incorporated, repeated and contested in the ordinary lives of women, in their practical relations to the world, others, and themselves. When Beauvoir defines femininity as the product of a historical dynamic, she does not forget to emphasise the extent to which this history is carried, reinforced, or displaced by each woman's way of being-in-the-world. For Beauvoir, the focus on 'situation' implies an attention both to social structures and lived experience, the description of the former calling for the description of the latter and vice versa.[5]

Between gender and subjectivity: lived experience

Emphasising Beauvoir's attempt to understand women's lived experience in the light of women's social situation, Young insists on the need to maintain, in addition to the phenomenological concept of the lived-body, a concept of social structure that would explain the gendered character of certain modes of being-in-the-world, identifying their social determinations.[6] Young defines social structures as 'the confluence of institutional rules and interactive routines, mobilisation of resources, and physical structures, which constitute the historical givens in relation to which individuals act, and which are relatively stable over time ... Social structures position individuals in relations of labour and production, power and subordination, desire and sexuality, prestige and status' (Young, 2005: 20). For Young, this means that 'membership in the group called "women" is the product of a loose configuration of different structural factors' (Young, 2005: 21). This concept of social structure allows Young to redefine gender in an anti-essentialist and materialist fashion that already characterises the work of Beauvoir. Gender designates neither an ahistorical essence, nor an individual identity. Rather, it is an attribute of social structures such as the sexual division of labour, the heterosexual norms and the hierarchies of power which together structure liberal and post-industrial contemporary societies. Gender, in this sense, refers to the multiple ways in which living bodies are socially positioned in relation to each other within particular historical institutions.

Articulating gender with the lived-body, Young's articles oscillate, in this way, between describing lived experience and analysing the social structures that account for it. For example, echoing Beauvoir, Young considers that having periods can be conceived neither as an obstacle *per se*, nor as a physical or even a moral deficiency. The experience becomes transformed into a handicap or a monthly nightmare only insofar as women are subjected to the pressure of a contradictory social demand that requires them to hide their bodily phenomenon while also restricting the material means for doing so (Young, 2005: 97–123; Beauvoir, 2010: 324–31). In a similar vein, Young describes pregnancy as an ambivalent experience, not only because women are both subject to it and the cause of it, but also because during this experience their unique 'pregnant' standpoint on their lived experience is systematically reduplicated and finally disqualified by medical discourses and practices that control, frame and objectify the pregnancy (Young, 2005: 46–61).

Articulating gender with the lived-body: terms and limits

Objections from a phenomenological perspective

When considered in the context of the social structures that shape it in a particular way, women's lived experience, contradictory and unhappy, can become the object of a collective project of social transformation. However, at this point, we could well ask whether the attempt to interpret lived experience through the reference to objective social structures is, in fact, convincing. In spite of the potential of Young's project for a critique of oppression, Young's articulation of the categories of the lived-body and the sociology of gender seems, from the phenomenological perspective initially adopted, to encounter two related objections. The first objection is the following: is it not the case that the introduction of the concept of social structures effectively clouds the very bodily experience that it was supposed to clarify? The second could be summed up as follows: is it not the case that the critical intent of Young's project effectively biases her description of experience from the very outset, by leading her to arbitrarily single out certain aspects of experience as particularly meaningful, to the detriment of others?

These two objections have been expressed by Dianne Chisholm in an article that takes up Young's project while modifying it substantially, as is suggested by its title, 'Climbing like a girl' (Chisholm, 2008: 9–40). In this article, Chisholm criticises Young first for having built a phenomenology of feminine incapacity by insisting on sociological gender and excluding the analysis of the feminine body's potentialities; second for giving gender the status of a direct cause of incapacity and forgetting that Beauvoir understands gender simply as a background of constraints;[7] third and finally for carelessly generalising the results of her phenomenological descriptions so that they fit perfectly with the explanatory schema she defends. According to Chisholm, the contributions which a phenomenology of female body experience can bring to feminist theory are opposite to the ones that Young suggests. Instead of analysing the way in which the female body incorporates gender stereotypes, a phenomenology of female body experience should try to clarify the way in which female body transcends its gendered situation, embodying forms of practical freedom that could speak to women's experience, allowing a woman to take hold of their world (literally, in the case of the mountain climber), and facilitating women's projects in the world. Inspired by the famous remark Beauvoir once made about hiking,[8] Chisholm bases her phenomenology of female body experience on the ethos and style of the free-climber Lynn Hill. Hill's practice of climbing is analysed as the paradigm of transcendence. She transcends both her gendered social situation – the social world of climbing being mainly masculine – and the existential situation defined by the potentialities and limits of her embodied subject.

Given the example Chisholm relies on, it is no surprise to discover that the five modalities of female motility that she identifies as existential categories are very different to those that Young focuses on (Chisholm, 2008: 20–33). Hill's climbing reveals that the female body can achieve what Beauvoir called the 'free movement of existence' by surging toward and grasping objects, a modality of movement that Chisholm sums up under the category of 'reach'. 'Reach' allows the female body to learn to overcome obstacles by facing them, an attitude

Chisholm refers to through the category of 'crux'. 'Crux' also makes clear that the female body can acquire its unity and become creative by training intensively and trusting itself, a modality Chisholm calls the 'flow'. Finally Hill's trajectory demonstrates that the female body can become familiar with the world around both by projecting itself practically in it, in a movement typical of the body's 'freedom', and by listening carefully to its own sensations and what they reveal about the world around, in an attitude Chisholm calls 'synaesthesia'. In this way, reach, crux, flow, freedom and synaesthesia describe the positive modalities of the female body, make visible possibilities of the female body which are in principle accessible to any woman. Indeed, Chisholm refuses to consider that Hill's example could be less significant than others because of the level of Hill's performances. She insists less on performance and more on 'trajectory', underlining the fact that Hill succeeds in developing a personal style of free-climbing, freely inhabiting her world and overcoming the stereotypes and scepticism of climbing circles. For Chisholm, this success is made possible by the process of training and habit-acquisition, through the practical intelligence of the body in action.

Social critique and the creativity of action

When we consider the significance of Chisholm's objections, we can see that they do not necessarily rule out the possibility of combining a description of the lived-body with a critical analysis of social structures. In her article, Chisholm herself gives a critical twist to her phenomenological description. She does not criticise oppressive social structures as such, but rather the tendency to reify them and analyse them independently of the subjective meaning they acquire in subjects' experiences and through their singular practices. In reproaching Young for ascribing too much import to the sociological category of gender at the expense of the phenomenological category of the lived-body, Chisholm refuses an objectivist conception of the social that she finds incompatible with the phenomenological approach. Read in this way, Chisholm's objections now lead us to ask whether Young's notion of social structure is in fact compatible with the spirit of phenomenological analysis and its insistence on the *creativity of action*.[9]

A brief suggestion of Young's, which appears at the end of the article 'Lived body versus gender', offers the beginnings of an answer to this question. Here, Young indicates that the theoretical project of articulating the description of lived experience with the analysis of social structures is the very project Bourdieu had in mind when he formulated the concept of *habitus* (Young, 2005: 26). The concept of *habitus* refers to the way in which global social structures are produced and reproduced through the movements and interactions of bodies.[10] It designates a system of lasting dispositions acquired by the agent through the process of socialisation, dispositions which are both the product of past social conditions and the condition for innovative social practices (Bourdieu, 1977). However, Young insists that Bourdieu's theory leaves itself exposed to criticism due to its tendencies to determinism and objectivism, which is why she considers Merleau-Ponty's theory of the lived-body, a primary source for the concept of *habitus*, to be more fruitful.[11] According to Young, by underlining the practical intelligence of the lived-body, Merleau-Ponty makes more room than Bourdieu for the creativity and plasticity of action, accounting for the latitude that social subjects have with regard to their action. In this way, and contrary to what Chisholm suggests in her analysis of Young's phenomenology of throwing, the creativity and plasticity of action that expresses women's freedom in fact plays an important role in Young's description of women's bodily experience, showing that Young, while paying attention to social structures, does not endorse an objectivist and determinist concept of the social.

For instance, in the article 'House and home' (Young, 2005: 123–54), Young returns to Beauvoir's analysis of housework and refuses to understand these activities as endless repetitions whereby the confinement of women in immanence is made explicit and reinforced (Beauvoir, 2010: 471–85). For Young, Beauvoir's diagnosis is insufficient, for several reasons: first, it ignores the process of re-signification and re-evaluation that takes place in all activities, even in housework. Housekeeping can also mean arranging a place, giving it new meanings and values, setting it up so that people who live in it can move freely and feel at home. Conceived in this way, the home becomes a place where one builds and preserves a living identity, and the set of activities that helps create such a space cannot be reduced, as Beauvoir would have it, to repetitive and unproductive activities. Young's point is not that housework is not repetitive and confining but rather that it need not necessarily be experienced as such, and that one needs to make visible these experiences from a properly feminist perspective.

Here, we are very far from Chisholm's view that Young wrongly instrumentalises her descriptions of women's activities in order to serve her own critical purpose, thereby overlooking the meaningful possibilities that such activities retain. But does this mean, conversely, that a phenomenology of feminine experience is condemned to celebrate in a non-critical fashion every particular feminine experience simply because every experience offers possibilities for re-signification and re-evaluation? The answer to this question is clearly negative due to the articulation Young proposes between lived experience and social structures. This articulation indicates that the experiences which a theorist tries to describe can be considered neither fully generalisable nor ahistorical. This is the second reason why Young returns to and revises Beauvoir's negative account of housework. If Beauvoir's diagnosis is judged inadequate it is also because the meanings of house and home in contemporary Western societies have undergone deep structural changes. In these societies, where housing shortages and housing crises have become structural problems, the idea of 'home' and its associated ideas have acquired critical value, complicating both the feminist discourses which reject the domestic sphere as a place of women's oppression in patriarchal societies and the Marxist discourses which tend to reduce the private sphere to a central component of bourgeois ideology responsible for the withdrawal of people from the political sphere.

These remarks do not solve once and for all the epistemological problems posed by Young's attempt to articulate social critique with her descriptions of lived experience. But they clearly show why her attempt is worthwhile. For Young, the appeal to lived experience is not simply intended to uncover certain theoretical assumptions made *a priori* and independently of experience. It aims, first, to uncover a layer of meaning that is generally ignored. At the same time, this detour also helps to understand certain sociological or political assumptions in a more complex and nuanced manner. The focus on lived experience makes visible not simply those negative or concealed experiences but also the ambiguity that characterises every situation in so far as it takes on meaning and significance at the junction of an individual experience and a general social situation. At the ontological level, this ambiguity is the flip side of the latitude or choice which all social subjects enjoy, even those in a situation of constraint. Such latitude allows subjects to re-interpret, if not transcend, their constraint. At the epistemological level, this ambiguity also plays a role: it refers to the fact that social critique can never fully achieve its goals, thereby limiting the attempt to produce a totalising and univocal theory. It could be argued that such a limit would have problematic implications in terms of political efficiency.[12] But, on the other hand, if the task of social critique is to give voice in the public sphere to experiences that are ignored, the legitimacy of the attempt depends on the extent to which it succeeds in presenting these experiences and their ambivalences. From this point of view, the phenomenological approach can be fruitful in that its account of the ambiguity of experience requires attention to the particularity and complexity of lived experience, thereby helping us avoid the pitfalls of political language which is often too ideological and too general.

Notes

1 For two different ways of solving the problem of the empirical reference point for a critical theory, compare the approach of Axel Honneth with that of Nancy Fraser (Fraser and Honneth, 2001 and Honneth, 2007b: 80–97).
2 On this point, see the concept of 'body image' (Merleau-Ponty, 1962: 98–9; 141 and 150).
3 On this point, see Merleau-Ponty (1962: 451–4), where Merleau-Ponty criticises the conception of freedom Sartre develops in *Being and nothingness* for being too intellectualist and too abstract.
4 On the different models of social critic and their assumptions, see Renault (2008a: 65).

5 It would be misleading to reductively interpret *The second sex* as an application of Sartrean philosophy to the question of women. It would be equally misleading to insist on the influence of Sartre's conception of the sovereign subject on Beauvoir's work. Although Beauvoir sometimes seems to endorse such a conception, especially when emphasising the value of transcendence, she nevertheless insists that social structures weigh women down, shaping their bodies and inhibiting their bodily agency. The idea of abstracting oneself from one's situation appears absurd from this viewpoint. In fact, Beauvoir mocks the idea of a sovereign subject, which she interprets as an avatar of masculine bad faith (Beauvoir, 2010: 661–5).

6 On this point Young's analysis departs from Toril Moi's. With Moi, Young admits that the concept of lived-body constitutes the starting point for a theory of subjectivity and ascribes weight to the multiplicity of individual experiences in their situational variety. But Young also maintains that the concept of the lived-body cannot alone facilitate the analysis of those social injustices that confront women, the identification of the root causes of such injustice and the suggestion of remedies. For Young, these tasks are of central importance (Moi, 2003; and Young, 2005: 12–26).

7 In my view, the articles gathered in the book *On female body experience* show that Young's perspective is not at all determinist. In 'Gender as seriality', Young argues that the social structures which allow women to be defined should be understood as a background for each woman's individual situation and not as the cause of her situation. The notion of background, linked to that of situation, is designed to show that these structures do not determine individual actions as a cause that would determine an effect but rather exercise an intermediate and limited influence on them (Young, 1997).

8 Beauvoir writes: 'If it were possible to assert herself in her body and be part of the world in some other way, this deficiency [her physical weakness] would be easily compensated. If she could swim, scale rocks, pilot a plane, battle the elements, take risks and venture out, she would not feel the timidity towards the world that I spoke about' (Beauvoir, 2010: 345).

9 Although I cannot give this question the attention it merits here, it should be noted that Merleau-Ponty provides the beginnings of an answer in his article 'The philosopher and sociology' (Merleau-Ponty, 1964: 98–113).

10 For a reading of Bourdieu's concept of *habitus*, see Christian Lazzeri's contribution to this volume (Chapter 9).

11 For an interesting reading of Bourdieu's account of *habitus* in the light of Merleau-Ponty's concept of the lived-body, see Crossley (2001).

12 It would be easier to say that housekeeping is a problem *per se*; or that women's emancipation *necessarily* entails the refusal of fashion imperatives; or that the recourse to plastic surgery is *always* the symptom of social domination. This is precisely the kind of statement Young tries to avoid when underlining the ambiguity of experience (Young, 2005: 123–55; 62–74 and 75–96).

PART IV
SYSTEMATIC OPPRESSION AND THE PRODUCTIVITY OF POWER

9

Conflicts of recognition and critical sociology

*Christian Lazzeri**

> Struggles for recognition are a fundamental dimension of social life.
> (Pierre Bourdieu, *In other words*, 1992)

THE concept of the conflict for recognition occupies a central place in Pierre Bourdieu's sociology, one as important as the concepts of 'field', '*habitus*', '*illusio*', 'symbolic capital', 'power' and 'symbolic violence', 'social space', or 'delegation'. One could even say that the concept of the conflict of recognition enables Bourdieu to establish a relation between these other concepts. It is implied by them and renders them intelligible in turn. It would in fact be difficult to understand the structure of what Bourdieu refers to as 'field' without recourse to conflict, difficult to grasp the modifications which affect the different forms of symbolic capital without once more bringing conflict into play.

Conversely, the relations between the different positions in social space, or between the different degrees of capital and symbolic power, specify the very conditions of conflict. In this sense, conflict is situated at the juncture of social structure and history and, in disciplinary terms, at the articulation of the analysis of structures and historical sociology.

There are many forms of conflict for recognition for Bourdieu: conflicts of revindication (for compensation or reparation), dealing with the processes of categorisation at work in the social world; or conflicts in crisis situations aiming to transform the structure of one of the different social universes that he calls 'fields'. These conflicts are subsumed under the category of 'symbolic struggles' intended to constitute or increase the symbolic capital of competing agents in a given field. One can even assert that, on Bourdieu's account, all conflict possesses, and can be explained in part by, a symbolic dimension. This is to say that the symbolic dimension of conflict is of interest for every theorist of recognition, an interest that must be all the greater for Bourdieu, who proposes a theoretical framework that allows us to conceive of the relations between individuals and social structures, and to come to grips with the conditions, stakes and logic of conflicts of recognition.

Systematic oppression and the productivity of power

If we turn to the *conditions* of these conflicts, the importance of Bourdieu's problematic is situated at a number of levels. The first consists in breaking with every account that immediately situates recognition within a reciprocity guaranteed by ethics and that eschews as much as possible the moment of the conflict, as is the case, for example, in Ricoeur, or in the later Derrida (Derrida, 1994a; Ricoeur, 2007). For Bourdieu, if recognition is inextricably tied up with conflict, it is because it cannot be understood without reference to the relations of power generated by the structure of fields or to the necessity for agents to free themselves from insignificance or social depreciation by establishing or supplementing their symbolic capital. The second level constitutes a critical reaction to the conceptions of collective mobilisation defended by rational choice theory, and consists in demonstrating that the damage done to the symbolic (and material) interests of social agents by relations of domination is not enough to ensure that these agents engage in conflicts for recognition when the cost of their entry seems acceptable. The perception that they have of the social universe, of the place that they occupy within it, and the recognition that they can obtain from it are largely determined by their *habitus*, which can lead them, irrespective of any question of cost, to renounce their hope for social recognition and adapt their preferences to their position.

Concerning the *stakes* of conflicts of recognition, Bourdieu distinguishes, as we have seen, two categories of conflict: classificatory conflicts, and conflicts that transform the field. The first consist, for individuals and social groups, in putting the different categories of social classification to work, recategorising them in their favour, or by transforming the hierarchical principles to their advantage. The second aims to transform as such the rules and hierarchies of the particular field in which they take place. The Bourdieusian theory of recognition asserts that those who dominate do not in principle participate in the same kinds of conflicts as those who are dominated. Whatever their interests, the latter do not in principle practically participate in struggles over hierarchy, but only in conflicts that redefine the structure of the field. In this sense, Bourdieu writes, 'the site [*lieu*] par excellence of symbolic struggles is the dominant class itself' (Bourdieu, 1984: 254) or 'the field of power' (Bourdieu, 1996: 215).

Finally, in relation to the *logic* of conflicts of recognition, Bourdieu has attempted to resolve two types of problems, keeping an equal distance, here as always, from both objectivist and subjectivist conceptions of collective mobilisation. On the one hand, he has tried to bypass the difficulty arising from the Marxist conception of class, reproaching Marx for the same reason Marx reproached Hegel, namely, for confusing the things of logic with the logic of things. One cannot, ignoring the role of the representation of class in its constitution, immediately identify the common, objective and implied interests of members of a social group – that is, of a merely theoretical 'class on paper' – the basis of their engagement in conflict – that is, as a mobilised class (Bourdieu,

1984: 101). On the other hand, Bourdieu has tried to bypass the difficulties that rational choice theory presents for collective mobilisation, difficulties which arise from the former's emphasis on the instrumental rationality of the *free rider*, that is, the individual's instrumental decision to abandon the cause, thereby threatening the mobilisation process.

Bourdieu argues, in keeping with his conception of *habitus*, that the solution to both of these difficulties must be discovered in the concept of the 'delegation' of power to an organisation or apparatus that provides the social group with a unified representation of its material or symbolic interests, along with a clear definition of its objectives. This mechanism of delegation leads members to identify with the collective identity of the group, thus assuring an allegiance of the former to the latter (Bourdieu, 2000b: 96, 101). It is this representation of their avowed interests, their identity, their demands, their unity and their force – and not only their common, objective, and implied interests – which allow the members of the group to pass from being a class of merely theoretical existence ('class on paper') to a real class, participating in conflicts, having overcome the attitude of the *free rider* (Bourdieu, 2000b, 146).

Critical sociology therefore demonstrates a certain interest in the construction of a theory of conflicts of recognition. It remains to be seen what it can teach us. What follows will concentrate strictly on the analysis of the *conditions* and *stakes* of conflicts of recognition. We will be concerned, here, with the theoretical dimension of Bourdieu's sociology, without being able to make use of the empirical studies which, however, constitute an indispensable component of Bourdieu's work (the structure of kinship, mythology, gender, education, language, State, political life, access to culture, scientific production, etc.). We will show that, contrary to the often naïve approaches of the philosophers of recognition, who tend to believe that stigmatisation, depreciation, or disrespect are enough to provoke agents to engage in conflict, the interest of Bourdieu's sociology consists in analysing in a precise manner the stakes and social factors which either prevent or promote conflicts of recognition. And yet, this gain in our understanding of such conflicts is negatively offset by an ambiguity with respect to the effects of the use of the concept of *habitus*. These effects draw attention to the fact that certain social groups confront, at least in theory, situations involving a *double-bind* that make it difficult to account for their engagement in conflicts of recognition in some cases, and their resignation to accepting their depreciated group-status in other cases.

This problem is coupled with an additional difficulty that concerns the extension of the concept of *habitus*, which is either presented as theoretically superior to the notion of material or symbolic interest that it governs, or engaged in competition with it. In any case, the problem that Bourdieu's approach poses is of interest for the theory of recognition, since the question of the conditions and stakes of conflicts of recognition must be answered in as precise a way as possible.

Systematic oppression and the productivity of power

The first section of what follows will briefly present a descriptive schema of the nature of differentiated social space by emphasising in particular some of the key concepts in Bourdieu's sociology. The second section will examine the relations between phenomena of domination and the struggle for recognition, while the third will evaluate the coherence of Bourdieu's theses.

Habitus, interest and recognition in the structures of the field

At the epistemological level, Bourdieu's sociology attempts to reconcile the objectivist approach to social structures (Durkheim, Marx) and the phenomenological approach (Schütz, Goffman) to the representations that agents have of their social world and of their own position in this world. Taking this starting point as a given, we can descend from the objective to the subjective, beginning first of all with the most general properties of social space in order to then examine the conception of the dispositions of social agents. Social space and the nature of the resources which are distributed within it will be defined first, followed by the notion of interest and its variants, and finally the concept of *habitus*, presupposing throughout a minimal familiarity with these concepts on the part of the reader.

Social space and resources

The notion of 'social space' can be defined as the expression of a relational conception of the social world. Breaking with the substantialist conception of social groups, it maintains that the whole of the 'reality' that it grasps resides in the mutual exteriority of its constitutive elements. Unconcealed and directly visible beings, whether individuals or groups, only exist and subsist in and by difference, that is, insofar as they occupy relative positions in a space of relations. This space, while invisible and always difficult to empirically perceive, constitutes 'the most real reality ... and the real principle of the behaviour of individuals and groups' (Bourdieu, 1998: 31). Social science must try to understand these social spaces in which the positions of social groups are differentiated. Now, the principle of this differentiation is nothing other than the structure of the distribution of kinds of capital – irreducible to economic capital – at work in the social universe under consideration. In a general sense, as *Language and symbolic power* (1993) notes, one can say that every position in a social field can be defined in relation to a multidimensional system of coordinates: it is for this reason that one of the fundamental and determining dimensions of the position of an agent (or a group) is the total *amount* of the capital (economic, cultural, social) that they possess, while the second dimension is that of the *structure* (composition) of its capital according to the relative weight of the different kinds of capital (economic, cultural, social, etc.) that make up this ensemble. It is precisely the existence of these aggregated or singular capitals that creates a range of differentiated positions in each field (economic, pedagogical, artistic, political, etc.), positions that only exist in relation to each other (Bourdieu, 1993).

The possession of capital allows individuals or groups of a given field to exercise power and influence within it, and therefore to be visible.

These different types of capital, material or otherwise, are all converted into what Bourdieu calls 'symbolic capital' when they are experienced and recognised in such a way that their possessors accrue an authority, a prestige, a reputation, or a form of charisma which guarantees for them the production of favourable acts of power in a determined field. They are in fact recognised within it through a perception which imposes the values of their distinctive properties (Bourdieu, 1998: 102–4). This symbolic dimension is therefore essential. The symbolic capital of an agent or a social group can only reside in their academic, economic, or cultural capital, or in an aggregation of different forms of capital.

Finally, since the amount of this capital together with the diversification of its structure defines the social position of agents, the latter, attempting to increase their capital, are always engaged in the process of reinforcing this position or of gaining access to a superior position. They strive to acquire 'positional goods', but these goods have a particular characteristic: the higher one rises in the social hierarchy, the *rarer* these positional goods become. Superior social positions cannot, in principle, be open to all. Such a striving thus assumes the form of a competition between individuals or social groups who confront one another in the search for the accrual, conservation, or acquisition of the different forms of capital (including symbolic capital) to which they can lay claim. As a consequence, competition in a given field depends upon an *effect of rarity* (Bourdieu, 1977: 64, 183). And yet, this 'objective' principle does not constitute the only possible explanation. Bourdieu complements it with a subjective principle, the *interest* of agents. This principle owes much to the traditions of philosophy and classical sociology; Bourdieu is inspired here as much by the analyses of Hobbes, Pascal, or La Rochefoucauld as he is by Kojève, Sartre, or Weber.

Interest

Interest appears in the first instance as an investment in the practices of a field to which value is accorded (one has an *interest in* [*intérêt pour*]),[1] and it is as a result opposed to indifference. This investment, this feel for the game of a field (for its rules and activities) nonetheless relies upon a principle of the selective fixation of interest. This principle is that of socialisation that operates on the basis of the 'narcissistic organisation of the libido, in which the child takes himself (or his own body) as an object of desire' (Bourdieu, 2000a: 199). It is on the basis of this attitude that these affective investments can be oriented towards other people and lead to the manifestation of an interest in the interest of others, thereby gaining access to a social universe now equal in size to the field. Now, contemporary societies are characterised by a differentiation of fields and by their increasing autonomy, such that their 'fundamental law' becomes irreducible – which is to say that each field possesses a specific principle of organisation for its activities that differentiates it from other fields. What determines the investment of the agents in the scientific, religious, political, or artistic fields is not the same as the investment that makes them compete in, for example, the economic field. This thesis therefore leads to a fragmentation and an historicisation of the concept of interest, since there are as many forms of investment as there are species of interest across the different fields. Such a thesis constitutes a reaction against the anthropological determination of the content of interest, such as it is presented in economic thought, which defines it solely as a *natural* tendency to maximise material profit (Bourdieu and Wacquant, 1992: 92, 95, 100).

This '*interest in*' [*intérêt pour*] is, in reality, inseparable from 'in one's "interests to" …' [*intérêt à*], that is, an interest related to a position that can be (or is already) occupied, and to the capital that corresponds to it; a particular profit is thus hoped for, one which is as much material as symbolic (Bourdieu, 1984: 475). The 'in one's "interests to" …', which can only be expressed once investment in the game of the field has commenced, represents the agents' own advantage, drawn from the position that they occupy.

How does the principle of socialisation work? It acts within the framework of primary (familial) socialisation through the – in general informal – educational practices that inculcate, in the child, beliefs and ways of perceiving and acting with regard to the social world. It is realised through pressure, requests, commands, warnings, corporeal interiorisation, calls to order and incentives for mimicry. These are the imperceptible transactions, psychological operations and attitudes encouraged and upheld, advised and channelled by the family by which the child incorporates the functional rules of a field. These exchanges account not only for the investment of children in the games of this field, but also for their desire to attain strongly valorised social positions richly endowed with symbolic capital (Bourdieu, 2000a: 165, 244).

Group interventions supplement those specific to the family, interventions on the part of peers and scholastic agents, who reinforce this process of behavioural inculcation adapted to the rules of the field.

Among the diverse factors which contribute to this result, there is one whose importance dominates the others: 'pedagogical work in its elementary form relies on one of the motors which will be at the origin of all subsequent investments: the *search for recognition*' (Bourdieu, 2000a: 166). It is this that engenders the behaviour by which the child finds themselves determined to adopt the point of view of others with respect to themselves, attempting to know and

Conflicts of recognition and critical sociology

perceive in advance the mode in which they will be evaluated by others: 'His being is a being-perceived, condemned to be defined as it "really" is by the perceptions of others' (Bourdieu, 2000a: 171).

This thesis of the social being as a 'being-perceived' is without doubt one of the most fundamental theses in Bourdieu's sociology. It explains how recognition valorises the performances, the capacities of agents and their interest in the activities of this or that field. It also explains, moreover, why they desire the acquisition of prestige, reputation, approval, esteem, respect, admiration, credit, or charisma (Bourdieu, 1998: 85–6). And yet, this socialisation, by recognition, of 'in one's "interests to" …' [*intérêt à*] accounts for the desire to possess important symbolic capital, not to *monopolise* it. In short, socialisation cannot account for the desire to possess recognition to the exclusion of others (or it does not account for the fact that socialisation inculcates a desire for this). In order to do so, a supplementary dimension must be added to 'in one's "interests to" …' [*intérêt à*] – it must be presupposed that it is an *exclusive* interest of enjoyment (egoism) by nature (not that this implies any attempt to reduce this interest simply to economic profit).

This is what Bourdieu seems to say when he writes that the 'anthropological root' of symbolic capital must be found in 'the principle of an egoistic question for satisfactions of *amour propre* which is, at the same time, a fascinated pursuit of the approval of others' (Bourdieu, 2000a: 166). We can see in this case that the search for prestigious statutory positions and the approval they receive when they have these positions only takes place within the framework of a general competition to obtain them. The competition between individuals or social groups to exercise symbolic power is thus a struggle for recognition, but it concerns a recognition of *superiority* of a 'monopolistic' type, as it does in Hobbes or Pascal. In a language very close to Kojève's, the struggle for recognition, Bourdieu writes, 'is competition for a power that can only be won from others competing for the same power, a power over others that derives its existence from others, from their perception and appreciation … and therefore a power over a desire for power and over the object of this desire' (Bourdieu, 2000a: 241; 2001: 21). Such a search even seems to account for altruistic behaviour: it allows the group to secure 'the sacrifice of "self-love"' on the part of the individual, to the profit of another object of investment that will satisfy this self-love in a different way (Bourdieu, 2000a: 166–7, 194). The objective of all of the 'officialisation strategies' of groups is 'to transmute "egoistic", private, particular interests … into disinterested, collective, publicly avowable, legitimate interests' (Bourdieu, 1977: 40).[2] This process is grounded in a 'universal anthropological law', according to which 'there is a universal recognition of the recognition of the universal', which is to say, of the submission to the rules of the group which allows 'altruistic' agents to acquire a personal symbolic profit (Bourdieu, 1998: 138, 141, 142–3).

Finally, it is worth asking whether there is not any competition involved in the desire to attain, in an exclusive manner, the social positions richest in symbolic capital ('in one's "interests to" ...' [*intérêt à*]). Such competition would have to take place between the account of rarity and the account of egoistic interest, each of which could displace the other. Is it possible to decide between these two kinds of explanations? Bourdieu oscillates from one to the other, which perhaps indicates that he sees their complementarity. Rarity indeed offers the opportunity for the exclusive enjoyment of a positional good and accounts for the situation of objective competition that results from it. And yet, it does not explain the fixation of desire on the monopolistic enjoyment of this good (since one can abstain from the desire for these rare goods) or the *sui generis* satisfaction that results from the victory over one's combatants. In order to account for the co-presence of these two explanations (sociological and anthropological), it would be necessary therefore to maintain that this rarity of positions in determined fields can only reinforce or exacerbate egoistic interest. We can now turn to the examination of the last concept necessary in order to understand conflicts of recognition: *habitus*.

Habitus

What is a *habitus*? This concept, inspired as much by Aristotle's *hexis* and Mauss' work on the taming or 'dressage' of the body as it is by the conception of temporality in Husserl and Merleau-Ponty, plays an essential role in Bourdieu: it functions to conceptualise the articulation of the individual and the social. At the same time, it is inseparable from a number of criticisms that Bourdieu addresses to philosophical and sociological objectivism and subjectivism alike. *Habitus* is first explicitly opposed to the mechanistic determinism of Durkheimian sociology, to Lévi-Strauss' structural anthropology and to the Althusserian version of Marxism, according to which social structures rigidly determine the comportment of agents (Bourdieu, 1990: 36-40). It is equally opposed to the Sartrean conception of freedom developed in *Being and nothingness* which makes the individual the absolute origin of choices, which are made against the background of social routine (Bourdieu, 1990: 42–6). This concept of *habitus* is also opposed to the 'intellectualist' conception of action that relies on a simple intellectual grasp of the rules of the social world and the opportunities found there (Bourdieu, 1992: 48; 107–9).

Habitus is, on Bourdieu's account, the principle of the conduct of an agent or group of agents effectuated by a social conditioning expressed in the form of an ensemble of *stable dispositions* that organise representations and behaviour (Bourdieu, 1990: 39–40). This conditioning is produced by both the rules of the fields in which agents are situated and by the position that they occupy therein. When a field possesses the rules of a specific game, these rules define the beliefs and permissible actions in this determined field, opening certain avenues for

Conflicts of recognition and critical sociology

acting and excluding others as inconceivable (acting on the basis of economic rules, for example, in the context of the religious field). Certain actions, deployed according to the rules of the field, are thus facilitated to a greater extent than those which conflict with them. In short, the practical education afforded by the rules of the field engenders dispositions to believe and act in accordance with them. From this point of view, it now becomes possible to respond to the preceding analysis, and to understand that the socialisation of interest and its fixation on this or that type of object depends in fact on the production of different forms of *habitus* by means of education in which recognition plays an essential role (Bourdieu, 1992: 110).

Finally, the principles of the perception of the social world incorporated in the different forms of *habitus* do not only objectively express the rules of the field, but also subjectively embody each social group's *point of view* on the field and on other groups. This is what makes possible the classification of each specific activity or social perception by reference to the position that it expresses while being at the same time 'classifying', since it consists in the categorisation of a social world and its various social positions according to a *particular* viewpoint. Social classification is one of the most frequent and ubiquitous of activities: the object of a practical rather than an intellectual mastery, it is common to all social groups. To classify is to define oneself by defining others and by emphasising what distinguishes the individual or group who classifies (Bourdieu, 1984: 191, 428–9, 549–50), an activity that draws attention to the social properties which are the most favourable and from which the common principles of classification are derived. These same properties are also apprehended through the *habitus* as the natural qualities of those that possess them. Finally, this classificatory activity is clearly inseparable from the competition that exists between social groups in a given field that preserves (or accrues) the rarest positional goods according to their chances of success. *Habitus* thus directs the behaviour of agents and social groups in relation to one another relative to the representations they form of one another.

This being the case, the classificatory schemata are not related to the most abstract properties (or forms of capital) that define social classes, but on the contrary to the *life-styles* that concretely express them – whence the subjective character of the perception of these differentiations, which is translated by classifications expressing *a* viewpoint on the field and on the concrete attributes of different social groups. What social groups perceive of each other primarily and in the first instance are the dramatised life-styles that they display and that accentuate *perceived, not real* distances between positions.

Systematic oppression and the productivity of power

Symbolic violence, recognition and conflict

For Bourdieu, conflicts of recognition rely on relations of contested domination. These conflicts are supposed to respond to the negative forms of categorisation on the part of those who command a power of classification. Theorists of recognition, above all those who are philosophers, seem to think that when social disrespect undermines the basis of *self-respect* and *self-esteem* required by agents for developing a certain degree of autonomy and a sense of their own value, these agents tend to contest practices or transform the social norms that engender these negative representations. Now, these norms are not natural but socially constructed. Agents need only become aware of the contingency of depreciative social classification for the rejection of this social rejection to manifest itself, by a kind of 'revolutionary *cogito*'. The principles or norms on the basis of which agents interpret the depreciative judgements that they are subjected to or according to which they formulate their demands for recognition would be readily and unambiguously available. In the end, everything takes place as the motivation for such resistance does not itself raise any particular problem, since motivation is supposed to exist as a kind of energy in reserve that needs only to manifest itself.

It is precisely this conception of engaging in conflicts of recognition that the concept of *habitus* allows us to contest. It involves, as we have seen, both objective and subjective aspects. From the objective viewpoint, *habitus* delimits the universe of social possibilities available to a group in keeping with its endowment of capital, from the possible social paths of its members, to the goods that they are able to appropriate. Consequently, it reconciles the representations and behaviours of the agents with the structure of the field, by defining, in a pre-reflexive fashion, the space of their preferences and possible actions. This leads the members of social groups who possess a meagre amount of economic, scholastic and cultural capital – and therefore a meagre amount of symbolic capital – to embrace a kind of *amor fati* or 'love of fate' with respect to the social structure and the position they occupy within it. Because they have no access to the intellectual tools that would allow them to contest the grounds of the distribution of economic and symbolic capital, they end up making necessity a virtue, tacitly accepting, as if it were self-evident, the naturalisation of contingent social choices that assign them to the least favourable place in a given field. In this sense, their only option is to refrain from demanding that which they cannot, in any case, have access to, resigning themselves to desiring only that which they already possess (Bourdieu, 1984: 379, 466).

From the subjective point of view, the *habitus* of the meagrely endowed finds itself manufactured by an unequal competition between the intersecting viewpoints of superior and inferior social groups. The affirmation of the identity of the most powerful groups relies upon a principle of social differentiation which rests in turn, as we have seen, on the rarity of the properties that classify them. Now, these properties only acquire their value through their opposition to the most common properties, credited with a lower value or with no value at all. In the former case, value is related to prestige and to the social approval based on the possession of the necessary capital and with the backing of institutions, and tends to become a shared norm. Bourdieu characterises this imposition as a form of social domination. And yet, it remains irreducible to coercion, since it is in fact the product of a violence of a markedly economic character: a *symbolic violence*, involving a *cost of power*. At issue is a 'soft violence', invisible and misrecognised, a violence that is chosen as much as it is suffered by those subject to it (Bourdieu, 2000a: 32).

Symbolic violence is defined by the fact that 'the dominated apply categories constructed from the point of view of the dominant to the relations of domination, thus making them appear as natural'. This can lead to a form of self-depreciation by the dominated (Bourdieu and Wacquant, 1992: 167). Because they only possess the most common properties, symbolic violence generates in them a negative self-representation but also a positive representation of the dominators that they produce by representing the latter as the dominators represent themselves (Bourdieu, 1984: 208–9). It is in this way that the common representation of their relations across the categories produced by the social elites is defined. This categorisation, which negatively qualifies the dominated, is inscribed in their *habitus*. It generates a recognition of this imposed perception, which is to say a submission to the implicit prescriptions that the categorisation includes. Bourdieu argues, for example, that the working classes are reduced to a certain number of social properties by the upper classes, a reduction that serves to draw attention to all of the judgements of distinction that characterise 'legitimate' life-styles: they are reduced to their physical force, their affective reactions, their intellectual inferiority, their hedonism, the vulgarity of their tastes and their incapacity to control themselves (Bourdieu, 1984: 497). He shows in *Masculine domination* (2001) that the transcultural masculine categorisation of women rests on a series of negative properties attributed to women (emotivity, weakness, instability, lack of self-control) that assigns them to a socially dominated position (Bourdieu, 2000a: 170–1). Because *habitus* is a generative formula for behaviour and for homogeneous tastes, it is thus the entire social being of the dominated that is negatively represented and perceived. The greater the number of social attributes lacking (attributes that the dominated consider important), the greater the intensity of the harm linked to the absence of recognition. On a number of occasions, Bourdieu makes us see that this absence is perceived as equivalent in importance to the loss of a natural right: it is, in short, a social death often equated with death (Bourdieu, 2000a: 223, 240).

This categorisation constitutes a form of 'soft' violence since it involves a degree of complicity on the part of the dominated and brings about an adaptation of preferences. A paradoxical acceptance of domination is at work here that reinforces this domination, since its mechanism is fictitiously inverted at the moment when what is in fact imposed is taken to have been chosen (Bourdieu, 2000a: 149–50). Bourdieu notes that it is particularly surprising that the established order, with its relations of domination, its privileges and injustices, is – with the exception of a few historical setbacks – perpetuated so easily, and that the most intolerable conditions of existence can so often appear as acceptable and even natural (Bourdieu, 2000a: 217). In short, what is most surprising, what poses a problem for the sociologist, is the fact that such a social order does not pose a problem from the viewpoint of the struggle for recognition itself (Bourdieu, 2000a: 1).

Given this, we must agree with Bourdieu that the most impoverished social groups, at least such as he describes them, cannot by themselves engage in the logic of conflicts of recognition. This is why Bourdieu often argues that

> the site *par excellence* of symbolic struggles is the dominant class itself. The conflicts between artists and intellectuals over the definition of culture are only one aspect of the interminable struggles among the different factions of the dominant class to impose the definition of the legitimate principle of domination, between economic, educational or social capital, social powers whose specific efficacy may be compounded by specifically symbolic efficacy, that is, the authority conferred by being recognised, mandated by collective belief. (Bourdieu, 1984: 254)

In other words, these conflicts only take place within what Bourdieu calls a 'field of power', that is, the site of competition between agents or institutions who possess the capital necessary to occupy dominant positions in a given field. The only conflicts of recognition that can motivate the dominated are the daily and disparate struggles over recategorisation.

A possibility exists nonetheless for the dominated to engage in conflicts of recognition, one which arises when the structure of a particular field is transformed. This results in the modification of the relations between hopes and opportunities such that the *habitus* that had been reconciled to these hopes and opportunities can no longer orient behaviour. At issue here is a *habitus* 'out of kilter' with the structures of the field. This inadequation, whose first effects are on the body, opens up in turn a critique of the contingency of social structures, allowing one to envisage the possibility of their transformation and the genesis of new principles in particular fields. This crisis situation enables 'critical prophecies' to transgress social boundaries and to define new expectations for recognition and new social categories (Bourdieu, 2000a: 266).

Again, this mobilisation is only possible because those who are deprived of the necessary capital can delegate their force and their speech to representatives or spokespeople who unify the group and provide it with a consciousness of its unity and a confidence in its capacities. Within the framework of this delegation, that is, in being represented, the dominated encounter a section of the dominant class which is itself dominated, a section engaged in the contestation of the field's organising principles: defrocked priests in the Middle Ages, artists rebelling against the dominant aesthetic principles in the artistic field, the aristocrat whose *habitus* is out of step with their political situation, marginalised intellectuals. This alliance can lead either to the genesis of new principles, or to the realisation that the previous principles were in fact contingent, which leads in turn to their delegitimation, where once their legitimation assumed a natural character.

The examination of these two levels of the conflict of recognition allows us to conclude that the various forms of domination cannot themselves engender a response from those subject to them. A response must be produced and publicised using the conditions created by the structure of fields, the positions occupied, the available capital and the *habitus* of the various groups. In short, the processes of social domination also find expression in the fact that they negatively influence the conditions of their contestation and must first be weakened in order to be contested. And it is without a doubt that the Bourdieusian theory encounters a difficulty on this point, concerning the divergent effects of the concept of *habitus* which seems to account for, at the same time and under the same relation, two opposing attitudes towards conflicts of recognition.

A problem in need of a solution

The difficulty that Bourdieu must face up to concerns the discrepancy between, on the one hand, the practices of acquiescing to domination that *habitus* produces in dominated social groups and, on the other hand, the empirical evidence of the irreducibility of symbolic struggles in a given field to the interactions between sections of the dominant classes alone, even when there is no crisis challenging the structures of the field. The relations between dominant and dominated social groups does not only reside in acquiescence by the dominated to their subordinate position, but are also traversed by tensions that give rise to conflicts on many fronts, as Bourdieu himself explains. Two examples involving classificatory struggle are particularly striking in this regard. The first is drawn from the ethnographic studies of the Kabyle and concerns the status of women in traditional Kabyle society; the second is related to the logic of conspicuous consumption by the underprivileged class which is intended to appropriate the distinctive signs of the upper class and the social value of some of their characteristics. These examples focus on the precise difficulty that Bourdieu must confront, while also raising a decisive problem for sociology and philosophy alike.

Systematic oppression and the productivity of power

With respect to the status of women, their submission, in this kind of society, seems more or less complete. Every negative representation converges on them: passivity, submissiveness, the absence of honour, weakness, the incapacity for self-control, etc. (Bourdieu and Passeron, 1990: 214). This categorisation is clearly expressed, and includes the devalorisation of female genitalia. Women accept this representation of themselves as the natural negative of the masculine, one which also determines the positive (feminine) view of the masculine and the view of the form that relations with the masculine must take. Moreover, to reject this domination would deprive women of the advantages of being accepted on the basis of their status, even when this status is accompanied by suffering. And yet, we find an explicit resistance by women to masculine domination in the emphasis on preferable feminine properties, in particular sexual properties, superior to those of men, and in the devalorisation of the sexual behaviour of men. This conflicting interpretation of the attributes and sexual behaviour of men and women resists the masculine interpretation and compensates for it with a positive recategorisation (Bourdieu, 2001: 19–20). Clearly, this resistance creates a problem: if *habitus* is structured by combining one's position in the system of field-positions, with capital endowment and with symbolic violence, the nature of submission is easily understood. Simply put, though, what is no longer clear is the origin of the resistance to domination and therefore the origin of conflicts of recognition between men and women. In the absence of any structural crisis in the field, where exactly do the resources necessary for the critique of masculine categorisation come from?

The other example is just as problematic: on the one hand, the working classes, imagining the upper classes in the same way that the upper classes imagine themselves, want to appropriate for themselves the distinctive signs characteristic of the upper classes on account of their positive value. Now, this effect of their *habitus* paradoxically engenders a desire for recognition through a change in status, which makes them engage in classificatory struggle by way of conspicuous consumption. This occurs because the working classes let the bourgeoisie impose legitimate norms for consumable goods and thereby find themselves dispossessed of the very means to define their own tastes. It remains the case that they engage in this classificatory struggle which is on Bourdieu's account a form of class struggle. However, this struggle is 'in disarray', lacking any collective control (Bourdieu, 1993: 197). On the other hand, the *habitus* of the dominated leads them to adapt their preferences to the chance of their realisation, rejecting what they cannot appropriate, claiming responsibility for this rejection and accepting the negative categorisation that affects them through symbolic violence. How can we explain the fact that the same *habitus* at the same time encourages and discourages engaging in a classificatory struggle, with the dominant class, for recognition? Must we assume that two distinct and conflicting forms of *habitus* are in fact involved, or that a motivation exceeding the *habitus* intervenes? Finally, how can we account for the fact that classificatory struggles, which are in principle reserved for sections of the dominant class, effectively extend to the dominated, in the absence of any structural crisis in the field?

Obviously contradictory forms of *habitus* can arise from the process of socialisation in conflicting social universes, affecting the same unique agent or social group. These conflicting firms of *habitus*, which Bourdieu calls 'split' or 'torn' (Bourdieu, 2000a: 160), give rise to a paralysis of action. This, however, is not what is at issue in the example of the Kabyle. Rather, we are dealing with a single and same *habitus*, since the valorisation of the status of the upper class (or men with respect to Kabyle women) is inseparable from a prestige whose enjoyment is exclusively differential: enjoyment only has significance insofar as it conflicts with the social properties of the dominated. The prestige of the dominant cannot be separated from depreciation of the dominated. If, however, this single and same *habitus* can generate conflicting behaviour, it can no longer explain either submission or contestation. Is it not therefore necessary to look beyond *habitus* to explain what it cannot entirely account for?

From Bourdieu's point of view, should we not then be arguing that the positions and properties symbolising social prestige are, in fact, objects of a monopolistic desire that the submissive and renunciative modalities of *habitus* cannot entirely explain? In which case, conflicts of recognition would fall within the province of a Hobbesian or Pascalian type of universal competition. If this is so, such conflicts would not only aim to escape social insignificance or undermine stigmatisation (a 'compensatory' recognition), but they would also aim to acquire the most advantageous classifications (a recognition by 'conquest') (Lazzeri, 2009). It is for this reason that Bourdieu asserts in *Pascalian meditations* that

> the social world is both the product and the stake of inseparably cognitive and political symbolic struggles over knowledge and recognition, in which *each* pursues not only the imposition of an advantageous representation of himself or herself, with the strategies of 'presentation' of self so admirably analysed by Goffman, but also the power to impose as legitimate the principles of construction of social reality most favourable to his or her social being. (Bourdieu, 2000a: 187, emphasis added)

Now, at issue here, Bourdieu says, are 'the particular individuals devoted to the vagaries of everyday symbolic struggle', up to and including the accredited professionals who write about social classes. For its part, *Language and symbolic power* explains that when differentiated social positions exist along with systems of hierarchically organised titles, which can be thought of as distinctive marks that attract symbolic capital, all agents 'resort to practical and symbolic strategies aimed at maximising the symbolic profit of naming' (Bourdieu, 1993: 240).

All agents are active in these conflicts and not only those most fully endowed with symbolic capital. In this way, everyday interpersonal conflicts of recognition, only accessible in principle to the dominated, would only be one particular case of this general competitive conception of conflicts of recognition. This is why *Pascalian meditations* can describe the function of the State as that of an apparatus capable of removing certain kinds of classification from the 'symbolic struggles of *all against all*' (to use an expression with Hobbesian resonances), so as to prevent these struggles from being interminably pursued and to satisfy those who are colluding the most closely with 'State nobility' (Bourdieu, 2000a: 241). What can account for the existence of strategies maximising symbolic profit in the symbolic struggles of 'all against all', if not the fact that *habitus* runs up against its own limit with respect to the exclusive interest that it cannot manage to completely govern?

Three consequences follow from this analysis of conflicts of recognition:

1 This active presence of individual interest competes with the principle whereby *habitus* governs conduct, and this produces instability in Bourdieu's argument: we never know which principle is best able to account for the behaviour of the dominated. This means that we must redefine the notion of domination in a more precise fashion: does domination only consist in submitting to a depreciative categorisation, or must it also make reference to the absence of participation in the struggles of classification? Depending on which of these definitions one opts for, we have recourse to a concept of domination which is either more or less extensive with, and whose consequences diverge from, resigned acceptance of social order to open contestation of it.

2 Within the framework of the first definition of domination where 'in one's "interests to" …' [*intérêt à*] plays an important role, every field is understood to be the theatre of ongoing conflicts of recognition. But from this it also follows that there is a distinction drawn between conflicts of reparation whose aim is to resist depreciation, and conflicts of conquest whose aim is to appropriate the classificatory properties of the dominant. In other words, conflicts of resistance inevitably tend to persist in the form of conflicts of monopolistic appropriation. Must the approval accorded to conflicts of reparation lead to approval of conflicts for monopolistic appropriation, implied by reparative conflict? And must the refusal to grant approval to conflicts of monopolistic appropriation lead to approval of reparative conflict?

3 Bourdieu cannot be satisfied with an analysis of conflicts of recognition that would begin with the concept of 'mutual recognition'. However, his whole analysis shows that it is just as unlikely that the conflictual social relations he describes could successfully analyse these conflicts. His conception of the symbolic struggle of all against all renders mutual recognition infeasible.

Conflicts of recognition and critical sociology

Mutual recognition can only be realised in only one unique manner through certain interpersonal relations that somehow miraculously escape the relations of domination, as in love for example. However, beyond this private sphere, theorists of recognition should abandon the idea of mutual recognition, that is, they should abandon a significant part of the ethical objectives that they are trying to achieve in their theories.

Beyond these internal difficulties affecting Bourdieu's sociology, it is clear that he bequeaths important problems to recognition theorists to which they must respond if they do not want to limit themselves to a merely formulaic account of conflicts of recognition.

Notes

* Translated by Jon Roffe.
1 The translation of *avoir l'intérêt pour* and *avoir intérêt à* differs from the official English translation of the relevant texts by Bourdieu. This decision has been made so as to emphasise a distinction, important to this chapter, between affective interest (where *avoir l'intérêt pour le foot* would mean 'to be interested in football') and economic or material interest (where *elle a tout intérêt à faire quelque chose* would mean 'it is in her interests to do something').
2 In this sense, it must be recalled that, for Bourdieu, the need for recognition is an 'indisputable ... anthropological fact' (Bourdieu, 2000a: 239).

10

Systematic misrecognition and the practice of critique: Bourdieu, Boltanski and the role of critical theory

Robin Celikates

IN recent years the sociology of critique, as elaborated by Luc Boltanski and his research group in explicit opposition to Pierre Bourdieu's objectivist conception of critical social science, has emerged as a new paradigm in social theory. Only now are the overlaps and differences with the Frankfurt School's tradition of critical theory coming into view. In what follows I explore this relation by defending three claims: (1) that Bourdieu's model of a critical social science rests on the assumption – empirically and methodologically problematic – of a systematic form of misrecognition which takes on the role traditionally played by ideology; (2) that the sociology of critique offers a convincing alternative to Bourdieu's model by taking seriously the actors' self-understanding, and thus the categories employed in their practices of justification and critique; and (3) that, drawing on Boltanski, a revised version of critical theory – elements of which can be found in the work of Axel Honneth – can play a crucial complementary role since these self-understandings and practices may suffer from what one might call 'second-order pathologies'. Such an understanding of critical theory offers a new perspective on the politics of recognition, on the level of both theory and social practice, by linking the 'micropolitics of recognition', negotiated within the field of everyday practices of justification and critique, to their 'macropolitical' conditions, that is, to institutionalised and structural forms of recognition and misrecognition.

In contrast to objectivist approaches which tend to understand social actors as 'judgemental dopes' (Garfinkel, 1984: 67–73) rather than as agents possessing reflexive capacities, the pragmatist sociology of critique rightly rejects the idea of a break between the supposedly objective viewpoint of the critical scientist and the unreflective perspective of so-called 'ordinary' agents. Instead, actors are understood as capable of those forms of critical reflexivity which scientific observers have often claimed as their monopoly. Indeed, being able to distance oneself from the immediate practical context, and critically reflect on it, is 'a capability whose existence must be presupposed if we are to account for the way the members of a complex society criticise, challenge institutions, argue with one another, or converge toward agreement' (Boltanski and Thévenot, 2006: 15).

While it is typical for approaches within the paradigm of critical social science to identify social structures and mechanisms at the macro level which account for the reproduction of the status quo, the sociology of critique follows the example of ethnomethodology by situating itself at the micro level and describing situated practices of critique and justification. Justified though this may be in terms of enlarging the theoretical perspective, this reversal tends to neglect the possibility that certain social conditions block the exercise or even the formation of actors' reflective and critical capacities. In order to account for this possibility, social theory has to focus – at a 'meso' or 'intermediate' level – on those social conditions, largely ignored by the sociology of critique, which can stand in the way of real-world practices of critique and justification. In contrast to Bourdieu's approach, however, the hypothesis that certain conditions block actors' reflective capacities does not imply that these actors find themselves structurally incapable – that is, incapable in virtue of the structure of the practice they engage in – of understanding this situation. In other words, such actors at not, as Bourdieu tends to imply, completely trapped in a naïve, pre-reflective position.

The 'pragmatic turn' proposed by Boltanski and others should not lead us to abandon the project of critical theory, as if all necessary criticism were already articulated within everyday practices of critique. The reflective capacities of 'ordinary' actors and their practices of justification and critique, which are convincingly reconstructed by the sociology of critique, constitute the social and methodological basis of critical theory. However, this should not lead us to attribute an epistemic authority to the perspective of the participants which is immune to being put into question from a theoretically informed point of view (see also Celikates, 2009a and 2009b).

Critical social science and structural misrecognition

According to a theoretical model that could be called 'orthodox', critical social science begins by substituting one question for another. Instead of asking why, in a particular case, people rebel or go on strike, it asks why such persons for the most part not only tolerate the status quo, but even participate in its reproduction, regarding it as natural and/or legitimate (Rosen, 1996: Introduction). Since there seems to be an obvious contradiction between the behaviour of people and their basic interests, we can reasonably suspect that ordinary actors misrecognise their objective situation and their real interests in a systematic, i.e. not purely accidental, manner.

In order to explain this phenomenon of systematic misrecognition critical social science points to the 'fact' that the agents do not really know what they are doing and are really prisoners of an ideology that masks their situation and their interests.[1] To be prisoner of an ideology means to be confined to a false form of consciousness that is both objectively necessary and necessarily false. This 'orthodox' notion of ideology does not only imply that actors do not know what they are doing, but also that they do not, and indeed cannot, understand how what they are doing and thinking contributes to the reproduction of the social order. The systematic misrecognition on the actors' part is then contrasted with insight into the 'real' mechanisms of social reproduction available to those who are able to diagnose forms of false consciousness, as it were 'from sideways on'. On this understanding, ideology can only be identified from an objective and epistemically privileged viewpoint which is situated outside of the ideological context and must be provided by social science.

The 'orthodox' conception of critical social science thus implies an asymmetrical opposition between science and critique, on the one hand, and the naïve perspective of 'ordinary' agents subject to structural forms of misrecognition, on the other. Consequently, social actors are seen as objects of critical discourse rather than as interlocutors in their own right whose self-understandings would provide more than just additional data. It is this dogma of asymmetry, and the associated methodological imperative of an epistemological break with the participants' perspective, which has animated the project of a sociology that is at once scientific and critical. It lies at the heart of Bourdieu's critical sociology. For Bourdieu, the break with the actors' self-understanding is both epistemological and methodological. It presumes a radical discontinuity between the perspective of the social sciences, on the one hand, and the perspective of participants, ordinary consciousness and common sense, on the other. This break is achieved by a double operation: the metatheoretical separation of science from common sense (as well as the epistemological disqualification of the latter) and the methodological imperative to struggle for scientific knowledge against common sense, vulgar opinion and ideology. Bourdieu and his co-authors squarely situate themselves in this Durkheimian framework when they characterise the first methodological principle of their approach as follows: 'The social fact is won against the illusion of immediate knowledge', requiring permanent 'epistemological vigilance' on the part of the sociologist (Bourdieu, Chamboredon and Passeron, 1991: 13). On this understanding, sociology is engaged in a continuous struggle with the 'spontaneous sociology' of ordinary agents and their self-understanding, with the 'spontaneous movements of naïve practice' that threaten to 'contaminate' sociological analysis (1991: 24). There is an irresolvable structural conflict between scientific sociological analysis and the

Systematic misrecognition and critique: Bourdieu, Boltanski

interpretations of actors, who are, in virtue of their immersion in social practice, incapable of distancing themselves from what they are doing, victims of a mere 'illusion of reflexivity' (1991: 24).

This conception of a form of misrecognition which is not contingent but structural, in that it is constitutive for the functioning of the practice in question and the reproduction of the social order, has played a decisive role in Bourdieu's work ever since his early analysis of gift exchange. The truth of this exchange – that it is, in reality, not a matter of disinterested gifts but a sublimated struggle for symbolic power and material advantage – cannot be recognised within the 'official' self-understanding that frames the perspective of the participants. What actors are (objectively) doing does not coincide with what they (subjectively) think they are doing. This misrecognition of the structure of their practice is necessary in the sense that it is one of the foundations of their practice: the practice in question, in this case the gift exchange, exists and functions 'because subjects do not, strictly speaking, know what they are doing', so that 'what they do has more meaning than they know' (Bourdieu, 1977: 79).

To account for this structure of misrecognition, Bourdieu speaks of a 'twofold truth'. In one sense, the gift really is and has to be what it seems to be – a generous act, without interest and calculation. However, this act is, in another sense, subject to the relentless logic and 'forceless force' of gift exchange (Bourdieu, 2000a: 188–202). This 'twofold truth' is only accessible from the standpoint of the observing sociologist because actors themselves are trapped with the half-truth which is all that is accessible to them from the perspective of a participant. According to Bourdieu, the contradiction between the 'subjective truth' of the participants and the objective analysis of the sociological observer is not limited to gift exchange alone; it accounts for the distinctive character of all symbolic practices. The self-mystification of such practices can only be unmasked by a 'general science of the economy of practices' (Bourdieu, 1977: 183).

This misrecognition, constitutive for the functioning of social practices, derives from a work of denial and repression that is interiorised by subjects in the course of their initiation into these practices by way of education or '*dressage*'. As 'second nature', the *habitus* which results from this formation allows actors to move in the social world 'like fish in water': we immediately and intuitively know which behaviour is appropriate and what we must do, and we usually do it without further reflection. Because the *habitus* conditions and structures our experiences, thoughts, evaluations and practices, it imposes strict limits on reflection and critique. Within these limits – which we could describe as 'the cave of practice' – we find the realm of *doxa*. The *doxa* of participants in a practice guarantees that they misrecognise the conditions of their thought and action, and do not ask any questions for which there is no immediate and 'official' answer. This immunity of practice – and of the entire social world more generally – to critical reflection and questioning is anchored, by way of *habitus*, in actors' self-understandings and secures the functioning and reproduction of the social order.

Within Bourdieu's framework, *habitus* and systematic misrecognition fulfil a function analogous to the 'orthodox' model of ideology in two respects. First, they are crucial elements in the reproduction of the status quo and must be analysed from a functionalist perspective. Second, for structural reasons, their functioning must remain opaque to the actors themselves, imprisoned in the *doxa*, and can only be unveiled by the sociologist who breaks with this incorporated and necessarily false consciousness (Bourdieu and Eagleton, 1994: 265–77; and Wacquant, 2002: 25–40). The quasi-ideological system of convictions and dispositions which make up the *habitus* is both necessary and sufficient from an objective viewpoint *and* false, because it rests on a fundamental misrecognition of its own conditions, causes and effects.

For Bourdieu, symbolic domination – a form of domination which successfully hides its dominating character – is solely based on the recognition accorded to it by the dominated, but this (mis)recognition is rooted in the 'disguised (and thus misrecognised) imposition of systems of classification and of mental structures that are objectively adjusted to social structures' (Bourdieu, 1993: 169) and that are effectively protected, in virtue of being part of the *habitus*, against being questioned. According to Bourdieu, actors are accomplices in the (re)production of their own domination, but it is impossible for them to come to an adequate understanding of this process and thus to transform it because it is viciously circular: '1. The system reproduces itself because it is misrecognised. 2. The system, by reproducing itself, produces the effect of misrecognition' (Rancière, 2003: 367). Having established the structurally limited nature of cognitive access to social reality on the part of 'ordinary' actors, the sociologist now 'installs himself in a position of the eternal denunciator of a system that is capable of eternally masking itself in relation to its subjects' (Rancière, 2003: 368).[2]

The sociology of critique and the recognition of 'ordinary' actors

In contrast to this underestimation of actors' reflective capacities and the associated overestimation of sociological knowledge which, as we have seen, are characteristic of Bourdieu's model of critical social science, the sociology of critique begins with the assumption of a basic symmetry between 'ordinary' agents and 'professional' sociologists, rejecting the methodological break with the perspective of participants and emphasising the reflexivity involved in and required by everyday social practices. We can represent the theoretical and methodological structure of this approach with the following four principles (Nachi, 2006: Chapter 1; see also Bénatouïl, 1999: 379–96):

Systematic misrecognition and critique: Bourdieu, Boltanski

1. The principle of symmetry: the rejection of the break which characterises the orthodox model of critical social science goes hand in hand with recognising 'the symmetry between the descriptive languages or explanatory principles used by the social sciences, on the one hand, and the modes of justification or criticism used by actors, on the other hand' (Boltanski and Thévenot, 2006: 11; see also Anderson, E., 1993: Chapter 5).
2. The principle of pluralism: the rejection of the idea of a vicious circle of misrecognition with the reproduction of the status quo goes hand in hand with recognising a plurality of modes of action – for Boltanski, these include violence, love, routine and justification – which are themselves viewed as internally plural, particularly the metaregime of justification.
3. The principle of reflective capacities: the rejection of the understanding of 'ordinary' agents as 'judgemental dopes' goes hand in hand with recognising their reflective capacities and, more generally, 'what people are capable of' (Boltanski, 1990a: Part 1).
4. The principle of grammars of agreement: the rejection of the idea that social rules are imposed behind the backs of ignorant actors goes hand in hand with recognising that actors themselves have to constantly negotiate and renegotiate these rules so as to coordinate their actions in concrete social contexts and to produce effective criticisms of each other as well as acceptable justifications.

In the conflicts of everyday life 'ordinary' actors furnish ample proof of their capacity to take up different viewpoints, distancing themselves from their situation and engaging in complex discourses of critique and justification. The fragility of the social order and the plurality of regimes of justification make it possible for actors, and indeed require actors, to conduct themselves in a reflective and critical manner. Actors must not only possess a habituated 'practical sense' but also a kind of mastery of 'the arts of living in different worlds' (Boltanski and Thévenot, 2006: 148) which allows them to orient themselves in heterogeneous social contexts and argumentative spaces that only partially overlap: 'The ability to detach oneself from the immediate environment, to remove oneself from the confusion of what is present ... constitutes the minimal ability human beings must have if they are to involve themselves in situations without getting lost in them' (Boltanski, 1990a: 74, author's translation).

Within the practices of critique and justification with their socially and culturally mediated repertoires of argumentation, agents can refer to a plurality of normative orders and regimes of justification (Boltanski and Thévenot, 2006: 235). Both the possibility and necessity of critique depend not only on this plurality and the conflicts that arise within it but also on the 'factual force of the normative' – the efficacy of normative expectations – and the 'normative force of the factual' – the permanent frustration of these expectations:

Systematic oppression and the productivity of power

> To be valid, critique must be capable of justifying itself – that is to say, clarifying the normative supports that ground it – especially when it is confronted with the justifications that those who are subject to critique supply for their action. Hence it continues to refer to justice, for if justice is a delusion, what is the point of criticising? On the other hand, however, critique presents a world in which the requirement of justice is incessantly contravened. It unmasks the hypocrisy of moral pretensions that conceal the reality of relations of force, exploitation and domination. (Boltanski and Chiapello, 2005: 28)

The plurality of regimes of justification and the permanent possibility of tensions between them opens up two avenues for social critique that are routinely taken by 'ordinary' agents in the course of their everyday lives. The first avenue, a kind of internal or reformist critique, accepts the regime of justification in question (and the kind of 'test' which goes along with it) and questions its application in a concrete situation. The second form of critique is more radical and questions the very regime of justification itself as inadequate to the situation at hand:

> The first [form of critique] is *corrective* in intent: critique reveals those features ... that infringe justice and, in particular, the forces mobilised by certain of the protagonists without the others being aware of it ... A second manner of criticising ... may be dubbed *radical*. In this instance, what is at stake is no longer correcting the conditions of the test with a view to making it more just but suppressing it and ultimately replacing it with a different test. (Boltanski and Chiapello, 2005: 32–3; see also Boltanski and Thévenot, 2006: 219–25)

These two forms of critique should not be understood as symptoms of a spontaneous and naïve sociology, as suggested by Bourdieu, but rather as a very elaborate kind of 'folk sociology' which also employs theoretical resources introduced into social discourse by sociology: 'All humans must be granted the same elementary capacities as social scientists when it comes to questioning ideologies and social representations. It must be acknowledged that what the social sciences produce is already included in society's hermeneutic circle' (Chiapello, 2003: 157).

From this description of the social world follows a methodological maxim which is both simple and demanding: 'follow the actors themselves.' In other words, sociologists must now take their lead from the interpretations and evaluations of 'ordinary' actors who alone possess relevant knowledge of the social world. No longer regarded as simple informants producing additional data, 'ordinary' actors are instead viewed as lay sociologists producing interpretations and explanations of their actions which are no less sophisticated than those offered by their professional colleagues (Latour, 2005: Introduction; Boltanski, 1990a: Chapter 13). In contrast to Bourdieu's model, the sociologist's understanding is interpreted as lagging behind. Her only chance to gain some ground is to take actors seriously, analysing their practices of critique and justification and avoiding a theoretical framework that turns them into 'judgemental dopes'. The sociology of critique tries to follow this maxim on three levels. On the level of 'pragmatics', it analyses actual practices of critique and justification. On the level of 'grammar', it analyses the rules and conditions to which actors must adhere if they are to successfully partake of these practices. On the level of 'topic', it analyses the repertoires of argumentation and modes of speaking employed by actors in different social contexts.

Despite the promising perspectives opened up by this approach, however, we must now ask whether the analysis proposed by the sociology of critique is sufficiently complex.

When the sociology of critique begins with the 'fact' of critique and justification, it makes two rather strong assumptions regarding the conditions of this 'fact'. The 'subjective' conditions of the practices of justification and critique equate to those capacities and competences which actors mutually attribute to each other and which the sociologist must also attribute to them in order to understand what they are doing. The 'objective' conditions equate to the existence of a 'metaregime' of justification and of a plurality of regimes of justification to which actors can refer when engaging in corrective or radical critique. But can we really presuppose that the subjective and objective conditions of the practices of critique – the starting point for the sociology of critique – are, in fact, given in social reality? Is it not the case that there exist certain social conditions under which actors' reflective capacities are blocked or constrained? The sociology of critique appears to exclude the possibility of an unequal distribution of, or structural restrictions on, the capacity to distance oneself from one's context and engage in critique. Yet a sociological approach which is sufficiently nuanced must take this possibility seriously. Similarly, regarding the 'objective' conditions of the social practices of justification and critique, a sociological approach must also consider the possibility that certain social contexts are successfully shielded from the pressure of justification and that certain hegemonic discourses of justification suppress alternative justificatory resources. Such possibilities significantly reduce the ability of actors to engage in the justification and critique of their own societies. In other words, the subjective and objective conditions of practices of critique may in fact find themselves restricted, and this possibility cannot be ignored if social theory is to retain its practical relevance (Honneth, 2008b: 84–103).

Critical theory and 'second-order pathologies'

The sociology of critique is thus confronted with a two-fold problem. Its focal point seems too restricted in that it limits itself to the critical discourses already part of 'society's hermeneutic circle' and this amounts to excluding forms of critique that are both more theoretical and more radical. As Boltanski himself concedes, actors are often 'realists' and adapt to what they take to be possible, at times 'closing their eyes' to factors which, from their perspective, are out of place. For critique to overcome this realist bias, it needs a critical theory that allows for the construction of an alternative position. Sometimes the only way to rid oneself of the yoke of reality and the predominance of 'realists' is 'to make reality unacceptable', that is, to show those actors concerned that a situation should be unacceptable from *their own* viewpoint, by means of a theoretical account or redescription (Boltanski, 2008; Boltanski, 2009; Boltanski and Honneth, 2009). Furthermore, as I have already indicated, the perspective of the sociology of critique does not appear to consider the social conditions of the exercise and formation of the reflective and critical capacities it assumes. Of course, the sociology of critique does not deny that actors acquire and exercise their capacities in given social contexts and are always subject to determined social conditions. But, owing to its 'situationist' orientation, its approach tends to reduce these contexts and conditions to mere resources which actors can employ rather than analysing such contexts as potential structural restrictions on reflective capacities and critical practices.

As Boltanski argues in an early article co-written with Bourdieu, the idea of 'linguistic communism', i.e. the belief in the (*de facto*) equal distribution of communicative capacities and the ability to make oneself heard, appears to be nothing more than an 'illusion' (Boltanski and Bourdieu, 1975: 2–33; see also Bourdieu, 1993: 43). As a function of their social position, actors possess, to radically varying degrees, a 'voice' and the social power to demand and produce justifications. Critical theory must therefore attempt to identify the quality of social conditions – or, following Axel Honneth, the relations of recognition – which actors require to form and exercise their reflective capacities. It is precisely this question which makes it necessary to move beyond the horizon of the sociology of critique so as to reintroduce the standpoint of critical theory without, for all that, abandoning the theoretical insights of the former's 'methodological egalitarianism'.

When certain social conditions block the formation and exercise of actors' reflective capacities or, in other words, when relations of recognition are asymmetric, ideological, or pathological (Honneth, 2007b: 323–47), we appear to face a case which can be called 'second-order pathology' that takes the form of a 'structural reflexivity deficit' on the part of the actors (Honneth, 1996: 369–96; Zurn, forthcoming; Fischbach, 2009: 155–9).

In such a situation, the first-order social conditions which appear to be normatively problematic – relations of injustice, exploitation, misrecognition, etc. – are not, in the relevant sense, accessible to those affected, be it because they are not experienced and recognised as such or because they are intuitively grasped but misinterpreted and consequently accepted as either legitimate or natural. Social theory should therefore ask why it is that certain situations are not experienced as unjust, alienating, or involving misrecognition, and why the perception of a situation as unjust, alienating, or involving misrecognition does not always translate into a corresponding collective consciousness, let alone into transformative collective action (Honneth, 2007a: 80–96; Renault, 2004; see also Lazzeri's contribution in Chapter 9 of this volume).

An answer to these questions would need to refer to those material and symbolic constraints which can prevent actors from engaging in practices of critique. In this sense, the ideological appearance of certain practices and institutions as legitimate and natural (i.e. their misrecognition by the actors involved), can be characterised as a second-order phenomenon. It effectively diminishes the probability that those opinions, dispositions and modes of acting which can be situated on the first level and which support these practices and institutions will be reflected on and criticised. 'Second-order pathologies' can thus be understood as blocking the assessment, critique and transformation of 'first-order pathologies'. It should be noted that the diagnosis of 'second-order pathologies' need not necessarily refer to a substantial conception of a 'normal' or 'healthy' social life. If one understands these 'pathologies' in a rather formal and 'negativistic' way, their diagnosis may be based in an analysis of the structural restrictions of actors' capacities resulting from certain social relations of recognition and misrecognition.

It is crucial to note that these restrictions are in almost all cases partial: when a capacity is restricted, that is, when its formation or its exercise is blocked, this does not entail that the person affected completely lacks this capacity but rather that, under certain social conditions, she only possesses it to a limited degree. In almost all circumstances we must attribute, at the very least, certain elementary reflective capacities to actors. Furthermore, they themselves are finally the judge of whether they really are confronting a 'pathology'. Certain social conditions are unacceptable when actors themselves reflectively understand them to be so, on the basis of their self-understanding. In order to begin, critical theory thus already presupposes a certain receptivity for its hypotheses on the side of the actors:

> If the proponents of a critical theory wish to enlighten and emancipate a group of agents, they must find in the experience, form of consciousness, and belief of *those* agents, the means of emancipation and enlightenment. If we can't find the appropriate experiences of suffering and frustration and the appropriate principles of reflective acceptability in the life and form of consciousness of those agents, Ideologiekritik cannot begin, and we have no right to call the agents 'deluded'. (Geuss, 1981: 65)

The critical and emancipatory task of social theory is thus to identify, analyse and criticise, in the context of a discourse with those affected, the social conditions that hinder or block the formation or exercise of their reflective capacities. On this view, critical social theory is a reflection on the (social) conditions of possibility of critique and, in this sense, a form of 'metacritique' (Boltanski, 2009).

Let me now turn to an example in order to give some substance to these rather abstract methodological remarks. In 'The souls of black folks', the African-American sociologist and writer W. E. B. Du Bois presents an analysis and a 'thick description' of the social and psychological effects of 'racial segregation', focusing on the loss of the capacity to see oneself with one's own eyes, that is, without the mediation of the misrecognising gaze of the white population. Du Bois links the 'strange meaning of being black' under these conditions to the fact that African-Americans are 'shut out' from the world of white people by a 'vast veil' (Du Bois, 1996: 100–1). The metaphor of the 'veil' implies that, beyond the more immediate effects of being excluded from certain activities and places (that is, political and social forms of exclusion), this exclusion also has a repercussive effect on the self-perception of the excluded and their way of experiencing the world. Unsurprisingly, Du Bois primarily takes the veil to be a testament to the blindness of the white population, but it also deforms the cognitive and perceptive capacities of African-Americans, preventing them from developing 'true self-consciousness': 'It is a peculiar sensation, this double-consciousness, this sense of always looking at one's self through the eyes of others, of measuring one's soul by the tape of a world that looks on in amused contempt and pity' (Du Bois, 1996, 102). This experience affects the psychic integrity of the subject: 'One ever feels his twoness – an American, a Negro; two souls, two thoughts, two unreconciled strivings; two warring ideals in one dark body, whose dogged strength alone keeps it from being torn asunder' (Du Bois, 1996: 102). The 'double self' is 'handicapped' and a repressive, prejudice-filled social atmosphere pushes it to permanent 'self-questioning, self-disparagement' (Du Bois, 1996: 102, 105). The 'prisoned souls within the Veil' live in 'two separate worlds' and their individual and collective 'double-consciousness' does not allow the epistemic and practical self-confidence that is basic for their agency (Du Bois, 1996: 147, 150). Under such conditions of institutionalised and structural misrecognition, actors are blocked from developing or exercising their reflective capacities, and this produces 'ontological wounds, psychic scars, and existential bruises' (West, 1999: 102). The permanent experience of being classified and treated like a 'quasi-person' with reduced cognitive capacities does not permit those affected to distance themselves from the social world on which they depend all the more because they are excluded from the dominant social ontology (see also Mills, 1998: Chapter 1).

As is well known, Du Bois thought that it would take a cultural avant-garde (the famous 'talented tenth') to initiate a process of emancipation by acting on behalf and in the true interest of the ill-educated masses. His solution reveals the temptations of elitism and the dangers of epistemological and political paternalism inherent in the diagnosis of structural reflexivity deficits and 'second-order pathologies'. Even though these deficits and 'pathologies' are not identified with an incapacity to reflect, Du Bois' problematic solution illustrates a dilemma which confronts critical theory in all its variants. As Henry Louis Gates remarks with regard to the critique of colonialism: 'You can empower discursively the native, and open yourself to charges of downplaying the epistemic (and literal) violence of colonialism; or play up the absolute nature of colonial domination, and be open to charges of negating the subjectivity and agency of the colonised, thus textually replicating the repressive operations of colonialism' (Gates, 1991: 462).

To be true to its emancipatory aims, critical theory must avoid the 'incapacitation trap', that is, the danger of further restricting actors' capacities with its diagnosis, but in so doing, it must inevitably introduce a tension into its theory (Bader, 2007: 258–9). The only way to make sense of this tension is to insist that the structural restrictions on actors' reflective capacities can only be diagnosed and critiqued in a dialogue between critical theorists and social actors themselves, a dialogue which already presupposes, to a certain degree, the very capacities that are restricted. At the same time, the 'methodological egalitarianism' and 'principle of symmetry' which are of fundamental importance for a non-paternalist and non-authoritarian account of critical theory should not hide the asymmetries in power, knowledge, influence and argumentative capacities which can be traced back to structural reflexivity deficits. In whatever manner such asymmetries are understood, their diagnosis cannot be validated from the supposedly privileged position of the observing sociologist; such asymmetries remain hypotheses awaiting empirical verification, in a discourse with those affected. The diagnosis itself – and, more specifically, its falsification and verification – is intimately connected to actors' self-understanding and cannot be assessed in independence of such understandings.

Instead of engaging in a substantial and normative critique of the self-understandings which it regards as false, critical theory should limit itself to identifying and analysing those restrictions on actors' reflective capacities which contribute to systematic distortions of the social process in which these self-understandings are formulated and reformulated. This makes it necessary to take the 'macropolitical' conditions of institutionalised and structural recognition into account (see also Deranty and Renault, 2007: 92–111). By focusing on those 'second-order pathologies' which block the social practices of critique, that is, relations of asymmetric recognition or of misrecognition, critical theory can be understood as a second-order critique: a kind of metacritique which aims to re-establish the social conditions of critique, so as to make them accessible to the reflective and transformative practices of actors themselves. 'What people are capable of' (Boltanski, 1990a: Part 1) is thus both the starting point and the aim of critical theory. The driving force behind this approach might well be best captured by the young Marx: 'Therefore, we can express the aim of our periodical in *one* phrase: A self-understanding (critical philosophy) of the age concerning its struggles and wishes' (Marx, 1997: 215).

Notes

1 For a characterisation of the orthodox model, see Anthony Giddens, who presents it as premised on understanding social action as 'the result of forces that the actors neither control nor comprehend' (Giddens, 1986: xvi). For an alternative, non-orthodox understanding of the critique of ideology see Rahel Jaeggi (2009: 63–86).
2 For a qualified defence of Bourdieu's approach, see Claude Gautier (2009: 419–45), as well as Christian Lazzeri's contribution to this volume (Chapter 9).

PART V
JUSTICE-TO-COME: QUESTIONING EQUALITY AND THE PRESUMPTION OF FINALITY

11

Habermas and Derrida on recognising the other

*Isabelle Aubert**

IT appears difficult to bridge the fundamental differences between Derrida and Habermas. However, given that both grant pride of place to the concept of the other person, it makes sense to compare their use of this theme.[1] Surprisingly, we will discover that two shared intentions motivate their interest in this concept. First of all, Habermas and Derrida are both concerned to unite two normative aspects of the other person: this other must be recognised *both* for his or her individuality and for the general characteristics shared with other human beings. Secondly, Habermas and Derrida are also concerned to prevent those conditions from arising which distort the relation to the other, and which suppress the other's singularity with overdetermining general characteristics. In this way, both affirm a double-edged normative requirement, which requires that norms be both universal and singular, applying to all equally while respecting the singularity of the other person.

That said, Habermas and Derrida develop this requirement in two opposite ways. Habermas includes the relation to the other within a universal norm of dialogical intersubjectivity, which is meant to guarantee symmetrical and reciprocal relations between people by ascribing equality to all particular viewpoints (Habermas, 1991a and Habermas, 1993: 19–111). In contrast, Derrida (1997a; 1997c; 2002b) emphasises the asymmetrical nature of the self's relation to the other, pointing out that the idea of ethical symmetry fails to properly account for the fact that the other *cannot* be understood as my *alter ego*.

As Axel Honneth demonstrates in 'The other of justice' (1995c), discourse ethics and deconstructive ethics appear as rival moral theories because of their contrasting accounts of the relation to the other. For Honneth, Habermas' deontological morality contrasts with the deconstructive insistence on irremediable conflict in ethics, a conflict born of contradiction between the principle of justice (or equal treatment) and the principle of benevolence (or unequal treatment in the form of infinite care for the other person).[2] This chapter will focus on the difference between Derrida's and Habermas' account of the ethical relation to the other. However, unlike Honneth, who wrongly domesticates Derrida's approach by reformulating infinite care as a possible complement to Habermas' theory (Honneth, 1995c: 319), this chapter aims to show that the deconstructive principle of asymmetry and the Habermasian principle of symmetry in fact require each other and, in this sense, the tension itself is fruitful. Honneth's attempt to subordinate Derrida's thesis to the Habermasian framework might be appealing for those who accept the priority of an ethics of justice with its emphasis on reciprocity, symmetry and equality. However, it does not account for the fact that Derrida questions these very norms. Consequently, instead of reducing Derrida's ethical writings to a 'phenomenology of moral experience' (Honneth, 1995c: 308) which could supplement and enrich the discursive framework, it will be shown that the tension between the perspectives of Habermas and Derrida is instructive when attempting to make sense of the recognition which the other person requires.[3]

To avoid privileging either Derrida's or Habermas' perspective, this chapter will choose a neutral entrance point, namely, the notion of the other person, which, despite its phenomenological connotations, plays an important role for each thinker. We will not only critique the presupposition of shared intersubjectivity which animates Habermas' account of the discursive relation to the other but also Derrida's Levinasian account of the absolute resistance of the other in the 'face'.[4]

In this sense, the aim of this chapter is two-fold. First, whereas Habermas can only include alterity within an intersubjective framework by rejecting Derrida's claim that the subject faces an other which is *not* his or her alter-ego (Derrida, 1978: 117), this chapter seeks to avoid a one-sided interpretation and instead explain why the tension between the two perspectives is productive. In so doing, our attempt will avoid Honneth's strategy of prioritising Habermas' work over Derrida's, which overlooks the tension between them. The chapter's second aim is to identify the relevance of each theory for the idea of recognition, the theme of this volume. It will be shown that Habermas conceives of the other within a horizon of mutual, symmetrical recognition, whereas Derrida reflects on the way in which the other's alterity exceeds any recognition which can be offered. In this way, resisting the temptation to privilege one account over another, we will explore the very different versions of interpersonal relationships and politics to which each account gives rise, arguing that both have their merits.

Habermas' intersubjective framework

The speech situation

The notion that the relation between self and other is symmetrical and horizontal (such that the other is considered as another 'dialogical self') is supported, in Habermas' work, by his anthropological and sociological account of the 'life-world'; the 'social bond of belonging' which pre-exists and situates intersubjective relations (Habermas, 1991a: 202). We are always and already situated in relations, and it is within this framework that the subject distinguishes his or her own sphere of action from another's. Subjects and others create such distinctions and relationships using the medium of language, animated by the shared intention of communicating with each other. The success of this movement relies on the performative roles that communicative recognition has for identity-formation and interlocutive relations. Where interactive recognition contributes to a continuous process of identity-construction and facilitates ethical self-understanding, the speech situation both presupposes and maintains distinct perspectives and identities. The use of speech in this way assumes that subjects are distinct and unique, while also communicating with each other in the performative stance of dialogical selves.

We can now raise the following questions: At what point in this shared communicative horizon can the subject lay claim to his or her singularity and uniqueness? How does he or she make such a claim?

According to Habermas, the stabilisation of my identity depends, at the outset, on intersubjective recognition relations (Habermas, 1994: 192). The self interiorises the dialogical model of interaction. The self is 'not the absolute inward possession of the individual', because it is constituted in a thoroughly relational manner (Habermas, 2003a: 11). The idea that individuals are intersubjectively entwined in shared ways of life implies an ethical and performative definition of individuality which negates the concept of a unique and separate individual: 'The self of an ethical self-understanding is dependent upon recognition by addressees because it generates itself as a response to the demands of an other in the first place' (Habermas, 1994: 170). For Habermas, the self takes shape through a reflexive relation to one's past and present which is informed by the perspective of the other. The individual does not, in this sense, own his or her past because 'the totality of a life project stands in need of confirmation by others, whether they be concrete or possible participants in interaction' (Habermas, 1994: 170).

For Habermas, the intertwining of individuals in the life-world provides a relational origin for both autonomy and vulnerability (concepts which initially appear to be antithetical) (Habermas, 1991a: 207 and 109). Against Habermas, and doubting his claim that intersubjectivity is so easily interiorised, one could instead suggest that both autonomy and vulnerability share a common heteronomous origin, namely, the social relation (where the self's 'law' comes from the other person). This suggestion promises to throw new light on Habermas' insistence that the self is dependent on the recognition of the other person. For Habermas, the self is dependent not only during childhood development, but also during adulthood because the ego itself 'retains an intersubjective core' (Habermas, 1991a: 170). To test the hypothesis that intersubjectivity might be penetrated by heteronomy, we must examine more closely the possibility of a truly equal and symmetrical relationship between partners, at the level of a theory of action grounded in linguistic pragmatics. Is Habermas correct in claiming that the excessive influence of the other on the ego can indeed be prevented by the framework of everyday communication?

Faced with this objection, the Habermasian response would probably be that we have not entirely grasped the impact of intersubjectivity and that we are neglecting the reflexivity upon self and other which is produced by performative language-use. Due to the inner structure of linguistic communication, each communicating partner, alternately a subject in the first *and* second person, experiences themselves in the dual modality of self and other. This 'performative attitude' produces two effects. First, due to the pragmatic rules of language and, notably, the use of personal pronouns ('I' and 'you'), the two interlocutors alternately adopt reversible roles and come to see themselves as sharing the same viewpoint (Habermas, 2008: 48). In this way, the speaker recognises another speaker as an alter *ego*. Role reversal neither confuses the two perspectives, nor assimilates the other's perspective to my own, but rather distinguishes between the two viewpoints. 'The communicative actor is encouraged by the bare structure of linguistic intersubjectivity to remain himself' (Habermas, 1994: 190). By speaking in one's own name, the addressee asserts his or her singularity, rejecting or accepting the validity claims raised in dialogue. The individual is irreplaceable, in that, as a speaker, the individual is responsible for what she or he has said. The other, in this sense, remains an *alter* ego: a second self who responds for themselves, and who is not identical to one's own self. As Habermas puts it, it is only in the 'performative attitude [that] one confronts the other as *alter ego*: only with a consciousness of their absolute difference and irreplaceability can the one recognise himself in the other' (Habermas, 1994: 48).

Thus the practice of communication does not force interlocutors to share a levelling and unitary vision but instead reveals the non-identical character of the other. Applying Adorno's account of difference to the human sphere, Habermas emphasises the prime importance of individual singularity. Habermas is concerned not to reduce the other person to the same, so as to include those differences which cannot be reduced to a common denominator. Whereas an observation about the behaviour of the other would distort 'the non-identical' which is vulnerable to objectification (Habermas, 1994: 48), communicative acts prevent an identity (or opinions) from being wrongly attributed to the other because these acts show the other to be someone who responds and possibly protests this attribution, thereby resisting assimilation and attesting to their unique nature (Habermas, 2008: 194).

However, it seems to me, for definitional reasons and in a precise situation, that careful attention to difference cannot always be achieved within Habermas' symmetrical conception of interpersonal relations. On the one hand, dialogue offers a rather limited access to the other. In *The theory of communicative action* (1984 and 1987), the dialogical schema reveals its own limits, in that it is not intended to correspond to the hermeneutical model of psychoanalytical understanding. If the performative attitude is the condition of possibility for respecting the other, then communicative action can only produce a limited knowledge of the other. Otherwise communicative action would be normatively overburdened. On the other hand, the idea that dialogue offers a limited access to the other is weakened when consensus is, in fact, achieved. The act of pursuing consensus presupposes the existence of important differences, but these are either forgotten or neglected when efficient action is pursued and some form of consensus produced. Communicative action does not appear to provide a way of preventing this tendency. In this sense, it is difficult to be satisfied with Habermas' assertion that 'linguistically achieved consensus does not eradicate from the accord the differences in speaker perspectives but rather presupposes them as ineliminable' (Habermas, 1994: 48).

Political tolerance as openness to others
The theories of action and social psychology constructed around Habermas' universal pragmatic principles provide a way of justifying the axiom of symmetry, which in turn allow differences to be expressed and included. It is also this axiom of symmetry which grounds discursive moral theory. However, at the level of politics Habermas' thought strikes a different sort of chord, revealing a disquieting attitude to otherness which is not initially visible in his moral account of universal pragmatics. New considerations come into play when accounting for the political and social integration of individuals who have not yet achieved the status of full interlocutors within a determined society or citizens who are relegated to the margins of the democratic process. Such individuals live their differences as a penalty or punishment. For migrants, the laws of their new society can be confronting; for the poor, socio-economic thresholds can be discriminatory; and for religious minorities, majority cultural opinion can be marginalising. It is unclear whether Habermas' political concept of tolerance can include these citizens in a way that preserves their difference and avoid a reductive and constraining assimilation to the surrounding norms.

Derrida would question this politics of tolerance, on the basis that it conceals a political attitude of paternalistic condescension toward certain worldviews, thereby invoking an 'intolerant core' by imposing conditions on what counts as 'tolerable'.[5] Habermas, however, claims that it is only by virtue of tolerance that the ideal of mutual understanding, the democratic imperative, can be extended to others. For Habermas, tolerance avoids paternalism in that it is both a juridical act and a political virtue of citizens. As a political virtue, tolerance is founded on the idea of reciprocal recognition among citizens, where citizens rationally accept each other's differences, knowing that their own differences are also accepted by others (Habermas, 2008: 248). As a hermeneutical model, in the broad sense of the idea, tolerance symmetrically situates citizens seeking to understand each other, so that the process does not require one citizen to unilaterally welcome another but rather applies the obligation of tolerance to both parties reciprocally, thereby transforming their relations to each other, to themselves and to the political community itself. If successful, tolerance overcomes the problematic political attitude of paternalism, in that newcomers or cultural minorities no longer need to assimilate or sacrifice their cultural identity to the dominant culture (Habermas, 2004: 37). For Habermas, tolerance can only be achieved if it is equally distributed between the different positions, so that *all* citizens in a community are involved in learning processes, seeking a common horizon of understanding.

However, with respect to religious difference, this normative account of reciprocal tolerance is so carefully qualified that it becomes, in my view, questionable. The differences between religious and secular citizens equate to a conflict between mutually exclusive worldviews, a conflict that Habermas concedes cannot be overcome (Habermas, 2008: 251–70). This contradicts Habermas' defence of the ideal of shared understanding which grounds his deliberative account of democracy. When two worldviews are mutually exclusive, Habermas recommends that we no longer engage in public debate about the different reasons for supporting or dismissing a worldview but instead respect the other's difference. This conclusion is surprising since it implies that some ethical values should *not* be subject to the very public debate which shapes the ethics of a political community. In other words, Habermas appears to be saying that ethical values *should* be subject to public debate, but that religious values should receive special exemption. This contradicts his attempt to undo the accepted division between private and public spheres in *The structural transformation of the public sphere* (1991b) and *Between facts and norms* (1998). That said, we should also acknowledge that the idea of reasonable disagreement over ethical values need not threaten the coherence of Habermas' theory if we limit this disagreement with the idea of tolerance, adjusting the consensus model so as to account for the complexities involved when a theoretical framework is applied to multicultural societies characterised by value pluralism (Habermas, 2008: 254). In the final analysis, disagreement would be indirectly regulated by the principle of political cooperation, a principle to which all reasonable parties must agree. In this way, the consensus model might be maintained, albeit in a weaker form.

Habermas needs to concede, however, that in order for reasonable disagreement to be justified within a deliberative democracy, he now needs what Derrida would refer to as a principle of asymmetry, that is, a relation to the other in which one welcomes that which one cannot understand. The ethical values of religious citizens cannot be expressed in the secular language of public debate, and this means that they find themselves situated *asymmetrically* in a deliberative context. Consequently, a further compensatory principle is required. Secular citizens are asked to engage an extra effort: they must tolerate what cannot be explained with public reasons, so as to reinforce political cooperation. The political virtue of mutual tolerance involves a duty of translation that is asymmetrically distributed among citizens. Not only is it doubtful that this act of translation can be achieved when the substantial core of religious belief cannot be translated into secular, public language, it also seems that Habermas can no longer claim that tolerance is a political virtue. First, from the viewpoint of political realism, the following question can be raised: Is the constitutional framework, which remains the guarantee of a public principle of tolerance, enough to encourage individuals to uphold public values? Second, at the theoretical level, a further difficulty arises: If we don't commit to a model of negotiation among interests, and if tolerance *exceeds* the cooperative quest (requiring toleration of values which are *not* shared (Habermas, 2008: 261), then the principle of toleration cannot be reduced to the deliberative principle, which implies recourse to a new set of principles for recognising the other. In my view, the irreducibility of toleration to deliberation reveals the fragility of Habermas' attempt to found his theoretical architectonic on the idea of symmetry.

An account of deliberation founded on symmetry is too general to account for a dynamic process of effective social membership, and reveals the structural weakness of Habermas' approach. First, it seems that the intersubjective starting point, which social psychology and social anthropology assume, cannot mask obvious asymmetrical relations in the political arena.

We have seen, then, that when it comes to determining norms for both secular and religious citizens, Habermas concedes the need for an idea of asymmetrical relations. This asymmetrical moment is not provisional, as Habermas believes. Instead, we have reason to fear that the political application of juridical universalism is limited in its capacity to face up to individual differences which, on Habermas' account, are accepted in a merely negative manner. We would like to suggest that the view that dialogue is capable of maintaining different perspectives rests on a condition that should be rejected, and that citizens in a liberal democratic state can lay claim to a stronger sense of civic solidarity (Habermas, 2008: 273). In a broader sense, the problem with grounding both social anthropology and the democratisation process on a hegemonic principle is that this principle tends to mask the reality and importance of asymmetrical relations.

In working out an alternative approach to alterity, we need to return to the psycho-social account of the relation to the other. As has been suggested, the problem with Habermasian intersubjectivity is that it is strongly identified with a model wherein subjects are positioned symmetrically as equals. However, as Jessica Benjamin's psychoanalytic theory of intersubjectivity has taught us, intersubjectivity need not depend on a symmetrical model of interrelations (Benjamin, 1997: 79–108). She writes: 'An intersubjective theory of the self is one that poses the question of how and whether the self can actually achieve a relationship to an outside other without, through identification, assimilating or being assimilated by it' (Benjamin, 1997: 80). With this definition, Benjamin responds to the objection that recognition 'falsifies the difficulties of difference' (Benjamin, 1997: 92). She explains that an intersubjective apprehension of the other should combine both a binary schema of recognition and a concept of negation (Benjamin, 1997: 98), and she claims that Habermas, while drawing on psychoanalytic studies, consistently neglects the tendency of the self to deny difference in an 'identificatory assimilation of the other' (Benjamin, 1997: 93). For Benjamin, this equates to a violent and destructive way of relating to the other.

By considering the external relation of the self to the other as symmetrical, Habermas presupposes an element that opens the way to the development of respect, following in part Kohlberg's moral psychology.

Derrida's appeal to asymmetry

Contesting the concept of intersubjectivity based exclusively on equality and symmetry, Jessica Benjamin's psychoanalytic approach calls into question the ethics of reciprocity, drawing on a variety of ethical modalities of relating to the other. According to Benjamin, when recognition is associated with the idea of reciprocity (where the other is another ego), it sees the influences that individuals exert on each other as positive. Benjamin's concept of negation implies an alternative form of recognition. Here, moral recognition appears as an ethical responsiveness which overcomes, in a paradoxical manner, the defensive reaction produced when the self's initial understanding clashes with a sudden awareness of the other's singular difference. Moral recognition, conceived in this way, would welcome the other's difference, compensating for the initial projection of one's understanding onto the other person. The obligation of moral recognition becomes, in this way, an effort to let the other express his or her difference. This is not equivalent to the concept of mutual recognition which Honneth develops in *The struggle for recognition* (1995a), but rather expresses the self's experience of an asymmetrical relation with the other, in which the recognition of difference is analysed from the viewpoint of only one of the two people involved (the self).

Although it is true that Habermas thinks that his account of tolerance in communication will allow different individual perspectives to be maintained and respected, the presentation of the other as a partner in discussion effectively pre-comprehends the other in a manner which is already normative: everyday communication allows speakers to see themselves *in the same way*, as rational and autonomous agents. These generic determinations can, in some cases, prevent a speaker from welcoming those features which are unique to the individuals involved, and which resist the speaker's comprehension. We now turn to Derrida, whose approach allows us to question the Habermasian view that fundamental moral values 'can be reduced to the relations of symmetry and reciprocity presupposed in communicative action' (Habermas, 1991a: 201).

An ethics of hospitality[6]

Derrida's reflections on ethics circulate around the principle that motivates Levinas' work. Before even considering the balancing of our viewpoints in a shared perspective, what matters is the possibility of welcoming the other as a unique individual without preconceptions or preconditions, in order '*to think, that is, to invent* what is necessary'. We must accept the *other's* principle, 'and give oneself over to this exposure to the other' (Derrida and Roudinesco, 2004: 58). In this way, Derrida questions the priority of the ideal of mutual understanding which Habermas assumes as an already given fact. In the experience where the self is surprised by the encounter with the other's face, Derrida discovers a new form of ethical attitude, namely, an opening to something radically other that cannot be reduced to 'mutual understanding'. The ethical weight Derrida ascribes to this experience can only be understood in terms of 'asymmetry': the self faces an other which eludes its grasp and which cannot be understood in terms of symmetry as another ego whose viewpoint the ego can understand through the aforementioned imaginative switch of perspectives.

The ethical attitude respects this connection between otherness and singularity, which is why Derrida calls it 'unconditional hospitality'. Unconditional hospitality is 'ethicity itself, the whole and the principle of ethics' (Derrida, 1997a: 50). As a pure principle, unconditional hospitality places limits on my action, preventing any movement that could condition the way in which the other appears. It thereby contrasts with the merely conditional hospitality which is synonymous with tolerance (Derrida, 2000: 25). Unconditional hospitality requires that the self be affected by the other, the foreigner, beyond any initial expectations of the encounter, and without the conditions implied by 'invitation' (Derrida and Roudinesco, 2004: 59–60). Welcoming the other's unexpected coming, we prevent ourselves from imposing our own rules on the other and violently overdetermining our relation with questions and procedures (Derrida, 2004). Unlike Habermas, for whom subjects are partners in a possible dialogue, Derrida presents the other as a foreigner who does not share my language, drawing attention to the self's *a priori* ignorance of the other and insisting on the ethically relevant limits of understanding. In contrast to Habermas, dialogue, for Derrida, unsuccessfully attempts to penetrate the other's secret: to encounter the other is to encounter the ineffable (McCarthy, 1991: 98). The other, always singular and unique, is 'the law of the exception' (Derrida, 2007: 87) which demands a specific response to every newcomer which need not take the form of a universal norm. The ethics of hospitality thus reflects on the unpredictability of the other's arrival, while also relying on a general confidence in our ability to aspire to the messianic order reflected in 'the experience of faith, of believing, of a credit that is irreducible to knowledge, and of a trust that "founds" all relation to the other in testimony' (Derrida, 2002a: 56).

That said, Derrida then points out that following the principle of hospitality alone would produce perverse effects, and he acknowledges the need to compensate such effects. In so doing, he articulates unconditional hospitality with the conditional hospitality of a juridical, symmetrising nature. The imperative of unconditional hospitality would imply a 'heteronomy [where] the other is my law' (Derrida and Roudinesco, 2004: 52). In the last analysis, a hierarchical inversion takes place between myself (the host or hostess) and the other (my guest). The unlimited nature of hospitality could have pernicious effects for me (the guest could be a murderer), hence the need for the rule of law; the restoration of reciprocal obligations (Derrida, 1997c). For Derrida, then, hospitality takes place as an articulation of these two opposing poles; between the unconditional and conditional welcome. Asymmetry must be moderated by reciprocity in intersubjective relations.

At this point, an objection could be raised with respect to the ethical principle of hospitality, in that the Derridean other seems to play the role of an icon. Of course, Derrida *is* aware of the significant threat of power when we find ourselves in the presence of someone else: every active attitude the self takes, even benevolence, implies a particular pre-comprehension of the relationship. However, one wonders why Derrida does not consider the reverse possibility, wherein the other constitutes an excessive influence on myself. Derrida's concern for the self to avoid interfering with the other can, in fact, give rise to a hyper-reflexive, even defiant, attitude with respect to my own behaviour, and this seems problematic. More confusion follows when we compare this concern with Derrida's assertion that it is only in friendship that the self can have more confidence in the other than in myself (Derrida, 1997b: 195). The situation wherein the other exerts excessive influence on the self is a background problem which Derrida does not resolve.

It then becomes rather difficult to understand what is meant by the imperative of asymmetry, particularly if the self is to respect itself and the other equally. Although a concept of equal respect is invoked by Derrida's conception of responsibility in *The politics of friendship* (1997b), it is hard to see how this concept of respect might allow Derrida to respond to the following two objections. First, given that Derrida acknowledges that some conditioning must compensate for the risks of unconditional hospitality, is it not the case that an asymmetrical welcome is *always* conditioned in some way, inevitably demanding the *conversion* of the other and his or her opinions to my conditions? We recall, at this point, that Habermas' concept of tolerance professes to prevent such conversion. Secondly, and consequently, doesn't the idea of asymmetry implicitly appeal to an intuitive practice of interpretation or hermeneutic, in that we cannot but welcome the other using our own values and structures of thought? In this sense, we wonder why Derrida would reject a dialogue which could open the way to reciprocity after the moment of asymmetry, facilitating a progressive and processual welcoming of the other.

Two kinds of justice

The difficulty in determining the right approach to the other in an evolving situation leads to a question that concerns the capacity of justice to respond, when the two versions of hospitality meet up in a dichotomous theory of justice. Justice is thought of, on one hand, on the model of asymmetry; it is the infinite duty the other imposes on me to welcome his or her singularity even when the welcome does not appear to be lawful. In other words, the full idea of justice exceeds law.[7] As Derrida puts it in *Specters of Marx*, the place for justice is the 'disadjustment ... that opens up the infinite asymmetry of the relation to the other' (Derrida, 1994b: 22). On the other hand, this non-presentable experience must be determined and presented in some way, in the vocabulary of law, that is, reciprocity and universality (Derrida, 2002b: 257).

The division of the concept of justice into two contrasting elements raises a methodological problem. On the one hand, the idea that immeasurable justice serves as an imperative for inventing new rights 'beyond the already identifiable zones of morality, politics or law' (Derrida, 2002b: 257). On the other hand, the imperative to create new rights effectively articulates immeasurable with calculative justice, making an important concession to Habermasian ideas of reciprocity and symmetry. The relation to the other, now moderated by law, is in practice only *occasionally* marked by the idea of asymmetry. This concession appears to endanger the very deconstruction which brings the idea of justice to life. Although the ethical injunction of justice exceeds juridical practice, this very excess can make deconstructive ethics vulnerable to being obscured by the generalisations that the everyday laws of justice imply. If the difference between the two forms of justice (immeasurable and calculable) is aporetic, and if maintaining this difference is the only way to preserve the purity of these respective forms, it is hard to see how focusing on juridical practice and equal treatment in similar situations will not eventually obscure a principle of difference centred on individual singularity. Doesn't the levelling character of law risk ignoring the asymmetrical character of deconstructive justice?

The strict application of Derrida's definitions leads, in this way, to all of the above questions. One aspect in particular remains theoretically problematic: the fact that Derrida does not think it necessary to moderate the aforementioned dangers of an ethics of self-sacrifice by framing it with a theory of responsibility. The question remains as to whether the call to maintain asymmetry makes sense outside of a context of equal respect which would soften the force of this appeal.[8]

Two similarities

Although both Habermas' and Derrida's philosophies take off from conflicting and mutually exclusive premises, each respectively reveals the need to include relations of symmetry and asymmetry, counterbalancing, in an important sense, the initial rigidity of their positions. One thing that must be said, however, is that intersubjectivity has an ambiguous relation with an asymmetrical principle, and conversely that Derrida's asymmetrical ethics can only be realised when it is articulated with an idea of equality. That said, the gap between the two perspectives remains, despite occasional intersections. For this reason, it seems to me that the two accounts of the relation to the other can only converge with the framework of a *temporal extension* of certain normative principles. Reflection upon the temporal development of the ethical and political community can alone permit Habermas' concept of alterity to meet with Derrida's (and vice versa).

Responsibility for those who are absent

Despite the aforementioned differences in approach, Derrida and Habermas share a common-sense approach to responsibility. Let us begin by recalling their divergent starting points. As with his notions of justice and hospitality, Derridean responsibility is born of a relation to the other (Derrida, 1997b: 230–1). Once again, responsibility is torn between two contrary imperatives which are together articulated without being reducible to each other, in such a way that the core of responsibility is, again, an 'experience and experiment of the impossible' (Derrida, 1992: 45). The self is both responsible for the particular other, and for *all* others. In contrast to this aporetic horizon, Habermasian responsibility involves a relation of symmetry between persons who are free and equal: the self is responsible for the other insofar as the other is also responsible for the self (Habermas, 2003a: 14).

Given this important difference between Derrida's and Habermas' account of responsibility, it is quite remarkable that both agree on one precise case, namely, responsibility towards those who are absent; responsibility towards 'certain *others* who are not present, nor presently living, either to us, in us, or outside of us' (Derrida, 1994b: xix). The agreement over responsibility for 'absent others' is not accidental but rather implies a broader view of responsibility itself. The similarity between the introduction to Derrida's *Specters of Marx* (1994b) and Habermas' *The future of human nature* (2003a) is instructive: both texts view responsibility as a duty of justice. Obviously, beyond their conflicting epistemic premises, one possible reason for their agreement on this point lies in their shared reference to a Kantian account. Both accept Kant's interpretation of respect which makes the other person the source of authentic, personal obligations.

This separation between the self and those who are not present (including those who are no longer living or who are yet to be born) leads Derrida, in *Specters of Marx*, to reflect on the temporal scope of justice. As Derrida explains, the problem is located in the gap or hiatus between, on the one hand, acts which engage us beyond our own lives and, on the other hand, a moral response to others that can only be given in the present and before living people. Extending the scope of justice is only possible if justice is motivated by responsibility towards others who are others of our own contemporary-others. For Derrida, the strict coincidence between our own present and short-sighted responsibility would annihilate all meaning in the political project – short-sighted responsibility would undercut the sense of politics in the present, in that it leaves unresolved the important question, 'where could we be tomorrow?' Using an expanded conception of the other (as a spectre or spirit), Derrida is able to ground the idea of a timeless responsibility which lends weight to the idea of a paradoxical justice beyond the lived present.

What position does Habermas take with regard to this expanded responsibility to absent others? In *The future of human nature*, Habermas warns against the possibility of a disproportionate dependence on future generations with regard to present generations. Habermas opposes what he calls a 'liberal eugenics', that is, the right to undertake genetic intervention on the genome of an embryo to produce a child whose genetic make-up can serve present generations. In so doing, he canvasses an idea of responsibility which, in my view, has two characteristics. From the idea of ethical self-understanding, mutually acquired by deliberating parties in a trans-subjective manner, Habermas derives the idea of an obligation of responsibility between living beings, a responsibility which is again symmetrical in that one is responsible before others who are equally responsible.

In comparison with a theory which includes a principle of asymmetrical responsibility, reciprocal responsibility makes it much harder to justify an increase in responsibility for future generations. For Habermas, the view that present generations could change the biological constitution of future generations is untenable because it projects a future situation where symmetrical equality cannot obtain between parents and their genetically modified teenager. Although natural social dependency between parents and their children can be resolved in time when parent and child become independent equals, this would not be possible in the case of genetic manipulation where parent – child reciprocity seems ruled out in advance. The genetically modified child would be forever instrumentalised, created simply to serve another person. As Habermas puts it, 'the assumption that there is, in principle, a reversibility to interpersonal relationships' (Habermas, 2003a: 63) would be threatened by the fact that the child has been genetically produced. Unlike social destiny, the child would be unable to reappropriate the paternalistic intention that has already shaped his or her body. Produced subjects would be irreversibly alienated from their bodies: 'A person ... who would be the sole product of a suffered socialisation fate would see his "self" slip away in the stream of constellations, relations, and relevancies imposed upon the formation process' (Habermas, 2003a: 59–60). In Habermas' ethics of human nature,[9] we discover another duty of responsibility on the part of the living towards future generations, a responsibility to foster the symmetrical and reciprocal liberty for all partners in a moral and political community. Although Habermas does not put it like this, we could say, in deconstructive fashion, that the living are responsible in an asymmetrical way for the conditions which will allow future persons to be truly themselves.

The meaning of democracy

The similarity between Derrida's and Habermas' account of the temporal extension of ethical responsibility implies a further convergence on the topic of the future conditions of the political community. Bearing in mind the discrepancy between their views on the nature of relations between people, expressed in the form of tolerance and solidarity for Habermas and hospitality for Derrida, the eventual intersection of their perspectives is surprising. An understanding very close to the general framework of democracy appears.

Insofar as Derrida recognises, with Habermas, the importance of the ideas of emancipation and reciprocity when accounting for the normative framework of democracy, it seems legitimate to draw similarities here between Derridean democracy and Habermas' account of the public sphere. According to Derrida's vision for the future of democracy, democracy should take place as 'a sort of heteronomic and dissymmetrical curving of social space – more precisely, a curving of the relation to the other' (Derrida, 1997b: 231), by which he means that democracy must work at including a larger space for difference, founded on the equality of the different liberties. For Derrida, the democratic imperative is equivalent to the idea of equality without comparability (Derrida, 1997b: 64). In comparison to this conception, Habermas wants to ensure that each potential speaker can express themselves (and be understood) in their own unique ways, insisting on the plurality of informal public spheres and drawing attention to the ways in which the standardisation of mediated discourse produces pathologies of political communication (Habermas, 2006).

If we focus now on Habermas' political philosophy, we are reminded that his account of the public sphere relies on the idea that only the plurality and free exchange of opinions can guarantee democratic vitality and ensure its legitimacy. On this point, Derrida's theory is surprisingly similar. Although Derrida expresses reservations about the current state of the public sphere, he agrees that it can only be effective if a 'right of reply' or a 'right of response' is encouraged and maintained (Derrida, 1992: 105). Far from being satisfied with the plural nature of opinions – a solution that might seem to follow from the thought of difference – Derrida's proposal sounds similar to Habermas' in that it takes each citizen to be a representative in dialogue, reciprocally related to other speakers, each with his or her own unique point of view.[10]

The close relation between Habermas and Derrida on the topic of ethical responsibility indicates that Derrida's messianic presentation of democracy-to-come shares certain elements with the utopian and processual character of Habermas' deliberative theory. It should not be surprising, then, that Habermas comes to accept Derrida's deconstruction, stating that: 'Derrida seems to be still inspired by the memory of the promise of radical democracy. It remains for him a source for the reticent hope in a *universal* solidarity that permeates all relations' (Habermas, 2008: 277).

This comparative reading of Habermas and Derrida makes it clear that the singular and universal character of the other person will only be fully recognised if we attempt to carefully articulate the other both as one who resembles me and one who is foreign to me. Although both authors agree that the figure of the other is ambivalent, their views are distinguished by a difference in emphasis between, on the one hand, an understanding of interaction as an ordinary everyday practice, and, on the other hand, an account of welcoming the other which respects the exceptionality and unique nature of his or her arrival. It is significant that these opposing premises paradoxically give rise to similarities, when they conceptualise living-together as a project or a point of temporal flight. Their shared reference to the Kant of the second *Critique* (1997) explains, in part, the convergence around this theme. In my view, it is more interesting to reflect on the way in which their conflicting premises of symmetry and asymmetry lead their viewpoints to intersect, showing that the multifaceted nature of relations with the other functions to transform both theories in important ways.

Notes

* I warmly thank Miriam Bankovsky for translating this chapter, and for her helpful comments.
1. Deconstruction can also be seen as a process that rejects the ontological fixation on identity, and insists on a definitional and moving otherness in *différance*. Here we will focus simply on Derrida's treatment of the other in the *person*.
2. According to Honneth, Derrida is the only postmodern philosopher to truly call into question the universalistic moral horizon (Honneth, 1995c: 307). Thomas McCarthy

expresses a similar interpretation (McCarthy, 1991: 123).
3. See Honneth's contribution to this volume (Chapter 2), where he explains that Derrida's work has led him to modify his view of ethics. However, he softens deconstructive ethics by including asymmetry within an intersubjective frame.
4. As Drucilla Cornell recognises, Levinas and Derrida can nonetheless be said to disagree with respect to the nature of alterity, suggesting that Levinas and Derrida both want to avoid reducing the other to the same but advocate doing so in different ways. Levinas 'declar[es] the other to be absolutely other' whereas Derrida 'recognis[es] that the other must also be an alter ego, irreducible to my ego precisely because it is an ego' (Cornell, 1992: 57). As Derrida states, in his critique of Levinas: 'If the other was not recognised as ego, its entire alterity would collapse' (Derrida, 1978: 156).
5. Lasse Thomassen develops a similar point in 'The Inclusion of the Other? Tolerance' (Thomassen, 2007: 69–94).
6. Here, we understand 'ethics' in a broad sense, so as to bridge differences in vocabulary between Habermas and Derrida. In so doing, we should be mindful that Habermas distinguishes morality and ethics, and that Derrida rejects the notion of morality by reflecting upon the conditions of possibility of ethics. However, given the objective of the chapter, these details are less important here.
7. 'If there is deconstruction of all presumption to a determining certainty of a present justice, it itself operates on the basis of an "idea of justice" that is infinite, infinite because irreducible, irreducible because owed to the other – owed to the other, before any contract, because it has *come*, it is *coming*, the coming of the other as always other singularity' (Derrida, 2002b: 254).
8. In this sense, it is understandable that Honneth might be tempted to read Derrida as attempting to welcome asymmetry into symmetry: 'With this line of reasoning Derrida has already gone way beyond the limits drawn today in the tradition of justice going back to Kant, because now the attempt is being made to integrate the two different moral perspectives in a single frame of orientation' (Honneth, 1995c: 315).
9. I will not deal, here, with the controversy over Habermas' expression 'ethics of human nature'. See Haber (2006: 253).
10. For consideration of a similar point, see Thomassen's *Deconstructing Habermas* (Thomassen, 2007: Chapter 5).

12

Honneth, Lyotard, Levinas

*Jean-Michel Salanskis**

MY guiding thread in this reflection will be a memory related by Jean-François Lyotard in homage to Pierre Souyri, his companion in militant life within the 'ultra-left' Marxist group *Socialisme ou barbarie* of the 1950s and 1960s. Lyotard recalls Souyri's assertion, in one of their sempiternal conversations, that the notion of justice aroused his suspicion (Lyotard, 1988: 68). Now, in their debates, it was Souyri who wanted to remain faithful to Marxism. The idea is therefore that the mistrust towards justice is a manner in which this particular style of militant philosophy, this critical conception of politics represented by Marxism, is expressed. In what, fundamentally, does this mistrust consist? I note two of its aspects:

1. On the one hand, the suspicion towards justice is a suspicion towards the possibility of bettering the world through the abstract and universal assertion of the 'ought'. It is claimed that the destiny of the world can only be interrupted by evolutions which belong to it by nature. The world cannot give birth to a worldly state that would turn out to be other than what follows from the logic of its historical development, conceived by analogy with natural process. Any attempt to guide it in a purely normative and rational fashion would therefore be completely off track. In Marxism, it is the description of the movement of productive forces, the transformation in relations of production, the 'politico-economic' dynamic of capitalism, and the conception of a logic of contradiction at work in capitalism which are the elements that produce this essential 'naturalist mediation'.

2. The reference to justice, on the other hand, is conceived as a reference to morality, whose error consists in privileging the individual. Justice, as a form of morality, understands what is possible in terms of the correction of individual acts, the realisation of a 'Good' being made to depend upon the cumulative practical quality of each party, aggregated according to an operation which respects the 'atomic' character of the contribution and the

hardships of each. Now, it is thought that the social and political question has principally concerned the inferiority and suffering of the 'disadvantaged classes' as a whole, an inferiority and suffering that must be understood to have been inflicted by the ruling classes. The central issue is thus settled over and above (and thus without reference to) individual responsibility, in the conflict of interests that governs all agents.

The aim of this chapter is thus to compare the thought of Axel Honneth with that of two contemporary French philosophers – Jean-François Lyotard and Emmanuel Levinas – from the point of view of this operator of the rejection of justice. The discussion will be organised around the two constitutive aspects that have just been presented.

It will not be a question here therefore of engaging in a comparative analysis referring to Honneth's evaluations of the thought of Jean-François Lyotard or Emmanuel Levinas (Honneth, 1995c: 289–383). These evaluations display a concern for demarcation, a characteristic at odds with the current reflection: I am instead attempting to situate Honneth, Lyotard and Levinas in relation to a post-Marxist situation or configuration that may be, *a priori*, what they have in common. I will nonetheless say some words about Honneth's evaluations at the appropriate moment: the approach adopted here, in my opinion, allows me to interpret the author's concern for demarcation.

I will go straight to the heart of this comparative discussion by considering, first of all, Axel Honneth, whose work motivates, for the most part, the collective work in this volume.

Naturalist mediation and moral politics in Honneth

Should we say that Honneth has snatched politics from the jaws of justice? Emmanuel Renault suggests, in many respects, that we should, and he insists, in *L'expérience de l'injustice* (2004), on the idea that something is lost if we limit politics to the search for and formulation of good norms on the basis of an *a priori* conception of justice. On the other hand, following Honneth, he affirms on the contrary that the process of perfecting politics unfolds, in the final analysis, by way of an increasingly comprehensive series of reformulations of rights, with an eye to the best apprehension of the conditions of recognition. In the final analysis, the horizon of transformation indeed appears to be juridical.

However, for the theory of recognition, it seems that this 'better right' cannot proceed from the work of experts and intellectual persuasion within the space of deliberative democracy: a certain struggle is also needed. What radically distinguishes the theory of recognition from a purely 'normative' political philosophy is the reference made to struggles for recognition, to the way in which social groups, confronted with disrespect, engage in conflicts, and call for a recognition that they had been lacking. This struggle functions to reveal or make apparent rights which are lacking, new guarantees for inclusion into law, whose necessity and meaning emerge from the struggle itself, from its actors and what they express (though expressed imperfectly and obscurely in the first instance).

Thus the question which arises is that of knowing whether the theory of recognition admits of a naturalist derivation of right, which would radically distinguish it from a political philosophy 'of justice', and would allow it to be included in our Marxist *topos*, under its original theoretical reference. In order to respond to this question, the meaning of two of Honneth's references must be considered: Hegel on the one hand, and Mead on the other.

The schema of the struggle for recognition, such as it emerges in the Hegel of the *Realphilosophie* as read by Honneth, can appear to be inclined towards naturalism. The mechanism that links one sphere of recognition to another, which readily unfolds through a transgression resulting from a failure of recognition, seems to impose the image of a process that prevails over all deontology, or integrates deontology as a moment. There is injustice within justice that is stabilised at a certain level, an injustice that, in accordance with the nature of things, engenders transgression and conflict which is overcome in a superior state of right. Transgressions must not therefore be regarded in a deontological fashion as unjust, but as clues, expressions, or manifestations of the insufficiency of norms. This insufficiency comes to light within a gradually unfolding intersubjective process, within the future which awaits it. Honneth appears to accept as such this naturalising description of a history that brings with it forms of justice, and whose relativity is marked, each time factually, in transgression. He only fears that, because it is formulated within the framework of a philosophy of consciousness, it is not, according to this explicit formulation, scientifically well founded, not adequately anchored in naturalism. He considers, for this reason, that Hegel cannot sufficiently explain the experience of disrespect which provokes and motivates such transgressions. And so, he invokes Mead, therefore, as a 'solution', insofar as Mead's anthropology gives every indication that empirical findings have been considered: Mead's solution casts light on the need for recognition, and the suffering that arises from its lack, as indisputable psychological structures of the human. Without such a reference, it seems that Honneth conceives of principles – principles to which the social world would conform in its 'revolutionary' process – as emanating from the effective ontological economy of the subject and the world.

It would also be possible, however, to emphasise another aspect of Honneth's position. In the first place, when he evaluates *a posteriori* the contribution made by Marx to a 'social philosophy' oriented around recognition, he renders a qualified verdict: Marx is reproached for having conceived of the proletariat's struggle as the struggle of one self-interest against others, struggles for wealth or power, Hobbesian in the end, rather than as struggles 'for recognition', revolts against disrespect. In keeping with this, he very openly condemns the economic interpretation of status and conflict that prevails in Marx, so as to contrast it with a moral interpretation. Of course, the opposition between the moral and the economic is not yet clear from the point of view of our discussion: what can be understood already, though, is that Honneth challenges the figure of an 'economic nature' rather than naturalism in general, and that the moral component which he wants to integrate into discourse is related, for him, to a psychological naturalism. This ambiguity is indeed irreducible, but in the context of this reference to Marx there is no doubt that the reference to the 'struggle for recognition', misrecognised by Marxist reductionism, well and truly takes on a moral, hence anti-naturalist, 'colour'. Moreover, one can ask whether the *appeal* to a moral dimension can ever conserve the naturalist character that might have been invested in a naturalist *conception* of morality.

In the second place, Honneth makes no secret of the fact that the perception of the self, and of the group in which one is subject to disrespect, is not an acceptable criterion as such for complaint, contestation and struggle. In order to remind his readers of this point, Honneth – as a German philosopher who well knows the importance of the example – invokes the account offered by a neo-Nazi about his militant undertakings. The neo-Nazi hones in on the experience of disrespect and contempt which many experience, offering a 'gift of recognition' to the disrespected as a way of recruiting, to the cause, those who have lost all hope.

It thus appears that Honneth does not mean to suggest that social and political action should be determined once and for all by a 'natural process of recognition' (effective, observable and evolving) so as to present it as the instigator of our judgements and legal formulations. In other words, Honneth does *not* mean that recognition, as a 'natural process' should not be itself subject to normative critique. It appears that his 'naturalism' in social and political matters finds here its limit.

That said, another element could tilt the balance in another direction. In *Disrespect* (2007a), retracing the way in which social pathology has been thought since Rousseau and Nietzsche, and coming up against the central and crucial problem of legitimising the diagnosis that a society is ill, Honneth insists on the need for what he calls an 'internal transcendence', a kind of 'lever' for social philosophy. He notes in fact that the philosophies that diagnose the illness of the social body have always had great difficulty in explaining *how* they ground such a judgement, and from *where* they derive their ideal of a healthy social body in relation to which they judge deviation. In principle, according to the definition given by Honneth himself, the health of the social can only be judged in relation to the 'possibility of the good life': it is a question of verifying whether the prevailing conditions permit everyone to achieve a path in life which is good, crowned with success. However, this definition returns us of course to the debate on the content associated with the idea of the good life and, in this respect, to possible obscurity. Clearly, for Honneth, the diagnosis of pathology need not simply rely on a conceptualisation of the good, which can be opposed to the world such as it is, as an abstract 'ought'. What is needed – in addition? – from his point of view, is what he refers to as 'internal transcendence', that is, a real place in the actual world that can carry the moral excess of the world, and can bring it about in the mode of development and not deontological correction.

In the Marxist schema, this internal transcendence was represented by the proletariat that, as we know, supports and designates a double description. On the one hand, it was one element of the balance of power constitutive of the capitalist present, 'struggling' towards victory and domination (the 'dictatorship'), animated by its own self-interest. On the other hand, however, it was the promise of the disappearance of wrongful discrimination within society, to the extent to which the wrong-doing suffered was in a certain sense 'absolute' rather than particular. The proletariat, in such a philosophical account, is in fact both internal and transcendent, transcendent in the sense of the universal and the absolute.

Now, one of Honneth's profound motivations – an explicit and declared motivation, once again – is to 'rediscover' such an 'Archimedean lever' with respect to 'social pathology'. Truth be told, the concept of 'social pathology' is situated at a naturalist level, and conceives of the political difficulty as one of illness rather than of moral error. The struggle for recognition is the sought-after heir of class struggle.

Nonetheless, there is an important difference: no 'limit' of the process of political therapy is indicated *a priori*. Everything leads us to believe that the mutual and interlinked development of struggle and right will always uncover a new form of disrespect that calls for the revision of the laws. It might be thought that the simple fact of opening the perspective of political progress to infinity in this way provides an exit from the naturalist framework: a wound in the world which would be purely natural and the result of natural causes, like the grand canyon, would have to be able to be simply reabsorbed at the natural and causal level (by being filled, in this example) once and for all. Why do we think that there will always be a new denial of recognition? Isn't it necessarily because the power of the 'radical evil' of liberty is conspicuous, because evil is thought as transcendent, beyond every historical economy, and because one opens the door to the arena of ethical reparation, and for this very reason, to an infinite delay?

Without claiming to have come to a conclusion about Honneth's naturalism, we could also ask to what extent he takes up once more the essential suspicion of Marxism with respect to every type of ethical approach in political matters.

On the one hand, the 'theory of recognition' indeed appears to be exactly what Marxism would refuse, the grounding of political endeavour in an aspiration for justice, itself grounded in an 'experience of evil' at the individual level: is the description of the misrecognised man, specifically the black man who undergoes the experience of his invisibility, anything other than a phenomenological schema that exposes the moral violation of co-humanity? Honneth, in his reflection on *invisibility*, seems to assume this phenomenological schema, according to which a manifestation of moral evil is possible only with reference to a first person, who is in this case the disrespected subject (Honneth, 2001: 111–26). In this way, he appears to cast light on the fundamental moral fault of our societies, which is that forms of recognition, which avert disrespect at all levels, are not produced, and that those subjects thereby exposed to disrespect lack the 'recognition' necessary to exist in a human manner. This fault always occurs through basically immoral behaviour, even if we identify it at the collective and social level. We, the ordinary individuals, are in the final analysis those who 'pass by' the black fellow-citizen or who do not accord any value to the social contribution of the manual labourer. When reading Honneth, against all odds and notwithstanding the obvious motivations of political activists, one very often has the sense, in the end, of discovering, in his writings, the admission that the famous 'political problem' is strictly moral, an admission which is prohibited in and by Marxism.

And yet this is clearly not what he is trying to convey, in the first instance because of the naturalist interpretation of the need for recognition derived from Mead, which, as we have seen on p. 193, counterbalances the moralising character of the account of the 'phenomenology of recognition'. We are supposed to judge in favour of a commitment to recognition because, in a quasi-scientific way, we understand that the subject can only be developed on the basis of a positive relation to the self, of a security accorded *a priori* to its praxis, and not on the basis of a sustained indignation in which our originary morality would be expressed.

At the strictly epistemological level, it seems to me that, for Honneth, politics is situated between justice and rationality rather than between justice and morality. Politics must produce a way of managing human things, in a manner favourable to the good life: the rules of justice have no other meaning and no other justification. The theory of recognition reveals at the same time the absolutely general conditions of the good life and an historical process for the immanent perfecting of institutions (the struggle for recognition). It is therefore a question of backing this process in order to produce laws which are more and more in keeping with the rationally disclosed conditions that present the good life as a kind of rational collaboration. In fact, at the culmination of his still-developing body of thought, Axel Honneth intends to argue that recognition is also the first condition for both knowledge and reason, and that the intersubjective structure of recognition is also the guiding presupposition of the collective exercise of science – in the final analysis, Honneth reunites, in a sense, with Habermas (Honneth and Voirol, forthcoming).

We have not been able to work out whether Honneth has, in fact, been able to rescue politics from the jaws of justice, by reference to a naturalist account of the good life, or whether he in fact assigns pride of place to 'political morality', within the framework of justice. He situates himself somewhere between the two in an ambiguous manner. We will now examine the same problematic nexus in Lyotard.

Justice, morality and nature in Lyotard

Lyotard's response to the question of naturalism will vary, depending on which stage of the long itinerary of his thought is considered: I will limit myself here, according to the general perspective of this reflection, to its post-Marxist stages.

Does the Lyotard of *Discourse, figure* (2011) conceive of a revolutionary series on a naturalist basis? He seems to describe it as a transversal operation of desire in its economic sense: an operation which folds, overturns, or suppresses the plane of signification and of recognisable 'good forms'. Does desire as *Trieb*, however, belong to nature? Certainly, the Freudian economic point of view invokes the concept of energy, which is the naturalist or naturalising concept *par excellence*. And the debate with Lacan can be understood through this lens: desire is once and for all (or always already) representational, semiotic and, serving as signifier, itself moves toward a sharing of language, text and culture. In *Discourse, figure*, the one exception to the view that *Trieb* belongs to nature occurs in the Conclusion, where desire appears as revolutionary only when its subversion is not equivalent to its consummation: when everything is returned to the death drive. This is what makes art possible, insofar as it dramatises and exhibits behaviours, rather than allowing desire in its imperceptible opacity to count as pleasure. This reference to art and its theatre is incontestably non-naturalist.

The Lyotard of *Libidinal economy* (1993) accentuates in sum the economic paradigm, increasing the value of the body: the signs he calls tensors are constitutive of a body called 'the libidinal band', a non-organic body that overflows its boundaries, linking onto or appending what is external to it. There is, if you like, a kind of naturalist atmosphere here, except that capitalism as an historical institution, Greek *isonomia*, or Latinate civil religion are also examples of the libidinal band. In the final analysis, Lyotard denounces the Marx who wants to purge nature of the infamy of culture and return it to the purity of a hidden naturality (which Lyotard refers to as 'little girl Marx'). In any case, his protest against the use of the notion of alienation in critical revolutionary discourse implies that there is no essential necessity commanding the defeat or overthrow of the old world. Nevertheless, the 'principle of intensity' is not equivalent to a principle of justice. Desire requires its fires, its consuming action and its flights beyond good and evil. Its movement is self-justifying. Is this not a way of presenting an account of 'nature'?

For the Lyotard of *The differend* (1988), the social and political problem consists in the fact that phrase regimens or genres of discourse are constantly included in the totalising *hubris*, driving the claim that these regimens or genres structure everything, with their procedures and their stakes. In these conditions, a wrong is done to a phrase which has not even succeeded in being phrased; a wrong is done to the phrase which is pending or which suffers delay, because what attempts to be said in it could not fall within the province of the dominant regime or genre, and cannot be inscribed within, or translated by, it. What takes the place of revolutionary series, to use a term that no longer has a place here, is the listening for or welcoming of what seeks to be phrased, and the invention of the idioms which will all this to occur. No form of nature can make itself bring to light the 'complement' of the old world. Suffering calls for the invention of an idiom, but this idiom remains contingent, a work of liberty, again involving an artistic mode of activity (but a sense of the word 'artistic' which would include inventions in science, philosophy or law).

The final Lyotard, of *Misère de la philosophie* (2000), *Lectures d'enfance* (1991a), *The inhuman* (1991b), etc., insists on the moment of silence, the inarticulate, and powerlessness before the phrase, sometimes identified as the moment of the affect-phrase. He describes in a melancholic manner the inevitable betrayal or coercion of this originary *infantia*, and tries to understand the upright or honest use of thought in terms of assuming responsibility for inextinguishable debt towards this powerlessness. It therefore seems that every figure for the revolutionary series disappears, even if, in this debt in life or in writing to the *infantia*, it is always, in a sense, a question of the same thing, namely protest against the hegemonic disposition of language and history. To this hegemonic tendency is opposed our indebted fidelity towards the *infantia*. In the very notion of the *infantia*, we could perhaps find a naturalist narrative for the originary trauma of existence – and yet the Lyotardian evocation makes only sparse use of naturalising language. In any case, though, the reference to a debt which can be entirely ignored, and, indeed, that we probably frequently ignore, serves to expunge any sense of natural development from this dissenting position. And it should no doubt be recalled here that, in *Heidegger and 'the Jews'* (1990), Lyotard associates and even parallels humanity's debt towards the helpless pre-humanity of the *infantia* with the Jewish debt – incomprehensible for the West – towards the law: this association denaturalises the originary traumatism itself.

But we also need to ask whether Lyotard, drifting[1] from Marx's revolutionary 'political philosophy', ends up authorising morality.

Clearly, Lyotard's early post-Marxist positions, those of *Discourse, figure* and

Libidinal economy do not encourage such authorisation: both in fact describe the political opening in terms of desire. And does not morality begin only when desire is no longer understood as a value?

With an eye to simplification, and in the interest of comparing Levinas with Honneth, we will limit ourselves here to discussing the question of justice and morality in the context of *The differend*, without taking into account Lyotard's final works.

A return to the question of justice can certainly be seen in *The differend*. Indeed, this book provides a means to reflect on judgement, on the impossibility of evading it, on the weakness of criteria and on the crises of legitimation. Is it not the case that the whole problematic of the *tort* or the wrong, which openly employs a juridical vocabulary, is symptomatic of the effort to reformulate the revolutionary hope in terms of justice? But the question which must nonetheless be posed more carefully is whether the 'political philosophy' developed by Lyotard in this late period goes so far as to specify a way of contesting the world grounded in a moral motion.

Emmanuel Renault uses the thought of the *differend* to argue in favour of the theory of recognition as he understands it, that is, as a dynamic justification for the struggles that are unfolding in the contemporary world (Renault, 2004: 39–41). And, in a sense, he is right to do so. There is a *differend* whenever the plaintiff suffers a wrong that simply cannot be formulated in the available language of justice. Furthermore, the examples presented by Lyotard are emblematic of 'leftist' politics: the Algerian Arab Muslim who suffers from having to be French or a citizen of the republic, or the proletariat who suffers from having to sell his labour power on the market (Lyotard, 1984). The accent placed on the concept of the *differend* can be understood in terms of an *a priori* contestation of the principle of justice, at least if this latter is conflated with the idea that institutional rules are absolutes.

The one exception to Renault's view that the *differend* cannot be formulated in the language of justice concerns the fact that Lyotard, in spite of everything, can only appraise or assess wrong-doing on the basis of a general reflection on the legitimacy of the present set of circumstances and linkage of phrases. If we are, in fact, to recognise that the tribunals of justice are insufficient or incompetent, we must reflect more carefully on the deepest problem with regard to justice: under what conditions is the phrasing of a phrase *legitimate*, or the phrasing of a phrase which follows a particular phrase, or the phrasing of a phrase in the 'space' of phrasing haunted by a particular genre, etc.?

Justice, therefore, instituted in any particular code or language of right, is indeed suspect, but it can only be rendered suspect from the point of view of a *justice of language*, which is Lyotard's object of reflection and philosophical investigation. Such a justice of language includes, *de jure*, all previous political systems, because the present circumstance of the phrase is in a sense the ultimate and unique category for any ontology that subsumes the totality of human experience. Now, at the level of the philosophical elaboration of such a 'justice of language', Lyotard looks for general, *a priori* and absolute principles, even if his book would refuse such a formulation. In any case, it is clear that this justice is no longer to be found, at least in any obvious way, in the posture of a Marxist immanentism: justice does not require that a certain modality of phrasing, today marginalised, must become majoritarian and dominant, according to an 'historico-natural mechanism' already underway. At first sight, justice of phrases requires that no regime or genre be forbidden, both for the present, and for the series of circumstances to come.

It is at this moment or in this way that we return again to the space of morality: the anti-totalitarian principle which requires that no genre (whether cognitive, speculative, or economic), 'seize power' over phrasing and the linkage of phrases by condemning to silence, suffering delay, or holding up the other potentials of phrasing. Is this principle (that the politics of *The differend* seems to be reduced to and summarised by) a principle of justice or a moral principle? In other words, is morality the driving force of this principle?

Of course, everything depends on the criteria given for justice and morality. In Lyotard, the question essentially takes the form of a debate with Kant and Levinas. The problem has already been examined by others (Corrine Enaudeau, Gaëlle Bernard and Olivier Dekens) in a precise manner, by reading with acuity and depth the texts in question (Enaudeau *et al.*, 2008: 345–64, 153–67 and 135–51; Dekens, 2002). I will content myself here with a rapid and synthetic summary that seems to me to draw up the balance sheet of the discussion they have undertaken.

Essentially, the difficulty in Lyotard is the following.

On the one hand, the anti-totalitarian principle, the principle of expecting or of welcoming of a particular set of circumstances, lays claim to an horizon of justice not subordinate to theoretical or economic genres. For this reason, we 'must' activate the transcendence of what is 'just' against the claim to reabsorb it within the true or the efficient, which are the two forms of ontological or immanent criteria. This leads to a reliance on Kant and Levinas, who are brought into direct contact in Lyotard's important article 'Levinas' logic' (Lyotard, 1989: 275–313). But this transcendence of the 'just' is a transcendence of morality: the just as practical reason, the faculty of pure maxims (Kant), or as the expression of subjectivation in response to the call of the other (Levinas),[2] are not first an account of a political justice, nor even justice in the juridical sense, but a sense of justice which is included in every form of morality, when it intervenes at a personal and informal level.

On the other hand, transcendence in both its Kantian and Levinasian forms carries at least the risk of being 'hegemonic' and thus faulty with respect to the anti-totalitarian principle (on which moral transcendence is meant to be based).

The existence of this risk is, in Lyotard's view, incontestable in the Kantian case, due to the reference to universalisation included in the categorical imperative. Lyotard also detects it in Levinas, though in a more uncertain and less categorical way, whether this be because the Levinasian lesson concerns an *ethical truth* which is potentially hegemonic with respect to truth more generally, or because this ethical truth could be interpreted as the promotion of a particular genre – the prescriptive – over all others.

Ultimately, Lyotard never manages to escape from this difficulty, as the book of conversations with Jean-Loup Thébaud no doubt reveals most clearly (Lyotard and Thébaud, 1985). Although he explicitly formulates the desire to consider the prescriptive genre on the same level as all the others, he can only state the anti-totalitarian principle in this genre and, furthermore, he comes to determine its content in terms of the prescriptive genre: every pre-emption of phrasing which would prevent the recurrence of the prescriptive regime or genre is forbidden. Politics would basically be the guardian of the prescriptive.

To this it would also be necessary to add that the Levinasian description of the priority of the ethical welcome to every thematic rendering of what is welcomed is the model according to which Lyotard conceives the welcome of a particular present set of circumstances: the content of the *Here I am!* in Levinas involves welcoming without predetermining or prejudging, and this idea is what is ultimately at stake in the 'respect for the particularity of circumstances' in Lyotard. For these reasons, it seems to me difficult to deny that Lyotard's thought takes place 'under Levinasian conditions'. And yet this does not mean that he does not restlessly search for a way to resituate the prescriptive regime and genre among a peaceful and heterogeneous juxtaposition of regimes and genres, within which no eminence is tolerated – whence the impossibility of resolving the difficulty, a difficulty which is perhaps also a great discovery: Lyotard would have made explicit a constitutive paradox of contemporary societies, their politics and their problem with values.

One final word on Axel Honneth's reaction to the thought of the *differend*. Surprisingly, he sees it as leading, despite itself, to something like a return to Habermas. Lyotard's 'justice of language', on Honneth's account, must be expressed as a justice between individuals, and must in the end coincide with the search for a respect of particular individuals, in dialogue and discussion, making possible the equal participation of all. For Honneth, the Lyotardian *differend* must in the final analysis be converted into a litigation, giving rise to a ruling which would necessarily correspond to a shared understanding, made possible by the newly introduced idiom.

In a sense this is correct, and such a reading is in any case preferable to the – numerous – readings that understand Lyotard's book as an apology for conflict. But such a regulatory horizon is not the politico-moral *telos* advanced by Lyotard. His problem concerns the potential obliteration of what is possible by an economy of phrases which asserts itself as the ultimate tribunal. The solution is the attention to a transcendent guardianship of the possible. It is not therefore a question of using language so as to succeed in treating people equally, but of rediscovering in language the capacity for every possibility.

Honneth's reading reflects in this case an immanentist bias. He can only grasp the thought of the *differend* in terms of a general economy in which it is included, and which extends as far as the concrete rules of human relations. For Honneth, as a result, the thought of the *differend* amounts to an accent put on the conditions of understanding and recognition required for dialogue, in a Habermasian-style procedural politics. But for Lyotard, what humans suffer from, and what creates problems in human history, is the misrecognition or constriction of the possibilities of language. The remedy is thus above all, or most profoundly, another mode of inhabiting language and its universes, an alternative mode which can only be understood and sketched out with reference to a transcendence: our freedom from alienation implies, in any case, that we cease to subordinate our experiences of regimes and phrase genres to finalising or totalising economies.[3]

Features of Levinasian politics

It remains to examine our problematic in Emmanuel Levinas. To formulate our questions afresh: is politics, and in particular the path towards a good politics, even the best politics, understood in a naturalist fashion by Levinas? Does Levinas conceive of politics as a part of a trans-situational search for justice, and does he do so in the name of morality, sanctioning the recognised prevalence of the moral with respect to the political?

To answer these questions, it is necessary to recall first of all the manner in which Levinas sets out the triad of terms: *morality, politics* and *justice*. A central teaching of his philosophy is that justice is not morality. In fact, for Levinas, justice consists in the balancing of particular duties of self-sacrifice, in the rational calculation of an equilibrium between those particular ethical duties owed by each person, these being *de jure* infinite. Justice welcomes and takes on the real evaluation of situations, that is, ontology: it is in justice that language, logic, science and the thematic rendering of what is welcomed take on meaning. The moral domain is the experience of an Other as infinite obligation, a scheme in which the Other is equivalent to a call, claim, a demand for aid: the moral field is determined in a phenomenological manner by the description of what Levinas calls the *ethical relation*. The practice and study of justice presupposes the departure from this space, and the transgression of this experience or call in their strict sense. And yet, it is morality which commands justice, since the phenomenologico-narrative codicil of the *third* can be understood as follows. Insofar as my responsibility extends to infinity, and is always equivalent to responsibility for my responsibility, my *Here I am!* towards the Other which is interpreted according to a deafness with respect to the third – a second Other – and so on, in such a way that a balancing act is required following the ethical moment itself (Salanskis, 2006: 57–8).

As a consequence, the classical Marxist complaint (against a concept of politics exclusively formulated in terms of justice, which puts a moralising horizon back into politics) cannot apply to the Levinasian point of view. Although politics is conceived in terms of justice, it is this which allows it to distance itself from pure morality rather than pledge allegiance to it.

How, though, is the relation between justice and politics regulated, in Levinas? In two ways, it seems to me.

On the one hand – and this is the manner which is most likely to appeal to the French '*frisson*', to the *amour fou* for politics which reigned in our intellectual world throughout the twentieth century – Levinas thinks that politics is capable of providing a moral correction to justice. Justice, embodied in the universal rules which it enacts, is never entirely just. It always risks forgetting 'the tears of the Other', and thus political intervention could correspond to a necessary moral insurrection, one which recalls that every attempt to codify and regulate justice is only valid to the extent that it is rooted in the movement of self-sacrifice. It can even seem, on the face of it, as though Levinas justifies, in the present case, the inveterate 'illegalism' of political radicals (except that protesting against the immorality of the law and transgressing the law are not the same). In truth, in the deliberative politics of democracy (which understands social law as subject to indefinite revision through political debate), Levinas recognises a form suitable for this moral critique of justice by politics as he conceives it: on his account, the correction of the residual and inevitable immorality of laws should not take place through transgression and violence.

On the other hand, and although I am, perhaps, advancing claims which are more implied than explicitly formulated by Levinas, everything leads us to understand that political combat is a figure *par excellence* of the 'war of being' described at the beginning of *Totality and infinity* (Levinas, 2003: 21–7). This ontological war is the war of every being against every other, a war waged in view of perseverance or expansion (in view of harnessing space and time in one's favour). This 'tendency' which is read in being if we examine its procedure in an immanent manner, without reference to an horizon of transcendent justice, is the tendency of the *conatus essendi*: everything occurs as if being spontaneously and silently makes itself a value for everything which is, such that being already means aspiring to be more, spatially or temporally. What can be said at the level of the natural sciences, from physics to biology – somewhat like the way René Thom describes the *logos* of each thing as a dynamic regulation through which its form, or signature, is maintained and stabilised (Thom, 1974: 108), or again at the level of the zoological thought of species and their evolution in a

Darwinian fashion – resonates, in this way, with a certain vision of politics and its combat. When politics is conceived as the art of power, or when political struggle is conceived as the struggle for power, politics can then appear as the pure and simple prolongation of ontological war at the cultural, social, or human level. From this point of view, on the other hand, justice is the moderator and regulator of this politics of the self or of the *conatus essendi* which rages on, in such a way that this vision is as distasteful to the French sensibility invoked a moment ago as the previous one is appealing.

By presenting such a diptych of perspectives, we have also laid the foundations for a response to the question of Levinas' position with respect to political naturalism. Levinas quite clearly excludes the possibility that a good politics can be naturalist, in the sense that naturalism and ontology are one and the same. Naturalism thus always involves the methodological loss of the criterion of the good, a criterion which basically refers to the horizon of what is otherwise than being.[4] From this point of view, there is no doubt that the Honnethian idea of a struggle for recognition which would be deduced from anthropological nature, and which would be, at the same time, the lever for the improvement of justice, is strictly unacceptable. This facet of Honneth's position, elaborated, it is true, in a novel language and style, is what affiliates it with an Hegelian – Marxist naturalism, thereby making his philosophy incompatible with Levinas' thought.

Before moving on, allow me to note two other senses in which Levinas expresses his anti-naturalism: through his always explicit affirmation of the tribunal of history, and his demand for a thought of justice disengaged from history.

The first point is advanced in *Totality and infinity* (2003) and consists in the assertion that no power is accorded to historical process in its accumulated passing to expunge, and allow for the exoneration of, crimes committed against the Other within the historical drama. These crimes are and remain such that a statute of limitations (which specifies a maximum time after an event that legal proceedings based on that event may be initiated) cannot be applied. The time during which humanity may recognise, judge and, as far as possible, compensate for these crimes is unlimited. This must be so because, if it is not, then our conception of crime would cease to be fundamentally ethical, indexed to the trans-ontological and therefore to the trans-historical dimension of the 'for the Other'.

The second case, the idea that justice is in principle disengaged from history, is elaborated from the same perspective. Marxism, in the name of its naturalism and movement-ism, gave too much credence to the idea that – given that the wrongs done to human beings were collective and historical – both corrective struggle against such wrongs, and the very evaluation of this wrong, must gain a foothold in history. And yet, if such a point of view is adopted, then we are led to identify wrongs in relation to what aims to be tolerated, rejected, or desired in the human world: utopian hope or critical condemnation will only be considered valid insofar as it confirms an expectation or attests to a combat. Now, judging in this way amounts to succumbing to the fact of history, and to abandoning all 'eschatological' reference to right which, once again, is the exact opposite of what we are taught by ethical emotion.

As at the close of the discussion of Lyotard, we will here invoke in passing Honneth's evaluation of Levinas. I will recall three aspects that, in my view, are important.

The first, anecdotal in relation to the current approach, is that Honneth presents Levinas' ideas in the shadow of Derrida's: he comes to speak of the encounter with the face in order to understand Derrida's 'incalculable justice'. His reading is, to my mind, affected by this: it is harder for him to enter into the atmosphere which characterises Levinas' work, because he understands Levinas by way of Derrida. I note in passing, moreover, that he understands the philosophy and politics of the later Derrida as more continuous with the Levinasian 'for the Other' than it merits (at least to my mind).

The second aspect is that Honneth, without hesitation or ambiguity, notices that the entirety of politics and justice for Levinas is subordinated to the demands of the 'for the Other', which is not concealed by the simple reference to the sphere of a rationally conceived subjective dignity and the idea of 'equal treatment'. Honneth recognises that Levinas provides a principle that does not allow itself to be reduced to the universalisation of an egalitarian right, to a Kantian – Habermasian principle, as Honneth portrays it.

The third aspect is that Honneth, as he does with Lyotard, reduces the possible significance of such a principle to the level of the prerequisite conditions for dialogue among free individuals about laws. He understands Levinas' discourse to assert that a subject can only take part in debate if it is already sufficiently at home with itself and assured of itself, thanks to an unconditional love from which he receives his entire subjective capacity. The infinite demand for aid which singles me out in the face thus becomes for Honneth the need for unconditional love, which characterises every ego. Without the prerequisite satisfaction of this need, the ego could not play a part in the universalist game of the law. Nonetheless, this game prevails over love and love's range as soon as the subject is sufficiently redeemed.

In light of this third aspect, one cannot help but be struck by the radicality of Honneth's rejection of the Levinasian perspective. On the one hand, the demand for aid is seen from the point of view of already assisted ego, and not from the point of view of the person from whom the aid is being demanded: the entire effort to extricate the other as face is annulled. Assistance, reconceived as unconditional love, is no longer a requirement to help the Other which falls upon me, but rather the primitive need of the subject which makes possible the path to the good life. On the other hand, the morality of assistance is downgraded in relation to a normativity shared in the discussion of law according to the criterion of equal judgement, a sharing which normativity functions to introduce. In Levinasian terms, it is as if the primordial ethical signification announced in the dual scheme were rendered subservient and secondary in relation to the universalist stakes of justice. Honneth only understands the Levinasian message, once again, from an immanentist viewpoint of an economy of the world, whether at the psychological level – in asserting the foundational sub-structure of love – or at the social level – in privileging intersubjectivity as constitutive.

Conclusion

That said, the goal of this chapter was to evaluate our three authors from the point of view established at the outset, and not to respond to Honneth's evaluations of Lyotard and Levinas. With this in mind, a few points can be made in a synthetic fashion.

First of all, the attempts made by Honneth and Lyotard – the theory of recognition in the first case and the philosophy of the *differend* in the second – clearly have a family resemblance, both corresponding to an effort to stray from Marxism while retaining something essential from it, and expressing a similar suspicion with respect to the institutional tribunals of universal justice.

Secondly, what opposes them in this similitude appears to be clearly signalled by their use of Hegel and Levinas. Honneth maintains a link with the Hegelian idea of history, while Lyotard breaks with it. Lyotard only unites with the perspective of a politics of justice by taking up the Levinasian thought of ethics in his work, a thought which is held at arm's length by Honneth, while asserting certain themes that are consonant with it. Honneth and Lyotard would therefore be located between Hegel and Levinas, if in two different ways.

Such an attempt to situate these authors in relation to the common question of justice and naturalism interests me more than simply marking the polemical gap between Honneth and 'the French', at work in Honneth's interpretations of them. That said, as I hope to have shown, this gap remains relevant to the question of Honneth's position on our common problem.

Notes

* Translated by Jon Roffe. Thanks go to Ashley Woodward for his assistance with the translation of Lyotard's vocabulary.

1 Translator's note: The author is here making reference to Lyotard's *Dérive à partir de Marx et Freud* (1991c), partially translated as *Driftworks*. The title of this work, and the passage above, remains ambiguous, since Lyotard intends the drifting in question as both 'away from' and 'with', in keeping with the ambiguity of *dériver à partir*.

2 Translator's note: Following standard practice in Levinas translation, *autre* is translated as other and *autrui* as Other.
3 It might also be noted that, in this regard, Honneth's review neglects to distinguish between *phrase regimes* and *genres*. As a result, his version of the 'suffering of phrases' is not sufficiently related to the logical articulation of language, and too strictly related to its cultural or political aspects. Honneth sees this 'suffering' only as the destiny of the phrases expressed in a kind of minoritarian language.
4 Translator's note: The author is here referring to the title of Levinas' second major work, *Otherwise than being: or beyond essence* (1998).

13

Justice-to-come in the work of Axel Honneth and Nancy Fraser

Miriam Bankovsky

IN this chapter, I would like to draw on the interpretations of deconstruction offered by the recognition theorists Nancy Fraser and Axel Honneth to develop my own account of the relevance of deconstruction for a political theory of justice. Fraser and Honneth present novel accounts which question the view, popular within the Anglophone and German worlds, that deconstruction has little to offer the tradition of political theory. However, on a closer inspection of their interpretations, it becomes apparent that deconstruction is used and applied by Fraser and Honneth in a rather instrumental manner, no longer serving the more radical critical role which I believe Derrida intends it to play when he reflects on the inability of reciprocal norms of interaction to be reconciled with the specific ethical obligations which an individual has with respect to another person. Such reflections, in my view, support an account of the political which acknowledges the productivity of the tension between the idea of achieving reciprocal norms, on the one hand, and the idea of rendering to another person his or her due, on the other.

In developing my account of deconstruction's political relevance, I will proceed as follows. I will first explain the popular view of deconstruction, identifying the main reasons for Habermas' rejection of deconstruction in the 1980s, a view that tends to be uncritically inherited by mainstream political philosophy. I will then contrast this rejection with Fraser's and Honneth's novel interpretation of deconstruction as a principle of recognition, presented within Fraser's framework of justice as a principle of radical equality and, conversely, within Honneth's framework of authentic identity as a principle of unilateral care. I will then attempt to revive what I see as the critical dimension of deconstruction, suggesting, against Fraser and Honneth, that when deconstruction is identified with a principle of recognition, it no longer plays the critical role Derrida hoped it would fulfil. Deconstruction emphasises the inevitable failure of determined forms of justice to properly negotiate the general need for impartiality in the assessment of claims with the specific obligation to render to an individual his or her due. This failure to properly unite the general with the specific is not to be regretted, but rather should be seen as productive: it makes possible the essential transformability and perfectibility of the actual, without which the project of justice would have no sense. I finally reflect on the ways in which this deconstructive insight is implicitly assumed by the theories of justice and authentic identity which Fraser and Honneth defend, and I will encourage both to consider the pragmatic implications of the inevitable failure of their respective theories.

Habermas' early rejection of deconstruction

The prevalent view in the Anglophone and German traditions of political philosophy is that deconstruction has little to offer. This view is clearly expressed in Habermas' early 1980s critique of French philosophy presented in *The philosophical discourse of modernity* (1990a: 184–210). Here Habermas argues that Derrida reduces the linguistic function to power, persuasion and rhetoric, denying the ability of subjects to freely use reason to convince each other while, in the process, respecting each other's autonomy. For Habermas, Derrida neglects language's capacity to carry the weight of validity claims oriented toward mutual understanding (1990a: 205).

In a first step, Habermas professes his support for Adorno's faith in reason's capacity to perform its own critique. With Adorno, Habermas thinks that the self-critique of reason, that is, the critique of reason by rational argument, becomes caught in performative contradiction, since the critique is undertaken with reason's own tools. Reason's self-critique thereby reconfirms its own validity. Next, Habermas claims that Derrida does not share Adorno's or his own faith in reason's ability to perform its self-critique. Recognising that he cannot critique reason with its own tools without engaging in performative contradiction, Derrida chooses an evasive strategy, refusing to assess texts via discursive argumentation and instead assessing them aesthetically (1990a: 188). Deconstruction thereby avoids performative contradiction by levelling the distinction between philosophical argument and literary rhetoric, assessing philosophy in terms of its capacity to rhetorically persuade rather than rationally convince. Of course, for Habermas, this equates to a negative strategy, which 'robs' philosophy of its productivity, relieving it 'of the duty of solving problems' (1990a: 210). Defining moral personhood in terms of the capacity to engage in consensually oriented discourse or argumentation, Habermas concludes that Derrida, in denying the very possibility of rational consensus, is unable to contribute anything useful to the debate.

We see similar views expressed by Kantian liberals including the early Nancy Fraser (1984; 1991–92), Thomas McCarthy (1991: 97–120), Seyla Benhabib

(2006: 128–56) and Amy Gutmann (1994: 3–24) among others who, following in Habermas' footsteps, reject deconstruction for denying itself the means to enter into rational argumentation.

The story changes, however, with the work of Axel Honneth and the recent contributions of Nancy Fraser. While both thinkers share much with Habermas' deliberative framework, this does not prevent them from discovering, in deconstruction, resources to deepen their theories. It is to a consideration of these two respective interpretations that I now turn.

Deconstruction, recognition and justice

Fraser: deconstruction as a radical principle of equality

Fraser's relation to deconstruction can be divided into two stages. In her early period, she in fact sides with the popular view, seeing in deconstruction a withdrawal from the political (Fraser, 1984: 127–54; 1991–92: 1325–31). However, in a second stage, she attempts to counter this apparent withdrawal by 'politicising deconstruction', identifying what she sees as deconstruction's main political ideal, namely, 'the rough social equality' of all differences, that is, the equal value of different forms of identity (Fraser, 1997: 30). Fraser then reformulates this radical principle of equality as a practical political strategy which she refers to as 'transformative recognition', a strategy which has a specific role to play within her broader theory of egalitarian justice (Fraser, 1997: 11–40; 2004: 125–48; Fraser and Honneth, 2001: 7–109). I will begin with Fraser's reasons for dismissing deconstruction, and then turn to her politicisation of deconstruction's central idea.

The early Fraser (1991–92) has just one reason for thinking that deconstruction, practised by Derrida, is apolitical. Derrida exercises deconstruction as a quasi-transcendental analysis of the *necessary condition* of all position-taking, exposing this condition as unjustified force. Fraser is concerned that an analysis which exposes *every* position to be conditioned by unjustified force cannot provide the analyst with tools for distinguishing between different political positions themselves. As Fraser puts it, if *every* position is unjustified, then no particular position is more justified than another. Since political theory aims to explain why certain political positions are better than others, deconstruction cannot be of use.

In Fraser's view, Derrida identifies two kinds of force or violence which laws and policies wield and, hence, two different forms of critique. She believes that only the first form of critique is useful, and expresses regret that Derrida himself unfortunately pursues the second. The first kind of force is 'contingent' and 'socio-historical' and its critique is 'political' and 'empirical'.[1] Laws and policies in effect support social, economic and political forces which are often incorrectly posited as external to, or prior, to the laws themselves. Policies, for example, which regulate military service, family-based social-welfare support, and the benefits of tax or inheritance function to produce a social world which values heterosexuality over homosexuality. For Fraser, this first type of force is essentially transformable, and its critique is 'political', taking the form of historical and empirical enquiry. Focusing on the way in which positive laws and policies sustain social, economic and political relations, 'political' critique allows the analyst to identify a range of contingent but systemic processes which culminate in extensive social harms. For homosexuals, harm might include physical or verbal abuse, discrimination in the workplace, economic inequality, reduced life-choices with regard to having children, limited participation in decisions about one's partner and reduced self-esteem. For Fraser, 'political' critique is always useful. It promises to uncover the way in which social harms (including those as diverse as malnutrition, obesity, mental and physical illness, medical neglect, incarceration, environmental toxicity, unemployment, poverty and homelessness) become stratified in society in terms of gender, colour and class. 'Political' critique allows us to identify specific elements of this set of interrelations that we might want to overcome or transform (1991–92: 1328).

It is unfortunate, in Fraser's eyes, that Derrida prefers a second form of critique, which she describes as 'quasi-transcendental'.[2] Quasi-transcendental (or 'deconstructive') critique does not focus on those *transformable* forms of historical violence which positive norms and policies legitimise. Instead, it seeks to expose a type of *non-transformable* or necessary force which structures, *a priori*, the very form of law itself. In her reading of Derrida's 'Force of law' (2002b), Fraser argues that 'deconstructive' critique identifies two contradictory demands that norms, in their determined form, cannot resolve and, in so doing, this critique uncovers 'force' itself as the very condition for the determination of norms. On the one hand, norms must apply to all equally, subjecting everyone to its law; norms must provide the objective standard against which behaviour is judged to be appropriate or inappropriate. On the other hand, norms must render to each person their due, addressing the individual's specific needs and distinct interests. These two demands are contradictory, and cannot be resolved with the one law. Either the norm of action corresponds absolutely to the specificity of an individual's particular case (in which case it does not apply universally to all cases) or the norm corresponds to all cases (in which case it does not apply to the individual's particular needs and interests which make the case unique) (Derrida, 2002b: 248). Under constraints of action, a decision must be made. However, this decision involves a moment of indetermination, which rules out an objective justification for the determined norm. For Fraser, 'deconstructive' analysis is best described as quasi-transcendental: it reveals that every decision whatsoever is *necessarily* characterised by unjustified force insofar as it resolves an *aporia* which remains, in principle, irresolvable.

Consequently, deconstructive analysis is impotent when it comes to politics.

It leaves empirical and transformable forms of violence unchallenged by shifting attention instead to the non-transformable, quasi-transcendental violence of normative determination itself. This, claims Fraser, equates to a *retreat* from the political because it does not allow one to distinguish between the concrete, empirical positions themselves. Derrida 'replace[s] the project of politicising deconstruction with the project of deconstructing the political' which means that 'there is one sort of difference which deconstruction cannot tolerate: namely, difference as dispute, as good, old-fashioned, political fight' (Fraser, 1984: 142). For Fraser, deconstruction must be replaced by the first form of critique, namely, 'political' analysis which identifies social harms in need of transformation.

Interestingly, however, in the development of her later egalitarian theory of justice, Fraser returns to deconstruction to help her think through empirical strategies for correcting social harms. Fraser now attempts to express, in principle form, the practical import of its quasi-transcendental analysis. Deconstruction's main practical idea, states Fraser, is that all differences are of equal value. Different forms of identity being equally ungrounded, deconstruction commits to 'the rough social equality ... [of] constructions of identity and difference' (Fraser, 1997: 30). This politicised principle of deconstruction now exposes, as unjust, the system of value which leads to systematic subordination of the status of certain identities. According to its principle, deconstruction states that institutionalised harm exists when different identities are no longer granted equal status. For Fraser, deconstruction equates to 'transformative recognition'. By 'recognition', she refers to an ideal in which all identities are satisfied with the value that all other identities accord them. 'Transformative' refers to the strategy by means of which misrecognition is remedied. 'Transformative recognition' seeks to remedy the very evaluative structure responsible for the denigration of subordinate groups, changing everyone's sense of self, with a view to achieving mutually recognised intersubjective relations (Fraser and Honneth, 2001: 75). As 'transformative recognition', deconstruction supports a 'utopian cultural ideal of fluid, shifting differences (Fraser and Honneth, 2001: 106).

What does this strategy of transformative recognition entail? Fraser throws light on the concept with her example of the French political decision to prevent Muslim girls from wearing headscarves in public schools, comparing 'transformative recognition' to its less preferable alternative 'affirmative recognition' (Fraser and Honneth, 2001: 41–2, 81–2 and 226). 'Affirmative recognition' (or multiculturalism) seeks to allow minorities to participate in public education without requiring their assimilation to dominant norms. Affirmative recognition would produce legislation which simply affirms and includes those aspects of group identity which the group itself sees as essential. Responding to concerns that the *foulard* marks the subordination of women in Muslim communities, the 'multicultural' position notes that the scarf's meaning is highly contested in French Muslim communities and that permitting, rather than banning, the scarf is closer to the ideal of mutually recognised intersubjective relations. In contrast, a strategy of 'transformative recognition' would intervene in both dominant and minority cultures alike, seeking, over a longer term, to not only refashion French national values of equality, liberty and secular fraternity to make them more suited to their multireligious society, but would also seek to reconstruct orthodox Muslim values to suit a liberal-pluralist and gender-egalitarian regime. Over time, 'transformative recognition' (committed to the equality of differences) would remedy the status subordination of Muslim women, both within French society (by allowing symbols of religious difference within the public sphere), and within their own Muslim communities (by preventing the veil from also being a marker of sexual oppression). Deconstruction would aim, says Fraser, to identify and transform those deep-rooted values which are responsible for subordination, so as to undermine intolerance in the public sphere while enhancing the liberation of women in their own communities.

Clearly, then, Fraser locates the strategy of transformative recognition within the framework of a theory of equality. Deconstruction seeks to restore equality in the evaluation of different system components. Committed to the idea of 'parity of participation' in social life, deconstruction encourages those system manipulations which are needed to allow different identities to participate, as equals, in the public sphere.

To summarise this rather detailed explanation of Fraser's ambiguous relation to deconstruction, we can say the following. Regarding its political nature, deconstruction, as exercised by Derrida, is not immediately political because, by revealing all positions to be unjustified, it cannot distinguish between positions themselves. However, once reformulated as a political commitment, deconstruction sits comfortably within an egalitarian framework of justice because it defends the equal value of social differences (all differences being equally unjustified). Deconstruction thus equates to a radically egalitarian principle, which attempts to achieve equality among differences by supporting deep changes to the way in which identities value each other.

Honneth: deconstruction as a principle of unilateral care
Unlike the later Fraser, Honneth does not think that deconstruction's utility lies in its commitment to equality. On the contrary, deconstruction describes an opposite obligation, namely, the obligation to treat people *unequally* (Honneth, Chapter 2 of this volume). As dependent individuals, we have needs that must be cared for, and this means we may need political principles that respond to the specific needs of the indigent, thereby treating people unequally.

Rejecting Fraser's first (and negative) appraisal of deconstruction as apolitical, Honneth argues that deconstruction does, in fact, defend 'a normative conception', 'the positive outlines of an ethic' (1995c: 307). 'Instead of merely negatively explicating the indeterminacy of moral rules' (Honneth, 1995c: 307) in the mode of Fraser's first interpretation, deconstruction equates to a phenomenology of moral experience, reflected in relations of friendship and love (Honneth, 1995c: 308; Derrida, 1997b). This ethic, suggests Honneth, is best expressed as a notion of care or benevolence, 'an affective openness to the particularity of the other' (1995c: 307) by virtue of which we experience the weight of a responsibility to address the needs of the other person, without first considering whether the response is consistent with equality or the principle of equal treatment (1995c: 309).

In Honneth's view (and in contrast to Fraser's later interpretation), deconstructive care finds itself in *tension* with the principle of equality. Concerned with the intersubjective conditions for the realisation of healthy identity, deconstruction reminds us that an egalitarian framework does not acknowledge the different ways in which others can impact upon our lives, impeding or supporting our practical relations-to-self. Habermas' and Fraser's egalitarian frame may well acknowledge that being recognised as an equal on a par with others is an important part of self-development because it allows us to respect ourselves as the bearers of moral claims. However, for Honneth, the egalitarian frame ascribes insufficient importance to other intersubjective relations which also condition the development of 'authentic identity'. In particular, the egalitarian frame does not recognise the moral weight of those particular obligations arising from specific relations of interdependency. As individuals, we depend on loved ones to recognise our particular needs, and to offer sympathy, affection and love, allowing us to develop confidence in our perceptions of our own needs. Deconstruction supplements the egalitarian framework which unfortunately ignores the important place of asymmetrical relations of care, compassion and benevolence in the development of healthy individuals (Honneth, 1995c: 316).

Nor can it be said that Habermas' idea of 'solidarity' is equivalent to the deconstructive principle of unilateral care (see Habermas, 1990b: 224–51). For Habermas, solidarity describes the concern for the 'welfare of one's fellow man' according to which participants in consensually oriented argumentation recognise each other not only as equal persons but also as unique individuals, thereby incorporating an affective concern for the existential fate of other human beings into their shared life-world. However, in this relation of solidarity, everyone is recognised as a unique individual to the *same* degree, and this excludes the kind of privilege that the principle of unilateral care ascribes to one's fellow (Honneth, 1995c: 317). For Honneth, where, in Habermasian solidarity, subjects reciprocally attend to the welfare of the other, with whom they share the communicative form of human life, deconstructive justice draws attention to the irreducibility of care to the standpoint of equality (Honneth, 1995c: 316–17).

In direct contrast to Fraser, then, Honneth claims to take, from deconstruction, the idea that ethical and political principles *cannot* be reduced to a framework of equal treatment. Self-realisation, and not equality with others, is the most important ideal, and its achievement requires not merely norms which situate participants equally with respect to each other but also a deconstructive principle which demands that principles also respond to the needs of dependent individuals in an *unequal* manner.

Consequently, Honneth argues that the deconstructive principle of care plays a central role within a theory of justice which includes *plural* principles. Equality, deconstructive care and a third principle of merit together contribute to the development of practical relations-to-self which allow freedom to be realised. Confidence in the perception of one's needs is supported by the deconstructive, caring response of loved ones; respect for myself as an equal member of society is reinforced by the equal rights which this society affords me; and self-esteem, or the ability to value my contributions to social life, is supported by the rewards I receive when I behave in socially valuable ways (Honneth, 1995a: 172).

Derrida on justice: correcting Fraser's and Honneth's interpretations

The interpretations offered by Fraser and Honneth offer positive and practical alternatives to the popular rejection of deconstruction, a breath of fresh air for those who think that deconstruction *can* produce effects in political life. However, it must be said that neither appears to coincide with the way in which Derrida himself presents deconstruction's relation to justice. Both appear to make instrumental use of deconstruction, so as to further their own respective frameworks. In my view, this instrumental use of deconstruction threatens to overshadow the critical dimension of deconstruction.

This instrumental use of deconstruction is, in fact, explicitly affirmed by Honneth and Fraser alike. Fraser acknowledges that her account is 'unorthodox, as it denotes a specific institutional remedy for misrecognition' (Fraser and Honneth, 2001: 106), thereby departing from Derrida's striking claim that deconstruction *is* justice (2001: 75). Honneth also concedes that his use of Derrida is 'more or less instrumental' (Honneth, Chapter 2 of this volume) and that Derrida himself would not agree that deconstruction can be reduced to a principle of care. Less concerned with deconstruction's 'deeper mission', Honneth admits to taking from Derrida what is most useful for his own work, namely, a contribution to understanding the intersubjective conditions for the development of authentic identity. Both Fraser and Honneth believe that they need to change deconstruction in order to render it productive. What is it that they need to change? And is deconstruction really so unproductive in its original form?

Fraser and Honneth appear to identify deconstruction with only one of the two demands which emerge from Fraser's earlier reading of Derrida's 'Force of law' (2002b). In this text, Derrida argues that justice is not simply concerned with the principle of equality, that is, with norms or laws that apply to all equally. Justice also concerns rendering to each individual person his or her due in a manner which responds to the specificity and particularity of the individual, and to his or her particular needs and interests. Fraser reduces the concern for particularity to a framework of equality, effectively prioritising the demand to treat all equally over the demand to respond to the particular needs of dependent individuals.

In my view, Honneth also privileges the principle of equal treatment over the obligation to render to each individual their due. I fully realise that readers might find my claim surprising, given the findings of the previous section of this chapter, which demonstrated that Honneth equates deconstruction with a principle of care, a supplement to the principle of equal treatment. However, although it might initially appear that Honneth includes a principle of unequal treatment, that is, the obligation to respond to the particular needs of dependent individuals, on closer inspection we notice that he uses the deconstructive principle of unequal treatment to deepen a symmetrical (and egalitarian) account of moral persons, which establishes a quasi-universal account of 'authentic needs'. In spite of an initial attentiveness to the specificity of the other which the principle of care professes to support, Honneth's instrumental use of deconstruction terminates in an account of quasi-universal needs, which includes the need for forms of recognition which facilitate self-respect, self-confidence and self-esteem. In developing self-respect, all persons need to be recognised as the (Habermasian) moral equal of others; in developing self-confidence, all persons require the 'deconstructive' sympathy and affection of significant others; in developing self-esteem, all persons need to validate their worth in the eyes of their peers, who share their system of values. In this sense, the radicality of the 'deconstructive' idea of rendering to each individual person his or her due is considerably softened by its accommodation within a framework which once again situates moral persons symmetrically, defining them in terms of quasi-universal intersubjective needs which all share equally.

This leads me to conclude that both Fraser and Honneth believe that they need to privilege the principle of equal treatment over that of unequal treatment in order to find something productive in deconstruction. Consequently, neither thinker sufficiently appreciates the fact that deconstruction commits to both principles. Derrida makes the claim that deconstruction *is* justice precisely because it emphasises the productive tension between the demand to treat all individuals equally, on the one hand, while also attempting to respond to the particular needs of the other person, on the other.

I would now like to consider whether deconstruction really is so unproductive in its original form, that is, when the idea of responding to the particularity of the other person is *not* reduced to a framework of equality. As I just mentioned, Derrida's view is that what makes deconstruction somehow equivalent to justice itself is its commitment to maintain the tension between the idea of impartiality among all and the idea of responsibility for the particular person. Deconstruction, like justice, cannot be given a non-revisable, determined content in the form of a theory, because the latter cannot fully reconcile two conflicting demands in one determined form. The unique contribution which Derrida promises to bring to the debate is the idea that by giving a positive content to the resolution of these requirements, a theory of justice inevitably fails to do justice to either one of its demands. In its determined form, justice always fails in its task.

This means that an important part of any theory of justice or even of 'authentic identity' is the acknowledgement of the inevitable failure of theory to reconcile the aforementioned conflicting demands. This acknowledgement, in my view, should then lead to theory's subsequent commitment to the attempt to maintain a critical perspective on its own determined form, its history and its future. The idea that justice is *not* possible in a determined form is an essential element of any critical theory about justice's possibility, in the sense that a critical theory of justice must be attentive to its inevitable failures (see also Thomassen, 2007). Deconstruction allows us to see that the failure to fully determine justice's content is not regrettable, but rather the very condition for critique itself; the very condition for the ongoing attempt, by theory, to provide the tools to respond to demands for justice. Deconstruction, in this sense, allows us to understand the continual development of theories of justice as part of our finite condition, part of our way of engaging with inevitable theoretical and practical failure. This is why, as Derrida would put it, the pursuit of justice requires constant vigilance, the continual attempt to produce a better negotiation, responding to the failures of our theories and to the effects of their application.

By reducing deconstruction to a framework of equality (Fraser, by explicitly identifying deconstruction with a radical principle of equality; Honneth, by using deconstruction to develop a symmetrical concept of moral personhood, characterised by a quasi-universal account of human needs) both Fraser and Honneth overlook the very deconstructive aspect which makes theory *critical*, namely, the impossibility of determining justice's content in a manner which satisfies both of its demands.

A deconstructive and critical perspective

I will now explore what a deconstructive and critical perspective means for a theory of justice or a theory of 'authentic identity', like that of Fraser or Honneth. It would mean not simply working to construct an account of justice

Justice-to-come

or identity, but also engaging with the impossibility of the task. But what exactly does this mean?

In my view, it means, on the one hand, that the determination of the content of justice or of 'authentic identity' always remains a *possible project*, a possible future horizon, and this requires working toward achieving it. As the later John Rawls puts it, following the intent of Kant's practical ideas, we must assume that a reasonably just political society is *possible* because it cannot even be approached without this assumption (Rawls, 1996: 172, lxii). On the other hand, however, the deconstructive perspective reminds us that were justice to be exhausted by the various attempts to determine it, then the concept itself would lose its critical function, no longer serving as a creative source for reflection on the content of the idea of a public standpoint which creates justice between individuals. In this sense, deconstruction helps us to see why justice itself remains (and will always remain) a *project*. The idea that, as a *possible project*, justice is not possible in the present, tends to be either overlooked by political philosophers or recognised with regret at the end of a life-time of work. I am thinking, in particular, of both Rawls and Habermas, who both come to recognise, with some regret, the impossibility of determining the content of justice or of achieving rational consensus in the present (Rawls, 1996: liii, 398, 399, 401–2, 428, 429; Rawls, 2001: 86; Habermas, 1990c: 141; Habermas, 1996: 1518; Habermas, 2003b: 102; see also Thomassen, 2007; and Bankovsky, forthcoming).

The first point I would like to make, in this final section, is that both Fraser and Honneth implicitly concede that their theories of justice cannot provide absolute criteria for the negotiation of the requirements both to be impartial and to ensure that principles are sufficiently partial. Without realising it explicitly, both Fraser and Honneth incorporate a deconstructive concept of responsibility in which the negotiation of principles takes place without absolute criteria, and this leads both theorists to make use of a concept of 'progress'.

The second point concerns the pragmatic implications of 'responsibility'. The implication is that we must continually construct and reconstruct the content of justice and of 'authentic identity' in relation to changing problems. One can claim nothing more than that the theory offers a *better* negotiation of justice's demands, affirming that further revisions will be needed so as to respond to inevitable system failure. I will now try to explain each of these points.

Negotiating without criteria, and the idea of progress

Honneth's theory is premised on the *possibility* of instituting mutual recognition relations, in which we happily recognise ourselves in ways that others also recognise us. However, Honneth's theory also implicitly includes the deconstructive idea that mutual recognition relations are *impossible*. Again, this is not a failing on Honneth's part, but rather expresses something about critical theory itself. In Honneth's theory, there are at least two ways in which justice presents itself as both possible and impossible.

The first concerns the inability to provide criteria for deciding between conflicting claims raised in relation to the three different spheres. Honneth does not provide clear criteria for determining which of the needs (for legal recognition, civil recognition, or affective recognition) should take priority. It is unclear on what basis a decision is to be made when an appeal to recognise the particular value of one's contribution to civil society conflicts with either a claim to equal treatment (raised in the legal sphere) or with a claim to recognise one's individual needs (the affective sphere). Returning to the example of France's decision to ban the veil in public schools will throw light on this difficulty. Within the sphere of civil society, the veil might well have value within a young girl's Muslim community (the sphere of civil life), a value which grants her a sense of self-esteem. However, the veil might also be experienced by young Muslim girls as a marker of a subordinate position in their Muslim community, a form of recognition which produces a lack of self-esteem, and on whose basis a demand for recognition could be made. Within the public sphere, the public school, French law requires that the veil be removed, so that the *same* laws apply to all, reportedly allowing school attendees to access a sense of self-respect, recognising themselves through the eyes of their peers as an equal member of society. Finally, within the affective sphere, a young Muslim woman might express the need to decide, for herself, whether or not she wishes to wear the veil, so that she can control the way in which she belongs to the wider French society. To develop self-confidence in one's ability to perceive one's needs, her will should be recognised by family, civil associations and other members of society, so that she can recognise herself in the eyes of others. At work, here, are at least three or more different claims: 'Allow me to wear the veil, it is an important part of belonging to my community' (sphere of civil society); 'Protect me from subordination within my community' (sphere of civil society and/or legal relations); 'Apply the same laws to all' (sphere of legal relations); and 'Recognise my own need to choose for myself' (affective sphere). It is unclear which principle or principles should take priority here. As Fraser puts it, Honneth's account 'lacks sufficient determinacy to adjudicate conflicting claims' (Fraser and Honneth, 2001: 225). When needs expressed in the affective sphere contradict the values of the civil sphere which, in turn rest uncomfortably with the laws of the legal sphere, Honneth's account cannot tell us which demand should take priority. With regard to equal respect, Fraser states that Honneth has no criteria to help him decide whether the law should manifest formal equality and 'facial neutrality' (as the French system maintains), or whether it entails the more demanding principle of equality of opportunity (as multicultural liberals maintain), or whether it requires an even more stringent, result-oriented standard, like Fraser's principle of participatory parity, which demands deconstructive, transformative recognition so as to achieve deep-rooted changes in the attempt to achieve equality of participation for all in the areas of life implicated by this situation (Fraser and Honneth, 2001: 225).

Honneth's own answer is that indeterminacy is inevitable, and that, when principles enter into conflict with each other, there are no universally acceptable solutions. In the above case, a negotiation best suited to the situation is required. In my view, and although he would not state it in this way, Honneth's solution resembles Derridean responsibility. On the one hand, we must commit to a decision. As Honneth puts it, 'We are responsible for finding a solution because we live under the constraints of action' (Honneth, Chapter 2 of this volume). But, on the other hand, we appear to lack the means for justifying the negotiation between the conflicting demands such that 'This decision is not justifiable in a more general way' (Honneth, Chapter 2 of this volume). For Honneth, it is an existential fact of our lives that in some cases we must simply make a decision, without absolute criteria for negotiating the demands appropriately. In the aforementioned case, Honneth believes that the French government made the *wrong* negotiation. He writes that 'insofar as we cannot know with certainty the reasons which motivate a number of young girls to wear the veil, we should not prohibit wearing it in the public sphere. If the desire to wear the veil can signify a form of oppression, be it familial or communitarian, it can also reflect a logic of emancipation or a desire to affirm one's autonomy' (Honneth, 2006). The important point, for our purposes, is that apart from saying that we must negotiate responsibility for the particular needs of young Muslim women with the demand to treat all persons equally, we cannot fully justify either banning the veil or allowing it to be worn. Moreover, it is highly likely that both decisions will produce unfortunate effects. On the one hand, banning the veil in French public schools may lead some Muslim families to school their girls privately, contributing to their further segregation and isolation. In many cases, it might also prevent a young French Muslim woman from benefiting from the recognition of her own community, central to her sense of self-esteem. It might also make Muslim communities in France less willing to accommodate French liberal values, if these are seen to stigmatise Muslim communities themselves. On the other hand, allowing the veil in public schools may exacerbate the subordination of young Muslim women, both in Muslim communities themselves (where, in some cases, the veil may mark out a subordinate position for young women) and in the French society at large (where, in many cases, French society is intolerant of expressions of Muslim identity in public life). In advance of an analysis of each negotiation's effects, one cannot be sure which negotiation is better. Honneth describes his position on the issue as 'agnostic' because, if I understand him correctly, it is non-partisan and not ideologically aligned, based merely on the empirical prediction that allowing the veil in public schools will produce less psychological and social harm.

Justice-to-come: Honneth, Fraser

In my view, there exists a second 'deconstructive' concession in Honneth's work, although, once again, Honneth would not explicitly agree to my claim. This additional 'deconstructive' concession is that not all values worthy of mutual recognition can, in fact, achieve mutual recognition. In other words, the ideal of mutual recognition *cannot* be fully satisfied within intersubjective relations. On the one hand, we need to commit to the possibility of instituting norms which allow parties to recognise themselves in the eyes of others, thereby supporting their own understanding of themselves and responding to experiences of disrespect, low self-esteem and lack of confidence. The possibility of instituting mutually recognised norms which support a positive sense of self for everyone effectively motivates our efforts to institutionalise practices worthy of recognition. However, the normative principles of each sphere (the obligation to respond to damages in self-confidence, self-respect and self-esteem) contain what Honneth refers to as 'surplus validity', claims which are worthy of mutual recognition but are not yet institutionalised in normative practice (Fraser and Honneth, 2001: 150, 151, 186, 187, 242, 264). It is certainly possible to conceive of a society in which surplus validity is overcome, a society whose norms are in complete accord with the needs, expectations and interests of all parties. This would be an ideal society, one in which everyone could recognise themselves in existing, intersubjective practices of recognition. However, Honneth implies that the existence of surplus validity is *inevitable*. Surplus validity cannot be overcome. He does not explain exactly why this is so, and it is here that we discover our second deconstructive idea: actual social norms will not be able to do justice to everybody's needs, interests, or rights because a tension exists between the claims themselves. Not all claims can be recognised, despite their inherent worthiness (Fraser and Honneth, 2001: 263).

The commitment to a society in which all claims worthy of recognition are successfully instituted leads Honneth to defend a concept of 'progress' in the quality of recognition relations (Fraser and Honneth, 2001: 174, 183–9; and Honneth, 2002: 508–11, 517–18). Faith in progress, faith in the possibility of a fully just society, motivates our efforts to achieve justice albeit in the face of the impossibility of recognising all claims worthy of recognition. Again in a deconstructive spirit, Honneth begins with an immanent diagnosis of specific forms of human suffering since this is the only viable way of trying to explain and respond to those validity claims which have not yet been instituted as valid social norms (Fraser and Honneth, 2001: 242). It is because justice is also impossible that it requires an internal diagnosis of its specific types of failure, and a continued 'expansion' of social norms that responds to this failure (Honneth, 1995a: Chapter 9).

'Impossibility', in the deconstructive sense, also marks Fraser's theory of justice. Fraser also commits to the possibility of determining the content of a critical theory of justice which she believes resolves the need to recognise the particular needs and interests of individuals and groups, on the one hand, with the need to apply impartial norms, on the other. However, in my view, her theory also includes the deconstructive idea that difference and equality cannot be fully resolved and, again, this failure is somehow necessary to the very concept of justice itself.

Fraser believes that she can unite the obligations both to respond to the individual needs of unique individuals and to apply impartial norms using the idea of 'parity of participation'. On the one hand, Fraser conceives of moral persons (to whom justice is owed) as unique, non-exchangeable individuals with different needs and interests. On the other hand, and using what she calls the 'deconstructive' idea of the equality of all differences, she conceives of all identities as equal. Unique, non-exchangeable individuals, whose concepts of identity do not also entail the subordination of another's concept of identity, should be considered as moral equals.

Fraser believes that it is because the framework of equality includes both the value of difference *and* the value of equality that it allows us to remedy injustices. It allows us to identify as arbitrary, contingent and in need of transformation, those institutionalised harms which are stratified in society in terms of identity differences (gender, colour, class ...). When such harms are publicly institutionalised (in norms regulating economic distribution, status recognition and political representation), then they treat a particular identity-difference unfairly, effectively preventing individuals characterised by that difference from participating *as an equal* in different spheres of life.

This framework certainly allows us to identify certain specific institutionalised harms which prevent individuals from participating as equals. In so doing, Fraser's framework allows us to design strategies (economic, cultural and political) which appear to target that specific harm most effectively. An analysis might reveal, for example, that the systematic harm which many homosexual men undergo is often more cultural than economic. Homosexuality crosses the economic class divide: Homophobia is not rooted in political economy because the position of homosexual men in the division of labour is not influenced primarily by their sexuality. Gay men do not tend to constitute an exploited economic class. Of course, there are certain economic advantages which heterosexual couples benefit from which are sometimes not available to homosexual men (family benefits, for example). However, these appear to stem primarily from the main form of harm which homosexual men suffer which, according to Fraser, is cultural, consisting in status violation. Gay men are more likely to be physically or verbally abused, to undergo discrimination in the workplace, and to suffer reduced life-choices with regard to marriage, having children, or making decisions about one's partner. Equipped with distinct categories which allow her to analyse specific forms of institutionalised harm, Fraser's theory thereby appears to resolve the idea of difference with the idea of equality, in a critical theory of society.

However, a tension nonetheless remains between the responsibility to respond to the unique and particular needs of individuals, on the one hand, and the requirement of impartiality among plural individuals, on the other. Fraser claims that empirical analysis of the way in which harms are distributed among identity types can support a claim that parity of participation is being impeded. However, she seems to assume that we know how to identify the groups involved, and what their distinguishing characteristics are. This brackets the question of injustice within groups, where identities might well go unperceived in the analysis. As Fraser herself comes to recognise, every frame produces exclusions, which may generate claims for further reframing. All attempts to identify and respond to harms involve determinations which themselves produce exclusions.

Like Honneth, when referring to the exclusions produced by determinations, Fraser uses a vocabulary which resembles Derrida's, speaking of justice as an ongoing 'project' which motivates a critique of the present without, for all that, being *achieved* in any present moment. Fraser writes: 'Any frame will produce exclusions. But the question arises as to whether these exclusions are unjust, and if so, whether there is a way to remedy them. Granted too, any remedy will produce its own exclusions, which may generate claims for further reframing, if the newer exclusions are seen as unjust. Thus, in the best-case scenario, we should envision an ongoing process of critique, reframing, critique, reframing, and so on' (Fraser, Nash and Bell, 2008: 150). In this sense, 'impossibility' remains a permanent part of the political landscape, and requires an ongoing practice of critique, facilitated by a certain practice of public engagement and criticism.

Reflections on a new pragmatic: responsibility for inevitable failure
How might we commit to the possibility of justice and of supportive structures of intersubjective recognition while also acknowledging, and attempting to remedy, the concrete ways in which theories fail to resolve the need for impartiality with the obligation to respond to the other person in the particular? In my view, the role which Derrida ascribes to justice requires that critical theory maintain a critical perspective on itself, its application and its development.

On the one hand, I am not suggesting that we rid ourselves of the constructive commitment to the possibility of justice. A constructive commitment is the condition for any attempt to achieve the goal of critical theory, namely, emancipation from enslavement. Without the constructive commitment, it would not be possible to begin thinking through ways of responding to the very different needs and demands of non-exchangeable individuals, along with the demand for impartiality among plural individuals. We have just explored the ways in which the theories of both Honneth and Fraser are formulated in terms of a constructive commitment, the first step towards this difficult task.

On the other hand, the deconstructive commitment to impossibility also means that a theory must retain a critical perspective on itself, continually asking itself whether the harms which it cannot respond to or which it also produces still allow it to claim that it negotiates justice's demands well. In this respect, it is important, as Fraser points out, that we encourage a critical approach to our present among our fellow citizens, who also include moral and political theorists. To negotiate the tension between impartiality and responsibility for the unique other, we need to support a social world in which citizens are prepared to make the effort to respond to the inevitable failure of their norms of interaction to properly render to each person their due. As Fraser puts it, framing disputes appears to be a permanent part of the political landscape and will never be resolved definitely, and this means that we need spaces, institutions and an evolving vocabulary to allow unforeseen issues to be raised and considered (2008: 150).

This means that subjects of critical theory must engage fully with the constructive task, comparing possible options for negotiations, comparing and assessing outcomes and harms, striving to ensure that their theory negotiates justice's demands in the best possible manner, while also engaging with the deconstructive insight, identifying concrete forms of failure, and working to remedy them in an ongoing process. This, says Derrida, is:

> anything but a neutralisation of the interest in justice, an insensitivity toward injustice. On the contrary, it hyperbolically raises the stakes in the demand for justice, the sensitivity to a kind of essential disproportion that must inscribe excess and inadequation in itself. It compels to denounce not only theoretical limits but also concrete injustices, with the most palpable effects, in the good conscience that dogmatically stops before any inherited determination of justice. (Derrida, 2002b: 248)

This is clearly an ethics of responsibility – both individual and collective – for the empirical harms produced by the force which law inevitably deploys. It is precisely the irreducible gap between justice and law which demands that we – the inheritors, users and creators of determined laws – take full responsibility for those particular forms of law which produce disadvantage and injustice. Deconstruction, with its attentiveness to 'impossibility', allows us to clarify why we – as social theorists, political scientists, sociologists, policy-makers and citizens – must take it upon ourselves to accept responsibility (individual and collective) for the empirical forms of force which determined forms of justice inevitably deploy.

It is with this idea that I would like to conclude this edited volume, defending the ongoing need for critical theory to maintain a critical perspective upon itself and its future development. Informed by both a constructive commitment to the possibility of achieving emancipation in the present, and a deconstructive attention to the concrete, empirical harms which determined concepts of justice or 'authentic identity' inevitably produce, I am now able to reiterate the promise expressed in the first chapter of this volume. Together, we hope that the contributions in this book will inform a continuing dialogue between recognition theory and contemporary French thought, so as to pursue the emancipatory goal of critical theory with a heightened sensitivity to the diverse facets of our intersubjective life.

Notes

1 With respect to the 'political' critique, Nancy Fraser directs us to the section in 'Force of law' where Derrida writes that we can find in deconstructive analysis 'the premises of a modern critical philosophy, even a critique of juridical ideology, a de-sedimentation of the superstructures of law which both hide and reflect the economic and political interests of the dominant forces of society. This would always be possible and sometimes useful' (Derrida, 2002b: 241).

2 With respect to 'quasi-transcendental' critique, Fraser directs us to the section in 'Force of law' where Derrida writes that the critical analysis which his work foregrounds 'concerns perhaps a more intrinsic structure ... [one that] a critique of juridical ideology should never neglect'. This critique highlights the constitutive relation of force and law 'not in the sense, this time, that law would be in the service of force [as per the first critique which Fraser names 'political'], but rather in the sense of law that would maintain a more internal, more complex relation to what one calls force, power or violence' (Derrida, 2002b: 241).

References

Althusser, L. (1971). *Lenin and philosophy and other essays*, trans. B. Brewster (London: Monthly Review Press).
Anderson, E. (1993). *Value in ethics and economics* (Cambridge, MA: Harvard University Press).
Anderson, J. and A. Honneth (2005). 'Autonomy, vulnerability, recognition, and justice', in J. Anderson and J. Christman (eds), *Autonomy and the challenges to liberalism* (New York: Cambridge University Press), pp. 77–100.
Anderson, T. (1993). *Sartre's two ethics: from authenticity to integral humanity* (Chicago: Open Court).
Bader, V. (2007). 'Misrecognition, power and democracy', in D. Owen and B. Van Den Brink (eds), *Recognition and power: Axel Honneth and the tradition of critical social theory* (Cambridge: Cambridge University Press), pp. 238–69.
Badinter, E. (2006). *Dead-end feminism* (Cambridge: Polity).
Bankovsky, M. (forthcoming). *Perfecting justice in Rawls, Habermas and Honneth: a deconstructive perspective* (London: Continuum).
Baugh, B. (1991). 'De l'individu à l'histoire: l'authenticité dans les écrits de Sartre', *Philosophiques*, 18(2), pp. 101–22.
de Beauvoir, S. (2010). *The second sex*, trans. C. Borde and S. Malovany-Chevallier (London: Knopf).
Bénatouïl, T. (1999). 'A tale of two sociologies', *European journal of social theory*, 2(3), pp. 379–96.
Benhabib, S. (2006). 'Democracy and difference: reflections on the metapolitics of Lyotard and Derrida' and 'Afterword', in L. Thomassen (ed.), *The Derrida – Habermas Reader* (Chicago: University of Chicago Press), pp. 128–56.
Benjamin, J. (1997). *The shadow of the other: intersubjectivity and gender in psychoanalysis* (New York: Routledge).
Berlant, L. (2000). 'The subject of true feeling', in S. Ahmed, J. Kilby, C. Lury, M. McNeil and B. Skeggs (eds), *Transformations: thinking through feminism* (London: Routledge), pp. 33–47.
Bickford, S. (1997). Anti-anti-identity politics: feminism, democracy, and the complexities of citizenship', *Hypatia*, 12(4), pp. 111–31.
Boltanski, L. (1990a). *L'Amour et la justice comme competences* (Paris: Métailié).
Boltanski, L. (1990b). *Distant suffering: morality, media and politics*, trans. G. Burchell (Cambridge: Cambridge University Press).
Boltanski, L. (2008). *Rendre la réalité inacceptable* (Paris: Demopolis).
Boltanski, L. (2009). *De la critique* (Paris: Gallimard).

References

Boltanski, L. and P. Bourdieu (1975). 'Le fétichisme de la langue (et l'illusion du communisme linguistique)', *Actes de la recherche en sciences sociales*, 1(4), pp. 2–33.

Boltanski, L. and E. Chiapello (2005). *The new spirit of capitalism* (London: Verso).

Boltanski, L. and A. Honneth (2009). 'Soziologie der Kritik oder Kritische Theorie? Ein Gespräch mit Robin Celikates', in R. Jaeggi and T. Wesche (eds), *Was ist Kritik?* (Frankfurt/Main: Suhrkamp), pp. 83–116.

Boltanski, L. and L. Thévenot (2006). *On justification: economies of worth*, trans. C. Porter (Princeton: Princeton University Press).

Bosteels, B. (2009). 'Thinking, being, acting; or, on the uses and disadvantages of ontology for politics', in C. Strathausen (ed.), *A leftist ontology: beyond relativism and identity politics* (Minneapolis: University of Minnesota Press), pp. 235–51.

Bourdieu, P. (1977). *Outline of a theory of practice*, trans. R. Nice (Cambridge: Cambridge University Press).

Bourdieu, P. (1984). *Distinction: a social critique of the judgement of taste*, trans. R. Nice (Cambridge, MA: Harvard University Press).

Bourdieu, P. (1990). *The logic of practice*, trans. R. Nice (Cambridge: Polity Press).

Bourdieu, P. (1992). *In other words*, trans. L. Wacquant (Chicago: University of Chicago Press).

Bourdieu, P. (1993). *Language and symbolic power*, trans. G. Raymond (Cambridge, MA: Harvard University Press).

Bourdieu, P. (1996). *The rules of art: genesis and structure of the literary field*, trans. S. Emanuel (Stanford: Stanford University Press).

Bourdieu, P. (1998). *Practical reason: on the theory of action*, trans. R. Johnson (Stanford: Stanford University Press).

Bourdieu, P. (2000a). *Pascalian meditations*, trans. R. Nice (New York: Polity Press).

Bourdieu, P. (2000b). *Propos sur le champ politique* (Lyon: Presses Universitaires de Lyon II).

Bourdieu, P. (2001). *Masculine domination*, trans. R. Nice (New York: Polity Press).

Bourdieu, P. et al. (1999). *The weight of the world: social suffering in contemporary society* (Cambridge: Polity Press).

Bourdieu, P., J.-C. Chamboredon and J.-C. Passeron (1991). *The craft of sociology: epistemological preliminaries*, trans. R. Nice (Berlin: de Gruyter).

Bourdieu, P. and T. Eagleton (1994). 'Doxa and common life: an interview', in S. Žižek (ed.), *Mapping ideology* (London: Verso), pp. 265–77.

Bourdieu, P. and J.-C. Passeron (1990). *Reproduction in education, society and culture*, trans. Richard Nice (New York: Sage).

References

Bourdieu, P. and L. Wacquant (1992). *An invitation to reflexive sociology*, trans. L. Wacquant (Cambridge: Polity Press).
Brown, W. (1995). *States of injury: power and freedom in late modernity* (Princeton: Princeton University Press).
Brown, W. and J. Halley (eds) (2002). *Left legalism/left critique* (Durham: Duke University Press).
Butler, J. (1997). *The psychic life of power* (Stanford: Stanford University Press).
Butler, J. (2000). *Antigone's claim: kinship between life and death* (New York: Columbia University Press).
Butler, J. (2002). 'What is critique: an essay on Foucault's virtue', in D. Ingram (ed.), *The political* (Oxford: Blackwell), pp. 212–28.
Butler, J. (2005). *Giving an account of oneself* (New York: Fordham University Press).
Caillé, A. (2007). *La quête de reconnaissance: nouveau phénomène social total* (Paris: La Découverte).
Canguilhem, G. (1991). *The normal and the pathological*, trans. C. Fawcett (New York: Zone Books).
Cavell, S. (1990). *Conditions handsome and unhandsome* (Chicago: Chicago University Press).
Celikates, R. (2009a). *Kritik als soziale Praxis* (Frankfurt/Main: Campus).
Celikates, R. (2009b). 'Recognition, system justification and reconstructive critique', in C. Lazzeri and S. Nour (eds), *De l'inclusion* (Paris: Presses Universitaires de Paris X), pp. 85–99.
Chanial, P. (ed.) (2008). La société vue du don: manuel de sociologie anti-utilitariste appliqué (Paris: La Découverte).
Charlesworth, S. (2000). *A phenomenology of working-class experience* (Cambridge: Cambridge University Press).
Chiapello, E. (2003). 'Reconciling the two principal meanings of the notion of ideology', *European journal of social theory*, 6(2), pp. 155–71.
Chisholm, D. (2008). 'Climbing like a girl: an exemplary adventure in feminist phenomenology', *Hypatia*, 23(1), pp. 9–40.
Cornell, D. (1992). *Philosophy of the limit* (London: Routledge).
Critchley, S. and A. Honneth (1998). 'Philosophy in Germany', *Radical philosophy*, 89, pp. 27–39.
Crossley, N. (2001). 'Phenomenological *habitus* and its construction', *Theory and society*, 30, pp. 81–120.
Dejours, C. (1998). *Souffrance en France: la banalisation de l'injustice sociale* (Paris: Seuil).
Dejours, C. (2003). *Le Corps d'abord: corps biologique, corps érotique et sens moral* (Paris: Payot).
Dekens, O. (2002). 'Le Kant de Lévinas: notes pour un transcendantalisme éthique', *Revue philosophique de Louvain*, 100(1–2), pp. 108–28.

References

Deranty, J.-P. (2005). 'The loss of nature in Honneth's social philosophy: rereading Mead with Merleau-Ponty', *Critical horizons*, 6, pp. 153–82.
Deranty, J.-P. (2008). 'Work and the precarisation of existence', *European journal of social theory*, 11(4), pp. 443–63.
Deranty, J.-P. (2009). *Beyond communication: a critical study of Axel Honneth's social philosophy* (Leiden: Brill).
Deranty, J.-P. (forthcoming). 'The political core of Merleau-Ponty's late philosophy', in F. Colman, H. Frichot and J. Reynolds (eds), *Global arts/local knowledge* (New York: Lexington Press).
Deranty, J.-P. and S. Haber (2009). 'Philosophie de l'histoire et théorie du parti chez Sartre et Merleau-Ponty', *Actuel Marx*, 4, pp. 52–66.
Deranty, J.-P. and E. Renault (2007). 'Politicising Honneth's ethics of recognition', *Thesis eleven*, 88(1), pp. 92–111.
Deranty, J.-P. and E. Renault (2009). 'Democratic agon: striving for distinction or struggle against domination and injustice?', in A. Schaap (ed.), *Law and agonistic politics* (Aldershot: Ashgate), pp. 43–56.
Derrida, J. (1978). *Writing and difference*, trans. A Bass (London: Routledge).
Derrida, J. (1992). *The other heading: reflections on today's Europe* (Indiana: Indiana University Press).
Derrida, J. (1994a). *Given time: I. Counterfeit money*, trans. P. Kamuf (Chicago: University of Chicago Press).
Derrida, J. (1994b). *Specters of Marx: the state of the debt, the work of mourning and the new international*, trans. P. Kamuf (London: Routledge).
Derrida, J. (1997a). *Adieu to Emmanuel Levinas*, trans. P. Brault and M. Naas (Stanford: Stanford University Press).
Derrida, J. (1997b). *The politics of friendship*, trans. G. Collins (New York: Verso).
Derrida, J. (1997c). 'Il n'y a pas de culture ni de lien social sans un principe d'hospitalité: entretien avec Jacques Derrida, propos recueillis par Dominique Dhombres', *Le Monde* (2 December), www.jacquesderrida.com.ar/frances/hospitalite.htm (accessed 21 August 2010).
Derrida, J. (2000). *Of hospitality: Anne Dufourmantelle invites Jacques Derrida to respond*, trans. R. Bowlby (Stanford: Stanford University Press).
Derrida, J. (2002a). 'Faith and knowledge: two sources of "religion" at the limits of reason alone', in G. Anidjar (ed.), *Acts of religion* (London: Routledge), pp. 40–101.
Derrida, J. (2002b). 'Force of law: the "mystical" foundation of authority', in G. Anidjar (ed.), *Acts of religion* (London: Routledge), pp. 228–98.
Derrida, J. (2004). 'Entretien avec J.-A. Nielsberg', *L'Humanité*, 28 January.
Derrida, J. (2007). *Gift of death and literature in secret*, 2nd edn, trans. D. Wills (Chicago: University of Chicago Press).
Derrida, J. and E. Roudinesco (2004). *For what tomorrow … A dialogue*

References

(Stanford: Stanford University Press).

Dodier, N. (1995). *Les hommes et les machines* (Paris: Métailié).

Donzelot, J. (1979). *The policing of families*, trans. R. Hurley (London: Johns Hopkins University Press).

Du Bois, W. E. B. (1996). 'The souls of black folk', in E. Sundquist (ed.), *The Oxford W. E. B. Du Bois Reader* (Oxford: Oxford University Press), pp. 97–240.

Enaudeau, C., J.-F. Nordmann, J.-M. Salanskis and F. Worms (eds) (2008). *Les transformateurs Lyotard* (Paris: Sens et Tonka).

Fanon, F. (2005). *The wretched of the earth*, trans. R. Philcox (New York: Grove Press).

Fanon, F. (2008). *Black skin, white masks*, trans. K. Appiah (New York: Grove Press).

Fischbach, F. (2009). *Manifeste pour une philosophie sociale* (Paris: La Découverte).

Foucault, M. (1980). *Power/knowledge: selected interviews and other writings* (Brighton: Harvester Press).

Foucault, M. (1982). 'The subject and power', in H. Dreyfus and P. Rabinow (eds), *Michel Foucault: beyond structuralism and hermeneutics* (Brighton: Harvester Wheatsheaf), pp. 208–26.

Foucault, M. (1984a). 'What is Enlightenment?', in P. Rabinow (ed.), *The Foucault reader* (London: Penguin), pp. 32–50.

Foucault, M. (1984b). 'Polemics, politics and problemizations: an interview with Michel Foucault', in P. Rabinow (ed.), *The Foucault reader* (London: Penguin), pp. 381–90.

Foucault, M. (1990). *The history of sexuality*, trans. R. Hurley (London: Penguin).

Foucault, M. (1991). *Discipline and punish*, trans. A. Sheridan (London: Penguin).

Foucault, M. (1994). 'The subject and power', in James Faubion (ed.), *The essential works of Foucault 1954–1984, vol 3: Power*, trans. R. Hurley *et al.* (London: Penguin), pp. 326–48.

Foucault, M. (2002). 'What is critique?', trans. L. Hochroth, in D. Ingram (ed.), *The political* (Oxford: Blackwell), pp. 191–211.

Foucault, M. (2008). *The birth of biopolitics: lectures at the Collège de France 1978–1979*, trans. G. Burchell (Basingstoke: Palgrave Macmillan).

Fraser, N. (1984). 'The French Derrideans: politicizing deconstruction or deconstructing the political?', *New German critique*, 33, pp. 127–54.

Fraser, N. (1991–92). 'The force of law: metaphysical or political?', *Cardozo law review*, 13, pp. 1325–31.

Fraser, N. (1997). *Justice interruptus: critical reflections on the post-socialist condition* (London: Routledge).

References

Fraser, N. (2004). 'Institutionalizing democratic justice: redistribution, recognition, and participation', in S. Benhabib and N. Fraser (eds), *Pragmatism, critique and judgment: essays for Richard J. Bernstein* (Cambridge, MA: MIT Press), pp. 125–48.

Fraser, N. and A. Honneth (2001). *Redistribution or recognition?: a political – philosophical exchange* (London: Verso).

Fraser, N., K. Nash and V. Bell (2008). 'The politics of framing: an interview with Nancy Fraser', in N. Fraser, *Scales of justice: reimagining political space in a globalising world* (Cambridge: Polity Press), pp. 142–59.

Garfinkel, H. (1984). *Studies in ethnomethodology* (Cambridge: Polity).

Garrau, M. and A. Le Goff (2010). 'Témoigner du différend ou politiser le tort: à propos des usages du concept de tort dans la théorie critique contem-poraine', in Claire Pagès (ed.), *Lyotard à Nanterre* (Paris: Klincksieck), pp. 257–85.

Gates, H. L. (1991). 'Critical Fanonism', *Critical Inquiry*, 17(3), pp. 457–70.

Gautier, C. (2009). 'Critique sociologique et sens commun', in C. Gautier and S. Laugier (eds), *Normativités du sens commun* (Paris: Presses Universitaires de France), pp. 419–45.

Geuss, R. (1981). *The idea of a critical theory* (Cambridge: Cambridge University Press).

Giddens, A. (1986). *The constitution of society* (Berkeley: University of California Press).

Gilligan, C. (1993). *In a different voice: psychological theory and women's development* (Cambridge, MA: Harvard University Press).

Griffin-Cohen, M. and J. Brodie (eds) (2007). *Remapping gender in the new global order* (London: Routledge).

Gutmann, A. (1994). 'Introduction', in A. Gutmann (ed.), *Multiculturalism: examining the politics of recognition* (Princeton: Princeton University Press, 1994), pp. 3–24.

Haber, S. (2006). *Critique de l'antinaturalisme* (Paris: Presses Universitaires de France).

Haber, S. (2008). *L'Aliénation: vie sociale et expérience de la dépossession* (Paris: Presses Universitaires de France).

Habermas, J. (1971). *Knowledge and human interests*, trans. J. Shapiro (Boston: Beacon Press).

Habermas, J. (1973). *Theory and practice*, trans. J. Viertel (Boston: Beacon Press).

Habermas, J. (1984). *The theory of communicative action: reason and the rationalization of society*, vol. 1, trans. T. McCarthy (Boston: Beacon Press).

Habermas, J. (1987). *The theory of communicative action: lifeworld and system: a critique of functionalist reason*, vol. 2, trans. T. McCarthy (Boston: Beacon Press).

Habermas, J. (1990a). *The philosophical discourse of modernity: twelve lectures*, trans. F. G. Lawrence (Oxford: Blackwell).

References

Habermas, J. (1990b). 'Justice and solidarity: on the discussion concerning stage 6', in T. E. Wren (ed.), *The moral domain: essays in the ongoing discussion between philosophy and the social sciences* (Cambridge, MA: MIT Press), pp. 224–51.

Habermas, J. (1990c). *On the pragmatics of communication*, trans. M. Cooke (Cambridge, MA: MIT Press).

Habermas, J. (1991a). *Moral consciousness and communicative action*, trans. C. Lenhardt and S. Weber Nicholsen (Cambridge, MA: MIT Press).

Habermas, J. (1991b). *The structural transformation of the public sphere: an enquiry into the category of bourgeois society*, trans. T. Burger (Cambridge, MA: MIT Press).

Habermas, J. (1993). *Justification and application: remarks on discourse ethics*, trans. C.P. Cronin (Cambridge, MA: MIT Press).

Habermas, J. (1994). *Postmetaphysical thinking: philosophical essays*, trans. W. Hohengarten (Cambridge, MA: MIT Press).

Habermas, J. (1996). 'Reply to symposium participants', *Cardozo law review*, 17, pp. 1477–557.

Habermas, J. (1998). *Between facts and norms: contributions to a discourse theory of law and democracy*, trans. W. Rehg (Cambridge, MA: MIT Press).

Habermas, J. (2003a). *The future of human nature*, trans. W. Rehg, M. Pensky and H. Beister (Cambridge: Polity).

Habermas, J. (2003b). *Truth and justification*, trans. B. Fultner (Cambridge, MA: MIT Press).

Habermas, J. (2004). 'Fundamentalism and terror: a dialogue with Jürgen Habermas', trans. Luis Guzman, in G. Borradori (ed.), *Philosophy in a time of terror* (Chicago: University of Chicago Press), pp. 25–44.

Habermas, J. (2006). 'Political communication in media society: does democracy still enjoy an epistemic dimension? The impact of normative theory on empirical research', *Communication theory*, 16(4), pp. 411–26.

Habermas, J. (2008). *Between naturalism and religion: philosophical essays*, trans. C. Cronin (Cambridge: Polity 2008).

Habermas, J. and R. Wolin (1992). 'Jürgen Habermas on the legacy of Jean-Paul Sartre', trans. R. Wolin, *Political theory*, 20(3), pp. 496–501.

Hale, M. (1924). 'Reflections by the Lrd. Chiefe Justice Hale on Mr Hobbes his dialogue of the lawe', in W.S. Holdsworth, *A history of English law*, 7 vols. (Boston: Little, Brown), vol. 5, pp. 500–187.

Hampshire, S. (2000). *Justice is conflict* (Princeton: Princeton University Press).

Hartmann, M. and A. Honneth (2006). 'Paradoxes of capitalism', *Constellations*, 13(1), pp. 41–58.

Hegel, G. W. F. (1977). *Phenomenology of spirit*, trans. A. V. Miller (Oxford: Oxford University Press).

Honneth, A. (1987). 'Ohnmächtige Selbstbehauptung: Sartres Weg zu einer

References

intersubjektivistischen Freiheitslehre', *Babylon: Beiträge zur jüdischen Gegenwart*, 2, pp. 82–8.

Honneth, A. (1991). *The critique of power: reflective stages in a critical social theory*, trans. K. Baynes (Cambridge, MA: MIT Press).

Honneth, A. (1992). 'Moral development and social struggle: Hegel's early social – philosophical doctrines', in A. Honneth et al. (eds), *Cultural – political interventions in the unfinished project of Enlightenment*, trans. B. Fultner (Cambridge, MA: MIT Press), 197–217.

Honneth, A. (1993). *Critique of power: reflective stages in a critical social theory*, trans. K. Baynes (Cambridge, MA: MIT Press).

Honneth, A. (1994). 'History and interaction: on the structuralist interpretation of historical materialism', in G. Elliott (ed.), *Althusser: a critical reader* (Oxford: Blackwell), pp. 73–91.

Honneth, A. (1995a). *The struggle for recognition: the moral grammar of social conflicts*, trans. J. Anderson (Cambridge, MA: MIT Press).

Honneth, A. (1995b). *The fragmented world of the social: essays in social and political philosophy* (Albany: State University of New York Press).

Honneth, A. (1995c). 'The Other of justice: Habermas and the ethical challenge of post-modernism', trans. J. Farrell, in S. White (ed.), *The Cambridge companion to Habermas* (Cambridge: Cambridge University Press), pp. 289–323.

Honneth, A. (1996). 'Pathologies of the social: the past and present of social philosophy', trans. J. Swindal, in D. M. Rasmussen (ed.), *Handbook of critical theory* (Cambridge, MA: Blackwell), pp. 369–96.

Honneth, A. (1999). 'Postmodern identity and object-relations theory: on the seeming obsolescence of psychoanalysis', *Philosophical explorations*, 3, pp. 225–42.

Honneth, A. (2001). 'Invisibility: on the epistemology of "recognition"', *Supplement to the proceedings of the Aristotelian society*, 75(1), pp. 111–26.

Honneth, A. (2002). 'Grounding recognition: a rejoinder to critical questions', *Inquiry*, 45, pp. 499–520.

Honneth, A. (2003). 'Foucault und die Humanwissenschaften: Zwischenbilanz einer Rezeption', in A. Honneth and M. Saar (eds), *Michel Foucault: Zwischenbilanz einer Rezeption. Frankfurter Foucault-Konferenz 2001* (Frankfurt/Main: Suhrkamp), pp. 15–26.

Honneth, A. (2004). 'Recognition and justice: outline of a plural theory of justice', *Acta sociologica*, 47(4), pp. 351–64.

Honneth, A. (2006). 'Entretien: sans la reconnaissance, l'individu ne peut se penser en sujet de sa propre vie', *Philosophie magazine*, 5, www.philomag.com/ (accessed 21 August 2010).

Honneth, A. (2007a). *Disrespect: the normative foundations of critical theory* (Cambridge: Cambridge University Press).

References

Honneth, A. (2007b). 'Recognition as ideology,' in B. van den Brink and D. Owen (eds), *Recognition and power: Axel Honneth and the tradition of critical social theory* (Cambridge: Cambridge University Press), pp. 323–47.

Honneth, A. (2008a). *Reification: a new look at an old idea* (Oxford: Oxford University Press).

Honneth, A. (2008b). 'Verflüssigungen des Sozialen', *WestEnd: Neue Zeitschrift für Sozialforschung*, 5(2), pp. 84–103.

Honneth, A. and H. Joas (1980). *Social action and human nature*, trans. R. Meyer (Cambridge: Cambridge University Press).

Honneth, A. and O. Voirol (forthcoming). 'The critical theory of the Frankfurt school and the theory of recognition', trans. J.-P. Deranty, in G. Rockhill (ed.), *Politics of culture and the spirit of critique* (New York: Columbia University Press).

Horkheimer, M. (1982). *Critical theory* (New York: Seabury Press).

Jaeggi, R. (2009). 'Rethinking ideology', in B. de Bruin and C. Zurn (eds), *New waves in political philosophy* (New York: Palgrave Macmillan), pp. 63–86.

Kant, I. (1997). *Critique of practical reason*, trans. M. Gregor (Cambridge: Cambridge University Press).

Kogler, H. H. (1996). *The power of dialogue: critical hermeneutics after Gadamer and Foucault* (Boston: MIT Press).

Kompridis, N. (2007). 'Struggling over the meaning of recognition: a matter of identity, justice or freedom?', *European journal of political theory*, 6, pp. 277–89.

Kruks, S. (1996). 'Fanon, Sartre and identity politics', in L. Gordon, T. Denean Sharpley-Whiting and R. T. White (eds), *Fanon: a critical reader* (Oxford: Blackwell), pp. 122–33.

Lacan, J. (2006). *Écrits: the first complete edition in English*, trans. B. Fink in collaboration with H. Fink and R. Grigg (New York: Norton).

Latour, B. (2005). *Reassembling the social* (Oxford: Oxford University Press).

LaVaque-Manty, M. (2008). 'Finding theoretical concepts in the real world: the case of the Precariat', in B. de Bruin and C. Zurn (eds), *New waves in political philosophy* (Basingstoke: Palgrave Macmillan), pp. 105–24.

Lazzeri, C. (2009). 'Conflits de reconnaissance et mobilisation collective', *Politique et sociétés*, 28(3), pp. 117–60.

Lazzeri, C. (2010). *La reconnaissance aujourd'hui* (Paris: Editions CNRS).

Lear, J. (2008). 'The slippery middle', in A. Honneth, *Reification: a new look at an old idea* (Oxford: Oxford University Press), pp. 131–46.

Levinas, E. (1998). *Otherwise than being: or beyond essence*, trans. A. Lingis (Pittsburg: Duquesne University Press).

Levinas, E. (2003). *Totality and infinity: an essay on exteriority*, trans. A. Lingis (Pittsburg: Duquesne University Press).

Lyotard, J.-F. (1984). 'Entretien avec Jean-François Lyotard', *Traces*, 11, pp. 5–22.

References

Lyotard, J.-F. (1988). *The differend: phrases in dispute*, trans. G. Van Den Abeele (Minneapolis: University of Minnesota Press).

Lyotard, J.-F. (1989). 'Levinas' logic', trans. M. Lydon, in A. Benjamin (ed.), *The Lyotard reader* (Oxford: Basil Blackwell), pp. 275–313.

Lyotard, J.-F. (1990). *Heidegger and 'the Jews'*, trans. A. Michel and M. Roberts (Minneapolis: University of Minnesota Press).

Lyotard, J.-F. (1991a). *Lectures d'enfance* (Paris: Galilée).

Lyotard, J.-F. (1991b). *The inhuman: reflections on time*, trans. G. Bennington and R. Bowlby (Cambridge: Polity).

Lyotard, J.-F. (1991c). *Dérive à partir de Marx et Freud* (Paris: Broché).

Lyotard, J.-F. (1993). *Libidinal economy*, trans. I. Grant (Bloomington: Indiana University Press).

Lyotard, J.-F. (2000). *Misère de la philosophie* (Paris: Galilée).

Lyotard, J.-F. (2011). *Discourse, figure*, trans. A. Hudek and M. Lydon (Minneapolis: University of Minnesota Press).

Lyotard, J.-F. and J.-L. Thébaud (1985). *Just gaming*, trans. W. Godzich (Minneapolis: University of Minnesota Press).

Mansbridge, J. and A. Morris (eds) (2001). *Oppositional consciousness: the subjective roots of social protest* (Chicago: Chicago University Press).

Markell, P. (2003). *Bound by recognition* (Princeton: Princeton University Press).

Marx, K. (1997). *Writings of the young Marx on philosophy and society*, trans. L. Easton and K. Guddat (Indianapolis: Hackett).

McCarthy, T. (1991). *Ideals and illusions: on reconstruction and deconstruction in contemporary critical theory* (Cambridge, MA: MIT Press).

McNay, L. (2008). *Against recognition* (Cambridge: Polity Press).

McNay, L. (2009). 'Self as enterprise: dilemmas of control and resistance in Foucault's *The birth of biopolitics*', *Theory, culture and society*, 26(6), pp. 1–23.

McNay, L. (forthcoming). 'Feminism and post-identity politics: the problem of agency', *Constellations*, 17(4), pp. 512–25.

McRobbie, A. (2008). *The aftermath of feminism: gender, culture and social change* (London: Sage).

Medearis, J. (2004). 'Social movements and deliberative democratic theory', *British journal of political science*, 35, pp. 53–75.

Merleau-Ponty, M. (1962). *Phenomenology of perception*, trans. C. Smith (London: Routledge & Kegan Paul).

Merleau-Ponty, M. (1964). *Signs*, trans. R. McCleary (Evanston: Northwestern University Press).

Merleau-Ponty, M. (1973a). *Adventures of the dialectic*, trans. J. Bien (Evanston: Northwestern University Press).

Merleau-Ponty, M. (1973b). *The prose of the world*, trans. J. O'Neill (Evanston: Northwestern University Press).

References

Merleau-Ponty, M. (1994). *Sense and non-sense*, trans. P. A. Dreyfus (Evanston: Northwestern University Press).

Merleau-Ponty, M. (1997). 'Philosophy and non-philosophy since Hegel', in H. Silverman (ed.), *Philosophy and non-philosophy since Merleau-Ponty* (Evanston: Northwestern University Press), pp. 9–83.

Merleau-Ponty, M. (2000). *Humanism and terror: the communist problem*, trans. John O'Neill (Piscataway: Transaction).

Merleau-Ponty, M. (2003). *Nature: course notes from the Collège de France*, trans. R. Vallier (Evanston: Northwestern University Press).

Miller, P. and N. Rose (2008). *Governing the present: administering economic, personal and social life* (Cambridge: Polity Press).

Mills, C. (1998). *Blackness visible* (Ithaca: Cornell University Press).

Moi, T. (2003). *What is a woman and other essays* (Oxford: Oxford University Press).

Nachi, M. (2006). *Introduction à la sociologie pragmatique* (Paris: Armand Colin).

Nielson, L. B. (2000). 'Situating legal consciousness: experiences and attitudes of ordinary citizens about law and street harassment', *Law and society review*, 34, pp. 201–36.

Oliver, K. (2001). *Witnessing: beyond recognition.* (Minneapolis: University of Minnesota Press).

Owen, D. (1999). 'Political philosophy in a post-imperial voice', *Economy and society*, 28(4), pp. 520–49.

Owen, D. (2010). 'Reification, ideology and power: expression and agency in Honneth's theory of recognition', *Journal of power*, 3(1), pp. 97–109.

Owen, D. and B. Van Den Brink (eds) (2007). *Recognition and power: Axel Honneth and the tradition of critical social theory* (Cambridge: Cambridge University Press).

Rancière, J. (2003). *Les scènes du people* (Paris: Horlieu).

Rawls, J. (1971). *A theory of justice* (Cambridge, MA: The Belknap Press of Harvard University Press).

Rawls, J. (1996). *Political liberalism with a new introduction and the 'Reply to Habermas'* (New York: Columbia University Press).

Rawls, J. (2001). *Justice as fairness: a restatement* (Cambridge, MA: The Belknap Press of Harvard University Press).

Renault, E. (2004). *L'expérience de l'injustice: reconnaissance et clinique de l'injustice* (Paris: La Découverte).

Renault, E. (2008a). *Souffrances sociales: philosophie, psychologie et politique* (Paris: La Découverte).

Renault, E. (2008b). 'The political philosophy of social suffering', in B. de Bruin and C. Zurn (eds), *New waves in political philosophy* (Basingstoke: Palgrave Macmillan), pp. 158–76.

Ricoeur, P. (2007). *The course of recognition*, trans. D. Pellauer (Cambridge, MA: Harvard University Press).

References

Rose, N. (1999). *Powers of freedom: reframing political thought* (Cambridge: Cambridge University Press).

Rosen, M. (1996). *On voluntary servitude* (Cambridge: Polity).

Rosenthal, S. and P. Bourgeois (1991). *Mead and Merleau-Ponty: toward a common vision* (New York: State University of New York Press).

Rousseau, J.-J. (1984). *A discourse on inequality*, trans. M. Cranston (Harmondsworth: Penguin).

Salanskis, J.-M. (2006). *Lévinas vivant* (Paris: Les Belles-Lettres).

Sartre, J.-P. (1948). *Existentialism and humanism*, trans. P. Mairet (London: Methuen).

Sartre, J.-P. (1957). *Existentialism and human emotions*, trans. B. Frechtman (New York: Philosophical Library).

Sartre, J.-P. (1958). *Being and nothingness*, trans. H. E. Barnes (London: Routledge).

Sartre, J.-P. (1963). *Saint Genet: actor and martyr*, trans. B. Frechtman (New York: Brazillier).

Sartre, J.-P. (1981). *The family idiot, Vol. 1*, trans. H. E. Barnes (Chicago: University of Chicago Press).

Sartre, J.-P. (1992). *Notebooks for an ethics*, trans. D. Pellauer (Chicago: University of Chicago Press).

Sartre, J.-P. (1993a). *Being and nothingness*, trans. H. E. Barnes (New York: Washington Square Press).

Sartre, J.-P. (1993b). 'La conférence de Rome 1961', *Les temps modernes*, 49(560), pp. 11–39.

Sartre, J.-P. (1995). *Anti-Semite and Jew: an exploration of the etiology of hate*, trans. G. Becker (New York: Schocken).

Sartre, J.-P. (2001). *Colonialism and neo-colonialism*, trans. A. Haddour, S. Brewer and T. McWilliams (London: Routledge).

Sartre, J.-P. (2004). *Critique of dialectical reason, vol. 1*, trans. A. Sheridan-Smith (London: Verso).

Sartre, J.-P. (2006). *Critique of dialectical reason, vol. 2*, trans. Q. Hoare (London: Verso).

Schaap, A. (2004). 'Political reconciliation through a struggle for reconciliation?', *Social and legal studies*, 13(4), pp. 523–40.

Shapiro, M. (2001). *For moral ambiguity: national culture and the politics of the family* (Minneapolis: University of Minnesota Press).

Skinner, Q. (1998). *Liberty before liberalism* (Cambridge: Cambridge University Press).

Stewart, J. (1998). 'Philosophy and political engagement: letters from the quarrel between Sartre and Merleau-Ponty', in J. Stewart (ed.), *The debate between Sartre and Merleau-Ponty* (Evanston: Northwestern University Press), pp. 327–54.

References

Taylor, C. (1992). *Multiculturalism and the politics of recognition: an essay.* (Princeton: Princeton University Press).

Taylor, C. (1994). 'The politics of recognition', in A. Gutmann (ed.), *Multiculturalism: examining the politics of recognition* (Princeton: Princeton University Press), pp. 25–74.

Thistle, S. (2000). 'The trouble with modernity: gender and the remaking of social theory', *Sociological theory*, 18(2), pp. 275–88.

Thom, R. (1974). *Modèles mathématiques de la morphogenèse* (Paris: Union Générale d'Editions).

Thomassen, L. (2007). *Deconstructing Habermas* (London: Routledge).

Thompson, E. P. (1963). *The making of the English working class* (New York: Random House).

Thompson, S. (2006). *The political theory of recognition: a critical introduction* (Cambridge: Polity).

Tully, J. (1993). *An approach to political philosophy: Locke in contexts* (Cambridge: Cambridge University Press).

Tully, J. (1995). *Strange multiplicity: constitutionalism in an age of diversity* (Cambridge: Cambridge University Press).

Tully, J. (2004). 'Recognition and dialogue: the emergence of a new field', *Critical review of international social and political philosophy*, 7(3), pp. 84–106.

Tully, J. (2008). *Public philosophy in a new key, vol. 1: democracy and civic freedom* (Cambridge: Cambridge University Press).

Tully, J. (2009). *Public philosophy in a new key, vol. 2: imperialism and civic freedom* (Cambridge: Cambridge University Press).

Wacquant, L. (2002). 'De l'idéologie à la violence symbolique', in J. Lojkine (ed.), *Les sociologies critiques du capitalisme* (Paris: Presses Universitaires de France), pp. 25–40.

Walker, N. (2002). 'The idea of constitutional pluralism', *Modern law review*, 65(3), pp. 317–59.

West, C. (1999). 'Black strivings in a twilight civilization', in *The Cornel West reader* (New York: Basic Civitas Books), pp. 87–118.

Williams, M. (1998). *Voice, trust and memory: marginalized groups and the failings of liberal representation* (Princeton: Princeton University Press).

Yar, M. (2001). 'Recognition and the politics of human(e) desire', *Theory, culture and society*, 18(2–3), pp. 57–76.

Young, I. M. (1990). *Justice and the politics of difference* (Princeton: Princeton University Press).

Young, I. M. (1996). 'Communication and the Other: beyond deliberative democracy', in S. Benhabib (ed.), *Democracy and difference: contesting the boundaries of the political* (Princeton: Princeton University Press), pp. 120–33.

References

Young, I. M. (1997). *Intersecting voices: dilemmas of gender, political theory and policy* (Princeton: Princeton University Press).
Young, I. M. (2000). *Inclusion and democracy* (Oxford: Oxford University Press).
Young, I. M. (2001). 'Activist challenges to deliberative democracy', *Political theory*, 29(5), pp. 670–90.
Young, I. M. (2005). *On female body experience: throwing like a girl and other essays* (Oxford: Oxford University Press).
Žižek, S. (2006). *The parallax view* (Cambridge, MA: MIT Press).
Žižek, S. (2009). *Violence: six sideways reflections* (London: Profile).
Zurn, C. (2000). 'Anthropology and normativity: a critique of Axel Honneth's formal conception of ethical life', *Philosophy & social criticism*, 26(1), 115–24.
Zurn, C. (forthcoming). 'Social pathologies as second-order disorders', in D. Petherbridge (ed.), *The critical theory of Axel Honneth* (Leiden: Brill).

Index

Note: 'n' after a page number indicates the number of a note on that page

action 8, 24, 27, 53, 63, 65, 72, 98, 106, 112, 122, 126n10, 127, 129–31, 138, 150, 151, 152, 157, 163, 165, 166, 198
  communicative 116, 178, 179, 183
  constraints of 37, 211, 220
  coordination of 102, 106, 120, 165
  individual 15, 63, 68, 114, 115, 137, 140n7, 177, 183
  norms of 4, 211, 224
  political 64, 92, 112, 114, 118, 119, 194
  social (or interaction) 5, 15, 19, 23, 29, 66, 69, 74, 75, 79, 80, 81, 85, 88, 89, 95, 113–121, 123–5, 125n1–2, 126n9, 155, 172n1, 177, 189, 208
  theory of 115, 116, 178, 179
  see also collective action
Adorno, T. 124, 126n13, 178, 209
affective relations see care
agency see freedom
agonism see freedom, agonistic; identity, agonistic
Althusser, L. 9, 13, 26, 45, 47, 48, 113, 150
anthropology 18, 41, 42, 44, 95, 114–16, 118, 120, 125n3, 127, 128, 129–30, 148, 149, 150, 159n1, 176, 181, 193, 204
Arendt, H. 89, 105
Aristotle 47, 150
asymmetry 11, 20, 30, 31, 32, 105, 123, 162, 168, 171, 183, 184, 186, 189, 190n3n8
  principle of 35, 38, 176, 180
  relations of viii, 18, 19, 22, 123, 168, 175, 181, 182, 185, 188, 214
  and responsibility 29, 30, 32, 35, 187
Aubert, I. 19, 38
authenticity see freedom, self-articulation, social or Hegelian; identity, authentic

autonomy see freedom

Badinter, E. 56
Bankovsky, M. 20, 38
Beauvoir, S. de 10, 15, 16, 54, 125n5, 128, 133–6, 138, 140n5n8
  see also existentialism
Benjamin, J. 57, 66, 182
Berlant, L. 56, 57
body, the see embodiment
Boltanski, L. 9, 16, 17, 57, 160, 161, 164–7, 168
Bosteels, B. 63, 65
Bourdieu, P. viii, 9, 17, 58, 60, 61, 64, 87n3, 111, 121, 125n11, 137, 138, 143–9, 160, 161–4, 166, 168
Brown, W. 15, 56, 57, 59, 64
Butler, J. viii, 10, 13, 41–2, 45–9, 62, 68

capitalism 28, 50, 51, 52, 68, 191, 195, 197
  capital 50, 143, 144, 146–57 *passim*
care 5, 9, 18, 19, 20, 22, 29–32, 35, 36, 66, 80, 124, 175, 176, 178, 208, 213–15, 216
  affective relations vii, 5, 19, 30, 31, 32, 33, 35, 37, 61, 67, 76, 80, 123, 124, 125, 126n13, 132, 147, 153, 214, 219
  friendship 5, 19, 31, 184, 214
  love 5, 19, 30, 31, 32, 35, 37, 51, 76, 77, 78–9, 80, 152, 159, 165, 205, 206, 214, 215
  see also self-confidence
Celikates, R. 17, 87n3, 126n11
Chisholm, D. 136–7, 138
citizen 6, 19, 45, 51, 63, 68, 85, 91, 93, 96, 97, 98, 100, 102, 104, 106, 107, 108n2, 179, 180, 181, 189, 196, 199, 224
civic freedom see freedom

Index

class 58, 61, 62, 64, 66, 71, 76, 114, 144, 145, 151, 153, 154, 155, 157, 192, 211, 222
   struggle 83, 114, 115, 118, 125n6, 156, 193, 195
   see also work, working class
collective action 32, 33, 56, 76, 118, 119, 169
   mobilisation 17, 60, 144, 145, 154
   social movements 3, 5, 7, 16, 107–8, 108n2, 117, 127, 128
colonialism 71, 81, 82, 83, 85, 98, 100, 127, 171
communication 9, 18, 32, 65, 85, 118, 126n10, 168, 177, 178, 182, 183, 188, 214
   language 9, 18, 19, 27, 29, 30, 31, 38, 41, 89, 92, 94, 96–100 *passim*, 100, 116, 119, 126n9, 145, 177, 178, 181, 183, 187, 198, 199, 200, 201, 202, 207n3, 209
   see also action, communicative
Connolly, W. 10
consent 33, 79, 94–100 *passim*
constitutionalism *see* legal relations
cooperation vii, 5, 6, 19, 32, 33, 35, 101, 104, 105, 180, 181
Cornell, D. 10, 21, 190n4
corporeality *see* embodiment
Critchley, S. 10
critical theory 4, 6, 7, 10, 12, 16, 19, 21, 22, 23, 37, 113, 114, 117, 118, 119, 121, 122, 124, 125, 126n10, 127, 128, 139n1, 160, 161, 167–72, 217, 218, 221, 223, 224, 225
   critical social science 160, 161–4, 165
   critical sociology 16, 17, 115, 122, 145, 162
   social criticism 59, 62, 69, 119, 123, 128, 132, 133–4, 137, 139, 166
   social philosophy 4, 70, 111, 112, 113, 121, 193, 194
   social theory 8, 9, 11, 13, 16, 17, 21, 37, 65, 66, 70, 76, 77, 111, 113–18 *passim*, 120–3 *passim*, 125n4, 160, 161, 169, 170
   sociology of critique 160, 161, 164–8

   see also practice, of critique; public philosophy

deconstruction *see* Derrida, J.
Deleuze, G. vii
deliberation 30, 102, 103, 104, 187, 189, 203, 210
   critique of 8, 9–10, 18, 22, 37–8, 38n2, 62, 65, 103, 105–6, 117, 120, 180–1, 192
   dialogue 8, 14, 84, 91, 96, 99, 101, 103–7, 201
   discussion 93, 103, 105, 107, 117, 182, 201
   ethics of 18, 30, 103, 105, 175
   monological 27, 28, 66, 85, 99, 103, 105
   see also action, communicative
democracy 28, 37, 50, 55, 57, 58, 61, 63, 83, 95, 97, 98, 103, 104, 112, 116, 117, 123, 179, 180, 181, 188–9, 192, 203
   see also sovereignty, popular
democratic freedom *see* freedom
dependency, human 15, 32, 35, 77, 78, 115, 116, 120, 123, 177, 187, 213, 214, 215, 216
   needs 5, 9, 14, 20, 31, 35, 37, 69, 76, 77, 159, 193, 196, 205, 211, 213–23 *passim*
   vulnerability 4, 10, 15, 16, 60, 61, 68, 69, 116, 122, 123, 124, 177, 178
Deranty, J.-P. 12, 15, 60, 64
Derrida, J. viii, 8, 18, 19, 20, 23, 38, 29–31, 32–5 *passim*, 36–7, 144, 175–6, 179, 180, 182–9, 188–9, 189n1n2, 190n3n4n6n8, 208–11, 213, 215–17, 223–5, 225n1n2
   deconstruction 9, 18, 20, 29, 31, 35, 62, 185, 189, 189n1, 190n7, 208–18, 224
   deconstructive justice 17, 22, 36, 37, 185–7, 190n7, 205, 208, 214, 215–19, 223, 224
   hospitality 183–4, 185, 186, 188
dialectic 45, 46, 47, 49, 50, 54, 74, 75, 76, 118, 119
discourse ethics *see* deliberation, ethics of

Index

disrespect 5, 16, 25, 56, 61, 71, 82, 124, 128, 145, 152, 192–6 *passim*, 221
  see also respect
dissent 21, 105, 198
  disagreement 21, 105, 106, 180
domination 7, 9, 13, 16, 17, 28, 46, 55–60 *passim*, 62–5 *passim*, 69, 74, 113, 114, 115, 127, 134, 140n12, 144, 146, 151–8 *passim*, 164, 166, 171, 195
  critique of oppression 3, 7, 9, 16, 17, 22, 36
  exclusion 14, 85, 87, 103, 149, 170, 223
  exploitation 82, 127, 166, 168, 222
  marginalisation 16, 17, 22, 127, 155, 179, 200
  oppression 3, 4, 7, 10, 11, 14, 16–17, 55–61 *passim*, 66, 69, 75, 127–33, 139, 213, 220
  powerlessness 55, 57, 60, 63, 127, 131, 198
  subjugation 3, 7, 13, 15, 16, 56, 58, 62, 78
  subordination 6, 9, 15, 44, 59, 99, 100, 135, 155, 212, 213, 219, 220, 222
  see also identity, distorted; injustice; invisibility; social pathology; subjectivity, subjection; suffering; violence
doxa 163–4
Du Bois, W. E. B. 170–1

emancipation 4, 13, 28, 36, 53, 55, 65, 116, 117, 120, 125, 131, 140n12, 169–71 *passim*, 188, 220, 223–5 *passim*
embodiment 4, 9, 10, 11, 15–16, 18, 21, 46, 63–5 *passim*, 111, 118, 120–3 *passim*, 128, 129–32, 133, 136
  bodily experience 34, 76, 116, 129–30, 125, 131, 132, 134–6 *passim*, 138, 140n5
  body, the 15, 27, 46–7, 58, 59, 63, 64, 119, 120, 124, 125n5, 126n12, 128–32 *passim*, 134, 135–8, 140n6n11, 150, 154, 197
  corporeality 15, 118, 148
  lived experience 10, 16, 21, 60, 61, 65, 114, 128, 130–4, 135–9 *passim*, 140n6n11
  see also phenomenology
epistemology 41, 112, 118, 127, 128, 139, 146, 162, 171, 196
equality viii, 5, 8, 9, 75, 84, 95, 97–102 *passim*, 175, 176, 178, 180, 182, 184, 187, 188, 208, 210–13, 219, 220, 222
  critique of 17–18, 19, 20, 22, 29–32, 35, 37, 64, 184–8 *passim*, 188, 201–2, 205, 206, 213–15, 216–17, 222
  reciprocity 5, 9, 18, 29, 30, 32, 33, 37, 67, 85, 102, 103, 104, 115, 118, 126n9, 144, 175, 176, 179, 180, 182–9 *passim*, 208, 214
  symmetry 9, 18, 30, 164–5, 171, 175–89 *passim*, 190n8
  see also justice, impartiality
ethical life 5, 102
  see also good life
ethical obligation 4, 10, 11, 30, 182, 202, 208–9, 213, 216, 223
  see also responsibility
exclusion *see* domination
existentialism 8, 23–6, 31, 37, 54, 61, 70–2 *passim*, 75, 80, 83, 84, 87n1, 112, 128, 133, 136, 170, 214, 220
  see also Beauvoir, S. de; Sartre, J.-P.
exploitation *see* domination

family 5, 66, 68, 148, 211, 219, 222
Fanon, F. 82–4, 87, 87n2
feminism vii, 7, 136, 138, 139
Foucault, M. viii, 9, 14, 15, 23, 27–9, 31–5 *passim*, 41, 42, 45–8 *passim*, 54–69, 88–92, 98, 101–3, 107, 111
Fraser, N. viii, 3, 4, 6, 9, 14, 18, 20, 21, 59, 86, 88, 128, 139n1, 208–19, 221–4, 225n1n2
freedom 4, 25, 28, 30, 32, 50, 55, 56, 61, 62, 63, 68, 69, 73–9 *passim*, 81, 83, 84, 88, 89, 91, 130, 133, 136, 137, 138, 139n3, 150, 202
  agency 28, 29, 55, 56, 62–5, 108n3, 127, 140n5, 170, 171
  agonistic 14, 69, 86, 87, 89, 103
  autonomy 46, 51, 61, 68, 117, 122, 123,

Index

148, 152, 177, 183, 209, 220
democratic or civic 14, 85, 87, 105, 106, 107
liberty 69, 75, 94, 95, 100, 101, 130, 188, 195, 198, 213
negative 33, 34, 35
realisation of 5, 26, 215
self-articulation 33, 34, 35
self-legislation 33
social or Hegelian 33–4, 35
French-German relations vii-viii, 10, 13, 22, 23, 26, 32, 37–8
friendship *see* care

Garrau, M. 15–16, 125n5
Gates, H. L. 171
gaze, the 41, 44, 132, 170
gender 46, 47, 48, 61, 62, 64, 66, 69, 101, 132, 134–7, 140n7, 145, 211, 213, 222
see also sexuality
genealogy viii, 89, 90, 91, 92, 96, 98, 100, 101
historical analysis 62, 73, 88, 103, 107, 114, 143, 210, 211
German-French relations *see* French-German relations
gift-giving 11, 12, 18, 19, 20, 31, 163, 194
see also Mauss, M.
Gilligan, Carol 18
good life 5, 6, 194–7 *passim*, 205
see also ethical life
governance 69, 106
practices of 88, 89, 90, 101, 102
Guattari, F. vii

Habermas, J. 33, 103, 125, 175–83, 185–9, 190n6n9, 216, 218
on Derrida 30, 208, 209–10
on Foucault 29
on French philosophy 10, 37
Honneth's difference with 8, 18, 19, 23, 26, 27, 29, 30–1, 35, 37, 38, 65, 111, 116–17, 121, 125n4, 205, 214
Honneth's similarity with 20, 29, 32, 112, 113, 197, 201, 202
on Lyotard 29, 30
on Sartre 26, 27

see also action, communicative; discourse ethics
habitus viii, 121, 122, 137, 138, 140n10n11, 143–6 *passim*, 150–1, 152–8 *passim*, 163–4
Hegel, G. W. F. vii, 5, 26, 41, 42, 45–7, 49, 50, 53, 54, 78, 116, 118, 120, 193, 204, 206
Hegelian approaches 3, 4, 6, 7, 8, 12, 13, 14, 16, 21, 71, 144
post-Hegelian thought 71, 144
Heidegger, M. 78, 80, 112, 113
Herder, J. G. 33, 34, 35
hermeneutics 50, 52, 112, 114, 116, 161, 166, 179, 180, 185
historical analysis *see* genealogy
historical materialism *see* materialism
Hobbes, T. 33, 98, 99, 147, 149, 157, 158, 193
Honig, B. 10
Honneth, Axel vii, 3, 4, 6, 7, 8, 16, 17, 20, 61, 66, 67, 78, 79, 84, 86, 88, 102, 128, 139n1, 160, 182, 193, 223
on Althusser 26
on authentic identity vii, 3, 5, 12, 68, 69, 87, 168
on deconstruction 18, 20, 29–31, 32–5 *passim*, 36–7, 38, 175, 176, 189n2, 190n3n8, 208, 210, 213–17
on Foucault 27–9, 31–5 *passim*, 67
on gift-giving and Mauss 18, 30
influence of French philosophy on vii, 9, 10, 13, 19, 22, 23–38
influence on theory in France 11–12
on Lacan 26
on Levinas 29, 30, 32, 33, 192, 205–6
on Lyotard 29–30, 192, 201–2, 207n3
on naturalism 192–7, 204, 206
on progress 21, 36, 84, 218–21, 223
proximity with Merleau-Ponty 15, 111–26
on reification 80–2, 87, 108n3
on Ricoeur 30, 31
on Rousseau 26
on Sartre 14, 23–7, 28, 31–5 *passim*, 70, 71–3, 77
on suffering 54–61, 63, 65

Index

see also Habermas, Honneth's difference with, and similarity with
Horkheimer, M. 4, 21
hospitality *see* Derrida, J., hospitality
Humboldt, A. von 33, 34, 35

identity 10, 45, 54, 58, 60, 74, 78, 82, 97, 101, 103, 104, 107, 127, 135, 177, 189n1, 210, 212, 220, 222
  agonistic 4, 11, 12, 14, 70, 85, 86, 107, 217–18
  authentic 3–8 *passim*, 12–16 *passim*, 21, 54, 61, 62, 69, 73–7 *passim*, 83–7 *passim*, 187, 208, 209, 214, 215, 217, 225
  distorted 64, 84, 116, 122
  group 7, 11, 95, 145, 152, 180
  non-identity 55, 62, 63, 85
  politics of 15, 55, 58, 64, 69, 83
ideology 15, 28, 41, 42, 45, 48, 49, 51, 55, 65–9 *passim*, 77, 82, 108n3, 139, 160, 162, 164, 166, 168, 169, 172n1, 220, 225n1n2
indigenous peoples 93, 96, 97, 98, 99, 101, 108n2
inequality 31, 32, 58, 59, 61, 62, 64, 65, 66, 123, 211
injustice 7, 17, 54, 56, 57, 59, 60, 64, 93, 98, 112, 114, 115, 116, 122, 123, 127, 128, 134, 140n6, 154, 168, 193, 222, 223
  see also domination; identity, distorted; invisibility; social pathology; subjectivity, subjectification, subjection, subjectivation; suffering; violence
interpellation 13, 26, 42, 45, 47, 48, 67
intersubjectivity 8, 14, 25, 30, 71, 72, 73, 77, 86, 111, 114, 115, 118–19, 124, 130, 176, 177, 178, 181, 182, 186, 206
  interpersonal relations vii, 15, 74, 78, 79, 81, 123, 159, 176, 179, 188
  intersubjective life 12, 22, 30, 130, 225
  intersubjective norms viii, 85, 88, 89, 102
  intersubjective relations 4, 5, 8, 18, 22, 28, 32–6 *passim*, 38, 66, 81, 177, 184, 212, 213, 214, 221
intolerance 52, 179, 213, 220
  see also tolerance
invisibility 42, 49, 146
  of the misrecognised 48, 196
  of oppression 51, 55, 59, 60, 63, 79, 153
  see also domination; identity, distorted; injustice; invisibility; social pathology; subjectivity, subjectification, subjection, subjectivation; suffering; violence

Joas, H. 111, 115
justice 14, 17, 19, 20, 21, 22, 31, 33, 36, 56, 85, 87, 92, 93, 94, 106, 107, 128, 166, 175, 176, 185, 191, 192, 193, 196–209 *passim*, 221, 222, 225
  deontology 175, 193, 195
  distribution 4, 6, 21, 56, 60, 63, 67, 102, 127, 128, 146, 152, 222
  impartiality 3, 6, 7, 18, 94, 217, 218, 222, 223, 224
  theories of 3, 6, 7, 9, 18, 23, 35, 102, 121, 127, 208–13 *passim*, 217, 218, 221
  see also deconstructive justice; equality; injustice
justification 160, 161, 165–8

Kant, I. 6, 33, 36, 90, 97, 99, 120, 187, 189, 190n8, 200, 201, 205, 209, 218
Kohlberg, L. 182
Kompridis, N. 14, 86

labour *see* work
Lacan, J. 13, 26, 41–5, 48, 50, 51, 53, 197
language *see* communication
Lazzeri, C. 17, 38, 87n3, 126n11, 140n10, 172n2
legal relations vii, 5, 32, 35, 57, 85, 219
  constitutionalism 92–100, 103–5, 108, 181
  legal institutions 67, 96, 97, 100, 194, 204
  see also legal practice
Le Goff, A. 14, 38
Levinas, E. 8, 9, 18, 19, 20, 23, 29, 30, 32,

[245]

33, 176, 183, 190n4, 191, 192, 199, 200, 201, 202–7
Lévi-Strauss, C. 111, 150
liberalism 6, 51, 52, 57, 83, 101, 102, 113, 134, 135, 181, 187, 209, 213, 219, 220
  see also neoliberalism
liberty see freedom
life-world 30, 33, 176–7, 214
lived experience see embodiment
love see care
Lyotard, J.-F. viii, 9, 20, 23, 29, 30, 38n2, 191, 192, 197–202, 205, 206, 206n1

McNay, L. 14–15
Malabou, C. 13
marginalisation see domination
Markell, P. 57
marxism 53, 54, 113, 116, 118, 119, 126, 139, 144, 150, 191, 193, 194, 195, 196, 197, 198, 200, 203, 204, 206
  post-marxism viii, 20, 192, 197, 198
Marx, K. vii, 50, 55, 70, 71, 114, 115, 120, 125, 144, 146, 172, 193, 194, 197, 198
materialism 12, 49, 113, 118, 119, 135
  historical 114, 115, 116
MAUSS see Mouvement anti-utilitariste dans les sciences sociales
Mauss, M. 18, 30, 150
Mead, G. H. 3, 8, 115, 120, 193, 196
Merleau-Ponty, M. viii, 10, 23, 111, 112, 113, 117, 118, 119, 120, 122, 123, 125n1n5n7n8, 126n9n10, 128, 129, 150
  on corporeality 15, 16, 123–4, 129, 130, 131, 132, 134, 138, 139n2, 140n9n11
misrecognition vii, 6, 9, 13, 26, 54, 59, 65, 122, 128, 153, 160, 162–5, 168–71, 194, 196, 202, 212, 215
  objectification 13, 14, 26, 44, 71, 78, 82, 83, 87, 135, 178
  reification viii, 12, 13, 14, 21, 26, 53, 57, 70, 71, 72, 74, 75, 78–81, 82, 87, 126n13, 137
mobilisation see collective action
Montesquieu vii
Mouffe, C. 10
Mouvement anti-utilitariste dans les sciences sociales 12, 18
multiculturalism 8, 108n2, 180, 212, 219
  cultural diversity 91, 92, 93, 95, 96, 100

naturalism viii, 193–8 passim, 204, 206
nature 15, 120, 124, 126n13, 197–8, 204
needs see dependency, human
neoliberalism 57, 61, 67–9
  see also liberalism
Nietzsche, F. vii, 47, 55, 58, 89, 194

objectification see misrecognition
ontology 19, 24, 26, 55, 57, 62, 63, 65–9 passim, 70–80 passim, 91, 111, 112, 113, 119, 120, 125, 129, 132, 139, 170, 189n1, 193, 200–4 passim
oppression see domination
other, the 8, 9, 18, 19, 20, 26, 33, 42–6 passim, 49, 50, 51, 55, 71–81 passim, 84, 85, 95, 103, 175–90, 200, 202–5, 214, 216, 217, 223
Owen, D. 14, 21

pathology see social pathology
Patton, P. vii-viii
phenomenology viii, 8, 10, 14, 15, 16, 27, 31, 32, 38, 41–5 passim, 48, 49, 62, 78, 111–14 passim, 117–22 passim, 125n7, 127–40, 146, 176, 196, 202, 214
  of suffering 14, 15, 54, 55, 57, 58–61, 65, 69, 116
    see also domination
  see also embodiment
pluralism 104, 107, 117, 180, 213
post-foundational approaches viii, 18, 29, 55, 62, 63, 64, 65, 111, 112, 113, 189n2
power viii, 4, 7, 9, 14, 15, 16–17, 22, 27–9, 32, 41, 44–8 passim, 54–9 passim, 63–9 passim, 85, 102–5 passim, 108n3, 115, 123, 129–32 passim, 135, 143–9 passim, 152, 153, 154, 157, 163, 168, 171, 184, 193, 195, 199, 200, 204, 209, 225n2
powerlessness see domination
practice 11, 88–9, 104, 114, 119, 120, 136,

Index

137, 147, 148, 162, 178, 185
  of critique 88, 90, 91, 160, 161, 165, 167, 168, 169, 171, 223
  legal 92, 93, 97, 98, 99, 100, 185
  praxis viii, 76, 86, 113, 116, 118, 120, 125n3, 196
  of recognition 4, 21, 105, 221
  social or institutional 5, 7, 14, 16, 19, 33, 36, 56, 68, 69, 89, 103, 107, 130, 134, 135, 138, 152, 155, 163, 164, 189
  see also governance, practices of
progress 5, 20, 21, 36, 71, 84, 97, 195, 218, 221
public philosophy 88–91, 107

race 44, 51, 61, 66, 83, 101, 107, 108, 170, 196, 199
rational choice *see* reason, rational choice
rationality *see* reason, rationality
Rawls, J. 33, 94, 103, 105, 218
reason 15, 16, 43, 44, 51, 91, 102, 103, 104, 105, 118, 121, 124, 181, 196, 200
  critique of 10, 29, 118, 124, 122, 191, 209–10, 218
  rational choice 18, 144, 145
  rationality 10, 50, 67, 122, 196, 202
  strategic 54, 56, 145
  see also reflexivity
reciprocity *see* equality
reconciliation 23, 82, 84–6, 87, 106
reflexivity 17, 33, 34, 121, 160, 163, 164, 168, 171, 177, 178, 184
  pre-reflexive experience 37, 129, 133, 166
reification *see* misrecognition
Renault, E. 11, 12, 64, 192, 199
respect 8, 9, 18, 19, 30, 32, 54, 56, 80, 84, 124, 149, 182, 184, 186, 187, 191, 209, 214, 215, 219
  for difference 9, 18, 19, 30, 52, 175, 179, 180, 183, 184, 187, 189, 201
  see also disrespect; self-respect
responsibility 17, 18, 20, 29, 30, 32, 35, 37, 45, 61, 68, 74, 75, 83, 178, 184, 186–8, 189, 192, 198, 202, 203, 214, 217, 218, 220, 223–5

  see also ethical obligation
Ricoeur, P. 11, 30, 31, 144
rights 5, 30, 32, 52, 67, 68, 82, 83, 102–6 *passim*, 153, 185, 187, 189, 192, 193, 195, 199, 205, 215, 221
Rousseau, J.-J. 8, 13, 26, 33, 194

Salanskis, J.-M. viii, 19, 20, 38n2
Sartre, J.-P. viii, 8, 13, 14, 23, 24–7, 28, 31–5 *passim*, 54, 70–87, 111, 112, 119, 139n3, 140n5, 147, 150
  see also existentialism
Schaap, A. 84, 85, 86
self-confidence 5, 32, 36, 170, 219, 221
  see also care
self-esteem 5, 6, 8, 32, 35, 36, 54, 56, 61, 76, 77, 80, 149, 152, 211, 215, 216, 219, 220, 221
  see also cooperation; solidarity
self-love 149
self-respect 5, 32, 36, 60, 152, 216, 219, 221
self-understanding 34, 90, 105, 160, 162–4, 169, 171–2, 177, 187
Sen, A. viii
sexuality 44, 47, 48, 68, 79, 80, 122, 123, 124, 126n12, 132, 156, 213, 222
  sex-gender distinction 46, 134–5
  see also gender
Skinner, Q. 88, 89, 90
social criticism *see* critical theory
social life 5, 6, 8, 22, 30, 32, 57, 68, 80, 81, 112, 114–18, 143, 145, 151, 153, 169, 177, 213, 215, 220, 222
social movements *see* collective action
social pathology 5, 7, 16, 20, 60, 61, 64, 72, 82, 115, 116, 119, 121, 122, 123, 132, 160, 168–9, 171, 194, 195
  diagnosis of 5, 20, 116, 119, 122, 123, 128, 133, 138, 162, 169, 171, 194, 195, 221
  hurt feelings 17, 55, 56, 57, 65
  suffering 7, 11, 14, 15, 54–65, 69, 82, 115, 116, 121, 123, 153, 156, 169, 188, 192, 193, 195, 198, 199, 202, 207n3, 221, 222
    see also phenomenology, of suffering

wound, the 52, 55, 56, 57, 170, 195
  see also domination; identity, distorted; injustice, invisibility; subjectivity, subjectification, subjection, subjectivation; violence
social philosophy *see* critical theory
social theory *see* critical theory
sociology of critique *see* critical theory
solidarity 5, 60, 107, 131, 181, 188, 189, 214
Sorel, G. 9, 70, 71
sovereignty 97
  aboriginal 97
  popular 96, 104
    see also democracy
  state 94, 97, 99, 100
  of the subject 96, 130, 140n5
status 3, 6, 14, 45, 59, 135, 145, 155, 156, 157, 179, 194, 212, 213, 222
  see also self-esteem
structuralism 29, 113, 114
subjectivity viii, 4, 5, 8, 13, 14, 16, 51, 69, 71, 79, 89, 103, 117, 122, 129, 134, 140n6, 163, 171
  subjectification, subjection, subjectivation 15, 21, 44–9 *passim*, 53, 85, 200, 211
    see also domination
  subjectivism 55, 57, 59, 62, 144, 150
subjugation *see* domination
subordination *see* domination
suffering *see* social pathology, suffering
suffer-mongering 15, 54, 55–7, 58, 59
  victimhood 15, 54, 56, 57
symmetry *see* asymmetry; equality
systems theory 27–9 *passim*, 116

Taylor, C. viii, 3, 4, 6, 8, 12, 14, 16, 33, 54, 84, 87, 88, 102
teleology 33, 84
Thévenot, L. 9
Thomassen, L. 9, 10, 18, 190n5n10
Thompson, E. P. 113, 114
Thompson, S. 17
tolerance 50, 51, 52, 179–82, 183, 185, 188, 190n5
  see also intolerance
Tully, J. viii, 4, 14, 17, 21, 85–6, 88–108

victimhood *see* suffer-mongering
violence 50, 51, 52, 67, 84, 127, 182, 183
  symbolic 50, 55, 58, 63, 143, 151–5, 156
  see also domination
vulnerability *see* dependency, human

Waldenfels, B. 112
Winnicott, D. 57, 66
Wittgenstein, L. 28, 88, 89, 99
work 46, 60, 61, 68, 69, 85, 91, 123, 124, 138, 192, 211, 222
  division of labour 115, 135, 222
  labour 58, 61, 67, 196, 199
  working class 153, 156
    see also class
working class *see* class; work, working class

Young, I. M. viii, 3, 4, 6, 7, 9, 10, 16, 18, 127–40

Žižek, S. 13, 41, 42, 48, 49–53
Zurn, C. 4

EU authorised representative for GPSR:
Easy Access System Europe, Mustamäe tee 50,
10621 Tallinn, Estonia
gpsr.requests@easproject.com

www.ingramcontent.com/pod-product-compliance
Lightning Source LLC
Chambersburg PA
CBHW071406300426
44114CB00016B/2203